PC Patrol Craft
of World War II

PC Patrol Craft
of World War II

A History of the Ships
and Their Crews

Wm. J. Veigele, Ph. D., USNR (Ret)

PC Patrol Craft of World War II

Published by

Astral Publishing Co.
P. O. Box 3955
Santa Barbara, CA 93130-3955

Hard Cover — First Edition — 1998

Address inquiries to Astral Publishing Co. P. O. Box 3955, Santa Barbara, CA 93130-3955.

Images used in this book are with the permission of the owners and authors as indicated in the captions of each image.

Library of Congress Cataloging in Publication Data
Veigele, William J.
PC Patrol Craft of World War II, $39.95, cloth
400 pages, photographs, figures, drawings,
Includes: references, index, appendices
1. Patrol Craft, 2. PCs, 3. Submarine chasers, 4. Navy, 5. World War II,
6. History, 7. Naval History, 8. Ship histories, 8. Navy crews

Library of Congress Catalog Card Number 97-78091

ISBN: 0-9645867-1-1

Printed in the United States of America

Dedication

I dedicate this book to those former young men who endured the hardships, difficulties, thrills, and dangers of life aboard the PC type of Patrol Craft of World War II.

Acknowledgments

I wish to thank my former shipmates on PC 793 and members of the Patrol Craft Sailors Association for their friendship and the exchange of sea stories when we held reunions.

Many persons and organizations contributed information, stories, photographs, drawings, and paintings for use in this book. They include Mrs. Pauline Allen, Mrs. Diane Kennedy Armstrong, Obadiah Armstrong, Harry Ayres, Robert Baldwin, Carter Barber, Bay County Historical Society, Brainard Belmore, Ralph Benefiel, Ron Bloomfield, David Brown, William Buffington, Joseph Craig, Robert W. Daly, Sr., William M. Defoe, John DiFilippo, Robert B. Dunlap, James O. Durham, Edward R. Emanuel, Arthur Fisher, Raymond E. Goin, Samuel L. Gravely, Jr., Greenpeace, Walter H. Haag, Jim Hunter, Mrs. Nancy Hyde, Institute for Great Lakes Research, Richard Janelli, Joseph F. Kelliher, Kenneth Kennedy, Donald M. Kerr, Leonard Kurtz, Myron H. Kurtz, Stanley Kusek, Allison M. Levy, Walter J. Mackey, Earl Mann, Mark Matyas, Nora McCarthy, James J. McMahon, Fred Morrisey, Webb L. Nimick, Herbert W. O'Quin, Raymond Page, Philip S. Padelford, Patrol Craft Sailors Association, Edgar C. Pease, Joseph J. Peck, Tom Pollock, Harold R. Raymond, Douglas L. Roberts, Ralph K. Roberts, Charles Sager, Kenneth J. Schwartz, Franklin P. Smith, Ken Tito, Wilfred Tlusty, John B. Tombaugh, William G. Truemper, Harold R. Walker, Mrs. Connie (Joseph) Whitman, and Albert W. Young.

Special thanks and my love go to my wife, Sue, for her patience and understanding while I spent hours on this book, away from her.

TABLE OF CONTENTS

Dedication

Acknowledgments

Table of Contents   7

Introduction   9

Prologue   13

Chapter One — The Need for and Deployment of PCs   21

Chapter Two — The Design of PCs   36

Chapter Three — The Construction of PCs   55

Chapter Four — PC Crews and Their Training   78

Chapter Five — Life Aboard a PC   100

Chapter Six — PC Exploits – General   137

Chapter Seven — PC Exploits – American Theater of War   151

Chapter Eight — PC Exploits – European, African, Middle Eastern Theater of War   170

Chapter Nine — PC Exploits – Asiatic, Pacific
Theater of War   202

Chapter Ten — PC Casualties   233

Chapter Eleven — The Naming, Decommissioning,
and Disposition of PCs   246

Chapter Twelve — The Patrol Craft Sailors Association   277

Epilogue   291

Appendixes
  A. Classes and Characteristics of World War II PCs   293
  B. Thirty Engineering Drawings Showing
      PC Design Details   297
  C. Sixteen Shipyards that Built World War II PCs   329
  D. PCs Built at Sixteen Shipyards   330
  E. Construction Program for
      PC 451 Through PC 1603   356
  F. Rates of Enlisted Men Aboard World War II PCs   358
  G. Decorations and Awards Won by PCs During
      World War II   359
  H. The Story Behind PC 1264   360
  I. PC Crew Casualties   366
  J. Patrol Craft Sailors Association Museum   367

Notes   368

Index   387

Fold Out – Sub Chaser (PC)

INTRODUCTION

Many books detail the actions of ships of the United States Navy and the men who sailed and fought them during World War II. Those books cover the activities, battles, and invasions in which the ships were engaged. The aircraft carriers, battleships, cruisers, destroyers, and submarines of the United States Navy brought great destruction to the Axis forces. In so doing they suffered heavy losses of ships and men. Therefore, it is reasonable and important that books written about the war have recounted the actions of these ships and their crews, their battles and victories, and their losses.

Less reasonable, though, is the exclusion from most books about World War II of the accounts of less glamorous ships that also did their part in the war. For example the auxiliary and other delivery ships that lugged war materiel to forward bases; hauled shells, bullets, and torpedoes to the battlewagons, tin cans, and submarines; and fed oil, water, and fuel to the carriers got less attention from historians than the ships they served. Similarly, authors have rarely mentioned the repair ships that kept the fighting ships operating and plugged the wounds of combat. Hospital ships, whose personnel nursed torn and broken bodies, were equally important but got less attention. Writers also neglected to record the activities of the many smaller vessels such as tugs, net tenders, yard craft, submarine chasers, and patrol craft. Years later, some writers remembered some small craft such as mine sweepers, PT boats, and landing craft.

One type of ship that authors almost completely ignored during and since the war, however, was the submarine chaser or patrol craft the Navy designated as PC. In 1957, Samuel E. Morison, the naval historian, noted this fact. In his *History of United States Naval Operations in World War II, The Invasion of France and Germany, 1944-1945, Volume XI*, Page 131, he stated that the Navy and historians did not recognize the roles of these PCs. He wrote, "The . . . PC's were the little lost sheep of American Naval Forces Europe, ..." This lack of notice and appreciation of PCs in the European area extended to all other theaters of World War II.

PCs were among the first new United States Navy vessels built and rushed to sea just after America entered World War II. Though not as heavily gunned as battleships, as speedy as destroyers, or as massive as aircraft carriers, PCs served with as much gallantry. They escorted convoys, hunted and destroyed submarines, sank small craft, shot down air planes, bombarded landing areas, and led landing craft to invasion beaches. They did this, and more, in every theater of war. PCs took part in every major invasion and many minor invasions from Sicily to Normandy and from the Aleutians to New Guinea and back to Okinawa. Though they were among the smallest of United States Navy ships, they inflicted losses on the enemy and suffered their own casualties. Despite the record of PCs, however, most books about World War II do not include discussions of or even mention PCs.

Since my almost two years on a PC during World War II, and over the intervening decades until now, I have searched books written about World War II. Particularly I looked for discussions of the exploits of PCs and tales of the actions of their crew members. Not much is available. A couple of books give the numbers of PCs, dates associated with their construction, and details of their characteristics. Not one of these books, however, gives all of that information. Fragments of the other information about and stories of PCs of World War II lay scattered throughout historical accounts of the war. Some are in one book, some in another. A few authors briefly mention isolated accounts of a handful of the ships. Here and there a writer mentions the actions of a few PC sailors. A handful of magazine articles about PCs appeared during and after the war. No one, however, has written a unified account of the PCs of World War II. No book describes the origin of PCs, their design and construction, the selection and training of their crews, what life was like aboard a PC, their war time sagas, the stories of the sailors who manned them, and the disposition of the ships during and after the war.

The United States naval history of World War II cannot be complete without descriptions of these PCs and tales of the exploits of the ships and their crews. They were good ships manned by good crews and made important contributions to the defeat of the Axis powers. Their actions, and the stories of the more than 50,000 young men, mostly Reservists with no prior sea duty, who served on them should not be ignored and forgotten.

Various private and public agencies have restored battleships, carriers, cruisers, destroyers, submarines, merchant ships, landing craft, and other vessels to honor those classes of ships and their crews. Ninety-five warships, many from World War II, are open to the public in the United States. No PC exists, though, as a historical artifact or a memorial. The PC Patrol Craft have been lost to history. This book will help rectify that oversight by telling the story of this one class of small ships of World War II.

This book unites many aspects of PCs of World War II in one place. From official and other sources I have compiled a list of all PCs of World War II, which shipyards built them, and the relevant dates and dispositions of the ships. This book contains descriptions and characteristics of the ships. Through my own recollections and records and interviews of, correspondence with, and reading the memoirs of former PC sailors, I have outlined the stories and exploits of many of the ships and their sailors. I have taken the accounts here from official records, my own experience, and the words other PC sailors. Also, the book contains photographs, drawings, and paintings made by PC sailors during World War II. Many of them are unique, came from private collections, and have never been published. With that material, this book memorializes those ships and preserves some history of PCs. It tells the stories of the men who sailed and fought them during World War II so that PCs and their crews will not remain a forgotten fleet.

I hope this book gives its readers a more thorough and first-hand account of PCs and the crew members who served on them during World War II. And I hope those former young men who sailed PCs can reminisce about and relive their experiences of five decades past and to know that they have not been forgotten.

Wm. J. Veigele

15 February 1998

PROLOGUE

Under an overcast sky in April 1944, sixty United States Navy sailors assembled on Pier One of the Commercial Iron Works in Portland, Oregon. Flicking up their collars, the men huddled in their pea coats against the cold wind that swept across the murky backwater of the Willamette River. They grumbled and griped about the routine of the Navy that had kept them standing there for half an hour.

"Attention," bawled a First Class Boatswain's Mate. Anxious for action, the men snapped to attention. Upon the Boatswain's next commands, the sailors shouldered their seabags and shuffled into three ranks. Then, one rank after the other, the men strode across a downward-sloping gangplank to a small ship that looked fresh and clean in her new coat of gray war-paint. Christened on 22 May 1943 as shown in Figure P-1, Navy officials would soon designate her USS PC 793. With them, those young men brought aboard their ship the enthusiasm and confidence of youth, the fervor of patriotism, a quest for adventure, and no previous sea duty.

Two weeks later, at the shipyard, white bellies of sea gulls floated in the sky as the birds wheeled over the ships, cranes, and other shipyard gear. They squawked at the men and women who were swarming over steel hulls of Navy ships that were in various stages of construction. Tons of preformed decks and superstructures swung down from cranes onto ships' skeletons. Burning welding rods flashed, and the buzz and snap of fused metal echoed from the hulls. Rivet guns roared and grinders screeched. Mooring lines, electric cables, air lines, and water hoses – the umbilical cords of ships yet to be born – snaked over the decks and down into the guts of the unfinished vessels. Odors of diesel fuel, oil, ozone, and the sweat of laborers filled the air. The stench of harbor flotsam and decayed sea life, which floated around and clung to the pilings of the docks in the calm water, hovered over the ships like a sea fog. The little vessels were rats' nests of activity. Whatever progress the workers made in the construction of the ships was all but undecipherable to those persons not working aboard the vessels.

The ship that would become PC 793 nestled away from the others. It was moored with its starboard side to Pier One, a heavy timbered dock that glistened from years of swabbing with grease, creosote, and tar. With the tide out the deck of the ship settled five feet below the pier. Civilians in festive clothing and Navy officers in blue uniforms with gleaming gold braid gathered on the dock. They chatted while the officers hugged their collars about their ears and the ladies clutched their coats close against their bodies to guard against the cold spring wind that swept across the shipyard.

Five officers stood in silence amidships athwart the ship, where sailors had removed the ship's boat. Of the five, only one officer sported a single ribbon on his breast, the American Theater Campaign Medal. He was the only officer with previous sea duty. Sailors in dress blues and sparkling white hats gathered on the main deck of the ship in two ranks, at ease, along the sides of the vessel. They did what sailors have done for centuries. They had hurried to their posts. Now, they waited. They joked, admired the ladies on the dock, and swapped scuttlebutt as the dignitaries gathered to start the ceremony that would convert hull 793 into USS PC 793, a United States man-of-war.

Except a few of the leading rated enlisted men, none of the young sailors had been to sea. For some, this was the first ship's deck under their feet. A few months earlier they had been students, farmers, tradesmen, clerks, and cowboys. Most of them had never seen an ocean or a body of water larger than a farm pond before entering the Navy. Now, they were sailors ready to man their ship and fight a war. All of them had been through Navy Boot Camp training and most had attended seamanship, gunnery, first aid, damage control, and firefighting training. Some had been to A, B, and C schools that had trained them for their rates as Radioman, Motor Machinist's Mate, Yeoman, Shipfitter, Gunner's Mate, and many other specialties needed on a PC.

"Attention on deck," the Boatswain bellowed. The sailors pressed their arms to their sides and stared straight ahead as seen in Figure P-2. A clutch of dignitaries groped their way down the sloping gangplank, the ladies helped by the officers. They clambered aboard the ship as a Navy band of a dozen brass instruments on the dock lit off with the strains of "Anchor's Aweigh." The music drowned out the clattering background noises of the shipyard. After the last notes of the tune drifted away, a Navy Chaplain intoned an Invocation. Then the ship's builder introduced Lieutenant Commander Ben W. Craine, USN, the representative of the Commandant of the Thirteenth Naval District. At 1405 hours, he drew a folded paper from his pocket, flicked it open, and read the commissioning orders for USS PC 793, as shown in Figure P-3.

As two sailors hauled on lines, the ship's colors flashed up the jackstaff at the bow and the flagstaff at the stern. The standards snapped in the breeze as though ready for adventure as the National Anthem resounded across the shipyard. The Commandant's representative ordered the seven-starred commissioning pennant hoisted. All the sailors' eyes fixed on the streamer, fluttering in the wind. Now, their craft was a United States Navy ship. They and the ship, of which they were proud "plank owners," would help make history.

When the new Commanding Officer of the PC assumed command of the ship, he ordered his Executive Officer, Lt. j. g. Gordon Secor to, "Set the watch." The boatswain's pipe sang, Signalmen on the flying bridge broke out the captain's colors on the yardarm, and the crew rendered honors with a snappy, "Right-hand Salute." The new skipper uncapped a gold fountain pen, stared around at his crew, leaned over the log desk, and inscribed in the log book its first entry:

> "The U.S.S. PC 793 was placed in commission on 10 May 1944 at Commercial Iron Works, Portland, Oregon. H. K. Mulholland, Lt., USNR, read orders assigning him as Commanding Officer and assumed command. Watch was posted. Starboard section on duty."

The Navy Commander stepped forward. He encouraged the men to sail a taut ship, battle the enemy, and uphold the two centuries of tradition of United States Navy honor. Reverend Richardson, a civilian clergyman, lowered his bared head and prayed in silence as shown in Figure P-4. At the end of the prayer, he looked at the crew, pronounced his blessings, and wished the ship and its crew "safe journey." Music rang again from the band, and the chattering dignitaries, ladies' high heels tangling in the cross pieces of the tilted gangplank, clambered up to the dock.

Between 1942 and 1945, Naval Reserve officers, like Lt. Mulholland, with no more Navy experience or sea duty than the crews they led, made 361 log entries similar to that of the one for PC 793. Their commands were, steel-hulled, 173-foot long, 450-ton, diesel-engine-powered PCs similar to the one shown in Figure P-5. Too small, and too numerous, the Navy did not dignify these ships with names. These small ships sported only the bold black letters "PC" and numbers painted on their bows and sterns.

When the ceremonies on PC 793 ended, the crew wasted no time. At 1430 hours all hands, who had swapped their dress blue uniforms for dungarees, turned-to to lug stores aboard. It was time to prepare for sea. Two days later, the men hauled ammunition and depth charges across the deck and stored the projectiles in ready positions and below-deck lockers. After final sea trials, degaussing to protect the ship against magnetic mines, calibrating of compasses, and last minute adjustments, the crew and ship would sail off on their shakedown cruise. With that training cruise over, the ship would then join the fleet.

Two months later those former students, farmers, city boys, and clerks aged seventeen to twenty-five, except three "old men" of thirty-five, had completed their shakedown cruise. Now they would prove that they were sailors. On 10 July 1944, the squawk box blared, "Set the Special Sea Detail." Twin diesel engines in the bowels of the ship roared to life. Gray smoke billowed from exhausts on the sides of the ship. The heavy odor of diesel fumes wafted over the decks. Workers on the dock cast off the ship's mooring lines that slithered through the water as seamen on the PC hauled them aboard. The ship's whistle screeched an alarm. The jack and the ensign slid down their staffs at the bow and stern, and the steaming colors soared to the gaff. Red and white stripes and white stars on a blue field flashed in the morning glow.

"All engines back one third," the Captain commanded, and the PC backed from its berth. "All stop," he ordered. As the ship lost sternway he said, "All ahead one-third. Rudder left ten degrees." Water frothed at its stern as the ship lurched ahead and spun around on a new course. As if eager to start its journey, the bow rose, and PC 793 steamed out through the mist that shrouded Puget Sound to join the war. From that moment on, sixty-five enlisted men and five commissioned officers would depend for their comfort, welfare, and safety on each other man with whom they shared their 173-foot long steel home.

In a similar manner, all the other PCs began their cruises. When they did, they started the story of the "Forgotten Fleet" of the three-hundred and sixty-one PC type ships of World War II.

Figure P-1. Christening of PC 793 on 22 May 1943 at the Commercial Iron Works, Portland, Oregon. National Archives photograph No. 19-N-45850.

Figure P-2. Commissioning Ceremony on PC 793 on 10 May 1944 at the Commercial Iron Works, Portland, Oregon. United States Navy photograph.

Figure P-3. Commissioning Ceremony on PC 793 on 10 May 1944 showing the reading of orders. Navy photograph. United States Navy photograph.

Figure P-4. Commissioning Ceremony on PC 793 on 10 May 1944 showing Reverend Richardson giving the ship and crew his blessing. United States Navy photograph.

Figure P-5. PC 551 goes through her paces off the Atlantic Coast. Photograph courtesy of Parade Magazine, circa 1942.

CHAPTER 1

The Need for and Deployment of PCs in World War II

Allied Strategy Against the Axis

After the Japanese attacked Pearl Harbor on 7 December 1941 the United States and its allies began planning a joint strategy for fighting the war against the Axis Powers. To develop this strategy, Allied civilian and military leaders met in Washington, D. C. from 22 December 1941 to 14 January 1942 in what became known as the Arcadia Conference. President Franklin D. Roosevelt and Prime Minister Winston Churchill acted as hosts at the conference for representatives from twenty-six countries that signed a United Nations Declaration to defeat the Axis.

The representatives decided that their priority was to protect England from defeat by the Nazi Third Reich of Germany and fight a holding war against the Empire of Japan in the Pacific. Their first goal was to ensure England's survival by prying open the sea lanes to England that Nazi U-boats were squeezing shut. The second goal was to transport armies and materiel to England and Africa that the Allies would use to blunt the German advance. Then the Allies would land forces in North Africa and eventually storm the shores of Europe. After that, they would wrench back the Pacific Ocean from the Imperial Japanese Navy and destroy the military might of Japan.

That strategy meant the lifeline of supplies to Great Britain, which had been operating since England had declared war against Germany, had priority to be kept open. Food, medicines, arms, men, and the essentials of life and war had to cross the Atlantic Ocean to England in merchant ships. Without these supplies from other countries, especially the United States, England could not survive.

The Battle of the Atlantic and Operation Paukenschlag

German Grossadmiral Karl Dönitz also understood Great Britain's needs and planned her defeat. He masterminded the U-boat (Unterseeboote) campaign to strangle Great Britain, which he labeled Operation Paukenschlag (Operation Drum Beat).[1]

The U-boat campaign was a strategy similar to that used in World War I with an all-out attack by submarines on the merchant vessels that supplied England. It almost succeeded in WWI, and Dönitz dreamed and planned for its success in the 1940s. His campaign started with five U-boats prowling the Atlantic coast, and they deployed almost without opposition or detection. For example, U-123 sneaked to within a mile or so of New York Harbor, and its Kapitan snapped night photographs of the glowing lights of Manhattan. During this period U-boats had an easy time sinking merchant ships.

Dönitz's immediate success in the first years of World War II alerted Winston Churchill that England had to defeat, or at least contain, the submarine campaign for England to survive. After the war he wrote, "The only thing that ever really frightened me during the war was the U-boat peril."[2]

In the early days of the involvement of the United States in the war, the U. S. Navy's antisubmarine force of ships, trained crews, and tactics could not stop the onslaught by German submarines. During the six months following the day President Franklin Roosevelt referred to as "A date which will live in infamy," U-boats sank almost six hundred ships in American waters. This number was half the United States' merchant fleet. In a few months a handful of U-boats sent hundreds of thousands of tons of shipping to the bottom.

In one month alone this attack had cost the Allies

400 tanks,
1,340 heavy guns,
740 armored vehicles,
6,000 rifles,
52,100 tons of ammunition,
10,000 tanks of gasoline, and
20,000 tons of stores.

Dönitz pleaded with Hitler for more submarines. Hitler agreed to Dönitz's request, but though he authorized more U-boats, he did not award their funding and construction until much later. His decision to delay submarine construction was because he expected that destroyers would protect the merchant ships. Hitler, therefore, geared German submarine construction to stay ahead of the construction of destroyers in the United States.

Hitler's strategy was reasonable, except that he did not know the United States would rely on new escort and antisubmarine warfare (ASW) ships until they could build more destroyers. Among these new ships would be patrol craft escorts (PCEs), patrol frigates (PFs), and destroyer escorts (DEs). However, the United States Navy had a problem. Though shipyards could construct these ships faster than destroyers, they still could not build them rapidly enough to counter the U-boat threat. The Navy needed even smaller ships that they could put to sea sooner to fill the gap until the PCEs, PFs, and DEs arrived. Among these smaller ship types were the 173-foot, steel-hulled PCs that the Navy still had not built. Meanwhile, the Allies needed other ASW and escort ships.

England Responds With Escort Ships

At this time the British nation consumed 750,000 tons of supplies more each month than reached them across the Atlantic Ocean. If they could not stop this bleeding of Britain's shipping arteries, the British people would starve, and their fighting machine would wither. They would then have to sue for peace with Germany and be at Hitler's mercy.

Desperate to prevent such a disaster, early in 1942, Winston Churchill rushed trawlers and corvettes to the United States. He dispatched twenty-two A/S trawlers,[3] ten "Flower" class corvettes, and fifteen RCN "Modified Flower" class corvettes to bolster the U. S. Navy ASW program.[4] The 1,000 ton corvettes were short, broad-beamed, and rough riding but seaworthy. Their sixteen knot speed made them suitable for slow convoys, and their 4-inch gun and depth charges provided effective weapons for attacks on U-boats.[5] Though these ships helped, the Navy needed even more ASW vessels.

America Arms

At home the American war machine ground away day and night every day. Flames soared from steel plants. Chips curled from lathes in machine shops. Smoke billowed from oil refineries. Shipyards glowed night and day. Young men marched into newly constructed camps and trained to become soldiers, airmen, marines, and sailors. Women, like the one in the poster in Figure 1-1, swapped skirts for coveralls and strode into factories and shipyards.

Serious rearming of the United States had begun and was consuming much of the material formerly used for civilian consumption. The lack of metal parts and electrical items frustrated civilian needs, but people responded and did with less. To help supply raw materials for military items, people scoured attics and garages to find and contribute aluminum, steel, and other metals to the war effort. Pots and pans, fences, tools, and even children's toys became guns and bullets and tanks and ships. Victory Gardens sprouted in back yards. Employment swelled. Prices skyrocketed. Gasoline climbed to 21¢ a gallon. A two-egg breakfast soared to 20¢. Even a glass of beer cost 15¢. Wartime prosperity had bred inflation. Despite the civilians' shortages and high prices, workers began to produce war equipment including merchant and Navy ships.

The Convoy System Was Revived

To help stop the destruction of Allied merchant ships, while America geared up to build more ships, naval leaders revived the convoy system of World War I. Canadian, U. S., and English Navy ships shared duties and responsibilities for escorting convoys along the Eastern seaboard of the Americas and from the new world to the old world. In January 1942, for example, the United States sent a fast convoy of troop ships to England escorted by battleships, cruisers, and destroyers that had the range to complete the journey. The Navy did not have enough escorts of that caliber for all convoys, though. So the Allies used ships of shorter range than the battleships and cruisers. They switched responsibilities With England for guarding the convoys at a Mid-Ocean Meeting Point (MOMP), or at Iceland, or off Ireland. This procedure helped but did not solve the problem.

Then too, many merchant ships lumbered along at less than fifteen or even ten knots and made easy prey for U-boats. Convoys with such ships needed smaller, more maneuverable, long-legged escorts. As evidence of the shortage of convoy escorts, only four U. S. Navy destroyers picked up a convoy of thirty-five ships near Iceland in February 1942. Despite constant sweeps and vigorous depth charge attacks on U-boats by the overworked destroyers, German torpedoes sank twenty-two ships in one day. Two days later, despite the efforts of the four destroyers, the U-boats sent four more ships from that convoy to the bottom. For the convoy system to succeed, the allied navies needed more escort ships to handle the coastal convoys. This would allow the Navy to use destroyers and longer range ships on the Atlantic convoys.

The Happy Time for U-boats

At this time, disaster for England crept closer. In January 1942, the Nazis operated ninety-three U-boats in the Atlantic and sank ships off the American coast at the rate of one per day. From December 1941 until June 1942, U-boat torpedoes and gun fire destroyed 495 ships. During the first ten months of 1942, U-boats sank 800 ships totaling 4,000,000 tons.[6] For all of 1942, a total of 1,200 ships went to the bottom.[7] German submariners called this the "happy time."

Early in 1943 as many as one hundred U-boats prowled the Atlantic, using wolf pack tactics (Rudeltaktik) with up to ten submarines in a pack stalking convoys. They slammed torpedoes into Allied shipping, almost strangling the war effort. In January 1943, for example, of nine tankers that sailed from Trinidad for Gibraltar, only two survived. Figure 1-2 shows Allied merchant ship losses during the end of 1942 and the beginning of 1943.

More than U-boats destroyed ships, however. From November through March freezing gale winds, driven snow, and heavy seas took their toll of ships and men. Those ships that did survive the stormy Atlantic crossings suffered from lost time en route, severe damage that required time in port for repairs, and the loss of men swept from their decks. Those calamities kept the ships from service and had the same effect as if the U-boats had sunk some of them.

Death Along the East Coast

As ship construction progressed, more merchant ships became available. What the Navy still needed, though, was more escort vessels to protect the convoys of merchant ships, tankers, and troopships that had to reach Great Britain. To defend these ships, the Navy sent big Coast Guard Cutters and destroyers with these convoys. That tactic, and the training of crews in antisubmarine warfare, helped to get the vital supplies to England. However it left few escorts to protect merchant shipping along the Atlantic seaboard and in the Caribbean. A few U-boats that operated in this theater[8] had an easy time. They littered the ocean bottom with twisted steel that once was ships and sent hundreds of men to their death, many with their lungs seared by burning oil. Often, viewers on the shorelines of the United States stared at ships that exploded and tankers that burst into fireballs. People watched men die only a few miles from shore.

The Eastern Sea Frontier Fleet

To defend against these U-boats along the coastline, the United States Navy continued the ship building program. Meanwhile, before these ships could slide off the ways, the United States deployed a variety of vessels. Rear Admiral Adolphus Andrews commanded these vessels in the Eastern Sea Frontier, the east coast naval defenses. He had twenty ships, a few Army Air Corps planes, and a couple of Navy blimps. This group was only a token defense against U-boats. Of his "fleet" Andrews wrote, "There is not a vessel available that an enemy submarine could not outdistance when operating on the surface."

These vessels, all of which U-boats could not only outrun but outgun, included eight World War I Eagle boats (PE), eighteen submarine chasers (the older designations, SC and PC, including PC 449 which saw action[9]), eleven gunboats (PG), five river gunboats (PR), and miscellaneous government and private small craft and yachts.[10] The Maritime Commission accepted these privately owned vessels and began converting them into warships by installing on them machine guns, depth charges, and sound gear when they could find it. These yachts ranged from thirty-footers to some that were hundreds of feet in length. Commander Vincent Astor (USNR), the millionaire, marshaled fifty vessels through the Cruising Club of America. The larger craft that joined Admiral Andrews' fleet came from other wealthy owners. They included financier Robert Herrick, banker Arthur Lehman, Henry Ford, Huntington Hartford of A&P fame, Joseph Davies, Mrs. Jesse Hall Du Pont, and William Kissam Vanderbilt.

The yacht that Vanderbilt contributed surprised her new Lt. Skipper. Lying in his bed, he pressed a nearby button and stared in awe as a fully equipped bar slid from behind bulkhead paneling. Pleased by this revelation, he pressed a second button. To his amazement and embarrassment he found his bed transported next to the bed in the adjoining cabin — in which, snoring peacefully, was his executive officer.[11]

The First of the PCs

Fortunately, in 1938, President Roosevelt had authorized a program to develop two experimental steel-hulled submarine chasers. One would have a flush-deck and use steam turbines. The other one would have a raised forecastle deck and use Diesel engines.[12] From eleven proposals, the Navy selected Sidney A. Vincent at Newport News Shipbuilding to design the ship with the raised forecastle deck that became PC 451. C&R designed a flush deck ship, the first of which was PC 452. By 1940, after some experimentation, BuShips selected the flush-deck design, but powered it with twin Diesel engines and designated it the PC 452 class.[13] The firm that built the first ships was the Defoe Boat and Motor Works of Bay City, Michigan.

Defoe received the contract for PC 451 in 1939 and finished it, with Diesel engines for propulsion, on 12 August 1940. This ship, shown in Figure 1-3, had a raised forecastle deck. All other PCs, such as PC 471, which Defoe launched on 15 September 1941 and was in the PC 461 class, sported a flush-deck.[14] In 1941 the company that built the first of the new PCs changed its name to the Defoe Shipbuilding Company. Defoe then built PC 452 in late 1941, but with an experimental steam engine.

Designers expected that steam engines would drive PCs ten knots faster and make them more maneuverable than those with Diesel engines. Also, at this time, the Navy needed trained Motor Machinist Mates to man the growing submarine fleet whose boats were powered by Diesel engines. Using Diesels in the new PCs would drain the pool of Motor Machinist Mates needed for the submarines, so the Navy decided to try steam engines in a PC. The steam engine, however, consumed too much fresh water, and the evaporators installed in the PC could not operate adequately to supply enough make-up water. After further tests, the Navy decided that steam engines were not practical on a small ship like the PC. All other PCs built during World War II by the United States used Diesel engines for propulsion.

The Navy Ordered More PCs

Admiral Andrews' little fleet included the first two steel-hulled patrol craft, PC 451 and 471.[15] In late 1941 the PC 472 and PC 473, also built by Defoe, joined the patrol craft fleet. The Navy ordered sixty more of these PCs but did not expect them until late in 1942. Until then it continued to press into antisubmarine service yachts and fishing boats, jury-rigged with a light armament and a few depth charges. The Navy used them for ASW patrol not as merchant ship escorts. Most of these small craft were not sea worthy or stable. They wallowed in swells and staggered in heavy seas, so they hugged the shoreline and operated only in good weather. U-boats outmaneuvered and avoided them and inflicted heavy losses on unescorted merchant vessels.

New Submarine Chaser Designations

On 8 April 1943 the navy assigned new designations to the submarine chaser family of ships. From then on all submarine chasers with wooden hulls became SCs. The new ship type,[16] the 173-foot steel-hulled submarine chaser or patrol craft,[17] became PCs (Peter Charlie in the phonetic alphabet of the 1940s).[18] The Navy assigned the SCs and PCs numbers but not names. This lack of names for the ships aggravated many men who sailed and fought them. It was a case in which the Navy failed to account for the love of a sailor for his ship and the pride experienced in referring to its name.

PC Production

Soon, experienced workers, beginners, men exempt from service, and many women swarmed into the shipyards the Navy had selected to build PCs. These men and women toiled during three shifts seven days a week to mass-produce these desperately needed submarine chaser ships. Workers, engineers, and managers teamed up to build dozens of PCs in the time it took to build a destroyer.

These ships sported a complete battery of three-inch guns, 40-

mm and 20-mm machine guns, and depth charges to fight U-boats. Besides depth charge racks and K-guns on the PCs, early in 1943 the Navy began adding mousetraps. These weapons were two launching racks for eight ahead-thrown 60-pound bombs, with four bombs per rack. Each bomb was loaded with thirty-three pounds of TNT.[19] Figure 1-4 shows the bows of three PCs each with mousetraps on its forecastle.

Shipyards turned out PCs in large quantities, on occasions so fast that some ships lay idle waiting for engines. When the ships were ready, despite some inadequacies in design and construction, the Navy rushed them to sea. Often, they were not complete and ships' companies finished some work, but the ships went off on their missions. Along the Eastern Seaboard and in the Caribbean PCs patrolled for submarines and swept the ocean around convoys.

Allied nations also received some ships that United States shipyards built, including PCs, and the United States Navy built some PCs that it later transferred to other countries. By the end of World War II the Navy had built and commissioned 361 ships on PC hulls.[20]

The Turning Point

Early in 1943 the convoy tactic, use of air cover from escort aircraft carriers, improved radar, and more surface escorts, including PCs, changed the situation in the Atlantic. Nazi torpedoes sank fewer ships, and the United States and British forces at sea not only kept U-boats from attacking convoys, they became the hunters. An item from a Caribbean Base stated, ". . . as more and more of the tough little escort craft [PCs] became available in this convoy-crowded area fewer and fewer merchant vessels went to the bottom with torpedo-blasted hulls."[21] These escorts, including PCs, harassed and killed U-boats in increasing numbers.

Acknowledging this change in the battle, and because of the Soviet Union's desperate need for our lend-lease supplies, Dönitz shifted his attention back to the convoys that crossed the Atlantic Ocean. In particular, the U-boats concentrated on the supply route to the Soviet Union through the port of Murmansk. This time Dönitz introduced the U-boat Rudeltaktik or Wolf Pack tactic in which as many as ten submarines would converge on and simultaneously attack a convoy. Despite the initial successes of Wolf Packs, the Allied ASW forces overcame them and defeated the submarines.

March 1943 was the turning point in the Battle of the Atlantic. By May, United States and Allied forces killed U-boats and their crews faster than the Germans could replace them. By then the Nazis had lost 40% of their undersea fleet[22] as shown in Figure 1-5. The Allies had stilled the "beat of the drums" of Admiral Karl Dönitz who wrote later about that time, "We had lost the battle of the Atlantic."[23]

By May 1945, U-boats had sunk 2,882 Allied merchant ships. Especially in the early years of the war this destruction came close to defeating England. Churchill noted this fact when he wrote, "The battle of the Atlantic was the dominating factor all through the war." Despite their success in the early years of the war, however, of the 1,150 U-boats built and the 842 of them that saw combat, few survived. Allied forces sank 779 U-boats and captured two. German crews scuttled or surrendered the remaining boats. Of the 39,000 men who manned them 5,000 became prisoners and 28,000 died in their "Iron Coffins."

Allied Naval successes against the U-boats were not without cost. German submarines sank, along with the merchant ships, 175 warships and sent many uniformed sailors to watery graves. In addition, researchers have estimated that the Allies involved twenty-five ships and 100 aircraft in ASW operations for each German submarine that was at sea.[24]

Hitler's Blunder

By the end of World War II, most of Germany's U-boats had come into service too late to overpower the Allied ASW efforts.[25] They did not achieve the goal of Admiral Dönitz to defeat Great Britain with a submarine campaign. The problem was because Hitler and Dönitz had not counted on the rapid development and construction by the United States of small escort ships. The deployment of these PCs, and later the PCEs, PFs, and DEs, helped defeat Operation Paukenschlag. Hitler's delay of U-boat construction to match destroyer construction in the United States was one of his gravest mistakes.

PCs Did Their Part

The use of PCs as escorts for convoys probably saved many ships and merchant seamen's lives. Though they received credit for sinking three U-boats, they helped kill others, damaged more, and kept many from attacking the convoys they guarded. In 1944, Capt. S. G. Fuqua, Medal of Honor winner and survivor of USS *Arizona* at Pearl Harbor, then head of the Escort Vessel Administration in Miami, lauded PCs for the damage they were doing to the enemy. With prescience, he also predicted that PCs would play a big part in the final victory over the Axis powers. They did this in all theaters of war and on missions beyond those for which their designers had conceived them. Despite the successes of PCs, however, the United States Navy, the government, and journalists neglected them in their accounts of campaigns and battles. Because of this lack of recognition, the crews called themselves the "Forgotten Fleet."[26]

These little ships, and their predominantly Reserve crews, did what the Navy had designed and trained them to do. They fought U-boats along the east coast of the United States, from Tompkinsville on Staten Island, New York to Key West, Florida, into the Caribbean, and down to South America. Then, when the Battle of the Atlantic subsided, they sailed off to other waters to continue the fight.

Figure 1-1. World War II propaganda poster, "We Can Do It," by J. Howard Miller. Year unknown. Courtesy of J. D. Ross, WWII Propaganda Posters, http://home.fish.net.an/jd/posters.

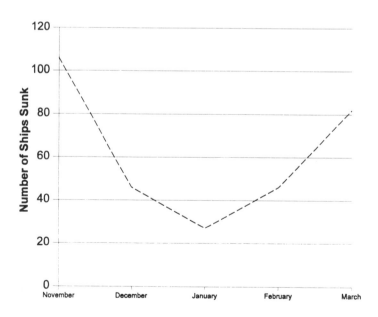

Figure 1-2. Allied ship losses in the Atlantic Ocean from November 1942 through March 1943.

Figure 1-3. PC 451 after completion. Photograph from Real War Photos.

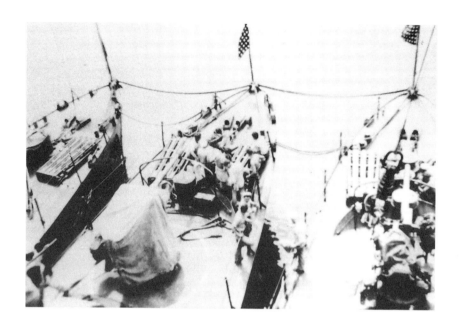

Figure 1-4. Three PCs showing the mousetraps on their forecastles.
Photograph courtesy of Ray Goin.

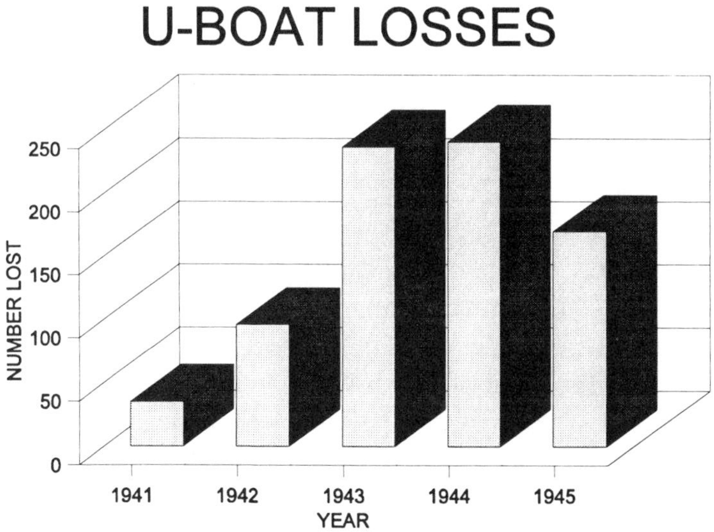

U-BOAT LOSSES

Figure 1-5. U-boat losses in World War II from 1941 through 1945.

CHAPTER 2

Design of PCs

The Navy Describes PCs

"These vessels have been designed for production in large numbers, yet of sufficient size and armament to carry an effective antisubmarine battery, and of such speed that they may perform escort and patrol tasks, relieving larger units for combat duties." This, in part, is how the United States Navy described PCs in 1942.[27] The comments continued. "Modern features of design, seaworthiness, speed, sound equipment, and maneuverability combine to make these vessels an excellent antisubmarine unit. . . . Submarine chasers [PCs] are excellent craft for A/S [Anti Submarine Warfare] operations. They are built for this single purpose. They can trail a submarine at its maximum speed. They have adequate communication facilities. They have been given the Navy's best sound equipment. . . . They are armed with guns suitable to combat a submarine on the surface. They are small and more maneuverable than a submarine. . . . Their size presents a small target for the submarine to evaluate."

These words gave an accurate portrait of PCs but it was a bit overblown from the point of view of the men who served on them. What was not accurate was the statement about combating a submarine on the surface. All hands on a PC feared such an encounter with a submarine. Most submarines mounted a gun that threw a shell farther and delivered a bigger wallop than did the 3-inch gun on a PC.

At close range, a submarine's bigger gun was deadly, and the submarine presented a small target to gunners on a PC. To counter this prospect of an unequal surface engagement, PC Skippers elected the tactic of charging toward a surfaced submarine to ram her. Slamming her bow into and ripping her keel over a submarine would damage the PC, but it could still stay afloat. On the other hand, a PC's peak tank and keel could collapse a submarine's conning tower and tear open the pressure hull of the submarine.

As stated in the Navy's description, PCs were fast and highly maneuverable. The writer of the Submarine Chaser Manual must have attributed these features to a PC's narrow beam, shallow draft, twin screws, and plenty of horsepower in its two Diesel engines. With the engines warm, a Skipper could ring up flank-speed from one-third speed and get to twenty-one knots in a couple of minutes. Then he could order, "Port ahead two-thirds. Starboard back two-thirds," and the craft would almost spin on an axis near the mast. In addition, PCs were seaworthy vessels, but they rolled, pitched, bounced, and flew like few other ships. Sailing a PC was, as their crews often bragged, "rugged duty." Samuel E. Morison wrote of the PCs,[28] "Their crews drove them to tasks far beyond their planned capacity, and under conditions of acute personal discomfort."

Design and Characteristics of PCs

A PC[29] distributed 450 tons along 173 feet 8 inches and, driven by twin screws, turned 21 knots at flank speed. For details see Appendix A. Figure 2-1 shows PC 461, the most typical class of PC. Figure 2-2 is a drawing of a PC. Figure 2-3 shows PC 543, which was in the PC 461 class but mounted a 3"-50 gun aft. For details of the design of PCs, when following the text in this chapter and elsewhere, the reader may refer to two sources. One is the thirty engineering drawings in Appendix B by Robert K. Baldwin, who was a nineteen-year-old sailor on PC 543. Another source is a set of plans by John Tombaugh for a PC, the information for which is in Appendix B.

Though the PC 461 class was designed for 20.2 knots, typical speeds of PCs were one-third speed 5 knots, two-thirds speed 12 knots, standard-speed 15 knots, full-speed 18 knots, and flank-speed 21 knots. Engineers squeezed another knot or two out of the ships with crow bars jammed in the engines' governors to hold back the revolving brass balls that limited the speed of the engines. This trick was not standard operating procedure (SOP) and was not done with the knowledge of the Officer Of the Deck (OOD) or the Engineering Officer. Nevertheless, it worked. Often when an emergency demanded extra speed, a liberty party was anxious to get ashore, or a couple of ships' Skippers drag-raced to port, the engineers hauled the crow bars out of the tool chests and applied their ingenuity.

The beam of a PC, near the bridge area was 23 feet, and it narrowed toward the stern. Her keel sank seven to ten feet below the water line. Fifty-three feet above the water, an inverted bell-jar-shaped, fiber, radar dome topped the raked mast. Early PCs, like many United States naval vessels, did not have radars, but the Navy installed them later. Different types of radars appeared, but on most PCs the radar was microwave type SG. Also, later in the war, the Navy installed LORAN navigation systems on many vessels including PCs.

Forecastle

Besides a windlass and other mooring gear, the forecastle of a PC held a 3"-50 gun and two racks of Mark XX mousetraps.[30] The 3"-50 gun was the United States Navy's standard, medium caliber, dual purpose weapon during World War II. It was singly mounted on an open pedestal, was fired manually, and used armor piercing, high explosive, and illuminating rounds. The mousetrap weapons were two fixed position launching racks for eight ahead-thrown 60-pound bombs, four bombs per rack, each bomb loaded with thirty-three pounds of TNT.[31] Typical launching racks are shown in Figure 1-4.

Rockets propelled the bombs to a range of 300 yards and for a flight time of eight seconds. The bombs landed in an elliptical pattern, armed as they descended, sank at a rate of twenty-two feet per second, and exploded on contact. These were fired when the ship came to an even keel position. Larger ships used Mark 10 Hedgehogs that were mounted on trunnions so they could be tilted to compensate for the roll of the ship.

Superstructure

The superstructure consisted of one almost rectangular structure. It housed the bridge (also called the pilot house), sonar gear, chartroom, radio shack, Yeoman's desk, ward room and pantry, a shipfitter's shack, and a one-man radar room. This room, which the radar operator jokingly called the Combat Information Center (CIC), was barely large enough for a console and a chair. The flying bridge, above the enclosed bridge, mounted a flag bag, halyards to run up signal flags, blinker lights, running lights, and three 20-mm Oerlikon antiaircraft machine guns. Details are shown in Figure 2-4 and Figure 2-5. Men on the flying bridge sought protection from wind behind canvas, chest-high, weather-cloths that wrapped around the forward part and the sides of the flying bridge. The cloths gave some defense against wind but not much against driving rain, snow, or sleet, or the waves that often broke over the flying bridge.

Bridge

The inside forward end of the superstructure housed the bridge with the wheel, a binnacle, an annunciator on the starboard side, a swivel chair for the OOD on the port side, and a log desk aft on the port side. Against the aft bulkhead on the starboard side sat the sound gear operated by a Soundman. Figure 2-6 shows the interior of the bridge. Shoulder-high steel shields protected the wings of the bridge, each of which held a pelorus for taking bearings, as shown in Figure 2-7. Officers conned the ship from the flying bridge in decent weather, but in the enclosed bridge otherwise. When coming alongside a dock or another ship, the conning officer often perched on the wing of the bridge on the mooring side of the ship.

Chart Room

A couple of steps down from the aft door of the bridge led to the chart room. This compartment housed the Yeoman's desk and file cabinet on the forward starboard side, the chart table aft of the desk, and the radio gear across from the chart table. A hatch between the Yeoman's desk and chart table opened to the weather deck. At the aft end of the compartment a door led to the ward room. To port a hatch opened to the ladder for below decks. These features made the chart room a cross roads area, and it was always one of the busiest places.

Ward Room

The ward room, aft of the chartroom, was the dining area and utility room for the officers. It also served as the Skipper's sea cabin. Here the "old man" (in his twenties) often stretched out on a leather sofa to grab a few minutes of rest, and with luck some sleep, while the OOD conned the ship. A dining table, barely large enough for five officers, a filing cabinet, safe, and several chairs completed the furnishings. On some ships, on one side of the table was a bench that made into a sofa and an upper bunk. To port and at the forward part of the ward room was the pantry. Here Officer's Steward Mates set out the officers' meals and perked strong pots of Joe, which filled the ward room with its fresh aroma. They lugged the officers' meals forward from the crew's galley in stacked steam pots.

Though the officers paid for their meals, most of the food the Stewards served them was the same as what the crew ate. Sometime the officers bought and kept private stores for themselves, but most often they had the same meals as the crews. Not always, though. On PC 617 during a long cruise in the Atlantic Ocean the cook used the last of the apples to make a few apple pies.[32] When the Stewards served the officers crushed pineapple for dessert one officer asked the Steward, "Mays, where is that apple pie I saw being baked in the galley?"

Mays stuck his head through the pantry opening and answered, "Sorry, sir, Cook says there ain't enough for the officers."

Outboard of the ward room area, on each side of the ship, hung a life raft and a first aid stretcher strapped to stanchions, ready for quick release. On the port side of the ward room a hatch opened to the deck. This hatch, like all topside exits to the deck, was rigged so that when opened the inside light turned off to keep the ship darkened at night. Red lights turned on in the ward room and other compartments when the white lights went out. Like on other ships, men who would stand watches on deck at night, and were exposed to white lights inside the ship, wore goggles with red lenses while inside to preserve their night vision.

Shipfitter's Shack

To starboard and aft of the ward room was the Shipfitter's shack, which was only large enough for a work bench with a vice, hand tools, and one person. Whoever worked there, straddled a hatch to the auxiliary engine room. Strapped to the outside bulkhead of the Shipfitter's shack were the gas bottles that fueled the Shipfitter's torches.

Deck Gear

The squat ventilator stack, aft of the superstructure, vented fresh air to the engine room and housed auxiliary machinery. Figure 2-8 is a sketch of that area. On deck behind the stack were a sixteen-foot wherry, two 20-mm Oerlikon antiaircraft machine guns, ammunition ready lockers, a 40-mm rapid fire Bofors gun, two depth charge K-guns, davits to lift depth charges, and two depth charge racks. A chest-high, steel, splinter shield or "gun tub" surrounded the Bofors. See Figure 2-9 for details. Outboard and aft of the 40-mm gun, the two K-guns exploded shells that lofted 300-pound teardrop depth charges into the air to port and starboard away from the ship. At the stern of the ship, on the fantail, stood two steel racks from which men rolled 600-pound "ash can" depth charges. A view of the stern of PC 546 is shown in Figure 2-10.

Below-Deck Compartments

Below the main deck, from bow to stern, were the peak tank, paint locker, crew's head, crew's quarters, ammunition storage spaces, fuel; oil; and water tanks, sound room, officers' staterooms, engine rooms, Gunner's area, mess hall and galley, depth charge storage compartment, and lazaret.

Designers seemed to have outfitted the crew's head on a PC for a crew of twenty, not sixty, enlisted men. It had two urinals, three seats, two showers, and three wash basins. Designers crammed all of this into a space so small that, when a different sailor used each of those stations simultaneously there was little room for anyone else in the compartment.

The crew's sleeping quarters were cramped. For example, the men of the deck department (all but the engineers and electricians), their double-deck bunks, lockers, foul weather gear, life jackets, battle helmets, canvas hammocks, and lumber for damage control shoring, were crammed into one compartment about twenty-five by fifteen by seven feet.

Officers fared better. They shared spaces the size of broom closets. Even the Captain's cabin was tiny, as shown in Figure 2-11, and he secured his privacy, not with a door on his room, only with a sliding curtain. Below the crew's area, the sound stack sat with its snout, the sound dome, that operators could extend out of the hull under the keel.

PCs did not carry much fresh water aboard (See Appendix A), and its priority was for use in the ship's machinery and for drinking and cooking. Designers had included evaporators, for distilling sea water to fresh water, in PC auxiliary engine rooms. Those evaporators worked in port, but at sea they did not work well under the severe rolling and pitching that the ships often endured. At sea, therefore, a ship's company could only wash its hands and teeth twice a day, and men rarely changed or took off clothing when they slept. After a few days it took a strong stomach to enter the crew's compartments, especially that of the engineers whose dungarees got soaked with oil and bilge water.

Engineering Spaces

Farther aft of officers' country, in the auxiliary engine room, two Diesel engines drove an electric generator each that fed a control panel to supply the ship's electricity. A ladder in front of the electrical control panel and next to a generator set rose to the hatch that opened into the Shipfitter's shack. This ladder was a favorite perch for a man on watch in the auxiliary engine room. He could sit on a rung, wedge his shoulders between the hand rails, and prop his feet on the generator. Doing this, he could ride out the motions of the ship without having to grasp handholds.

In the main engine room, two 1800 HP Hamilton (HOR), Fairbanks Morse, or General Motors Diesel engines drove twin screws, each with a hydraulic coupling and reduction gear. Figure 2-12, Figure 2-13, and Figure 2-14 show views of engine rooms. Figure 2-15 shows the propellers (screws), propeller guards, and other details. Appendix A lists characteristics of the propulsion system of a typical PC. The main engines belched their exhausts through the sides of the hull aft. Therefore, sailors called PCs "side burners." Other machinery in the engine room provided propulsion and services to fight the ship and give meager comforts to sixty enlisted men and five officers.[33]

40-mm Gun

Aft of the engine room hatch was the 40-mm Bofors gun in the circular chest-high splinter shield often called the gun tub. Clips of 40-mm ammunition were fastened to the inside of the gun shield, and men's helmets and telephone gear hung on the outside. When the 40-mm gun was not in use men huddled inside the gun tub as waves boiled over the deck of the ship and smashed against the metal. At night in port a sailor could scrunch down inside it and find a few moments of solitude on a vessel that was so crowded men never had privacy. Always, as they went about their duties or moved from one place to another aboard ship, they bumped and jostled each other. This happened even when the ship was tied to a dock.

Mess Hall and Galley

Immediately aft of the 40-mm gun was the entrance to the mess hall and galley, the interior of which is shown in Figure 2-16. The primary design purpose of the mess hall and galley was to provide a space for preparing and serving meals for the enlisted men. It also served as the social center for the crew. The mess hall held five long, green-topped tables bolted to the deck. These tables, with their attached benches, filled most of the space in the compartment. Fiddle boards hung from the edges of the tables. At sea the mess cooks raised them for almost every meal to keep food and utensils from sliding off the tables. Bunks for the Cook and mess cooks clung to the port and starboard bulkheads. Figure 2-17 shows men being served from buckets on one table and sitting at the other tables. Against the bulkhead are bunks in their triced up positions.

A metal cabinet on the forward bulkhead served as the pharmacy. The ship's store was usually a locker bolted to the bulkhead. From it, at designated times, the men could buy items for personal needs, say a pack of Lucky Strike cigarettes for ten cents or a bar of candy (pogey bait) for a nickel.

Gunner's Compartments

The next compartment aft was the gunner's area, where the Gunner's Mates kept small arms, ammunition, and other gear. They also had a small work bench on which they did minor repairs on the ship's weapons. This compartment was followed by the depth charge storage area.

Lazaret

The last compartment at the stern of the ship, the lazaret, contained the emergency steering mechanism, extra ship's lines, and other miscellaneous gear. Buried under this equipment one might also find a few cans of beer or bottles of liquor that sailors had smuggled aboard ship for emergencies.

General Appearance

Lines, life rafts, ammunition ready lockers, and upright canvas hatch-covers broke the otherwise smooth lines of the ship's flush-deck. PCs were sleek, simple, clean, uncluttered, and graceful. With a sharp prow, as seen in Figure 2-18, they looked like men-o-war, like small destroyers. Friedman wrote,[34] "It [the PC] was well liked because it handled like a destroyer." In 1942 in the Saturday Evening Post, the author of an article about PCs wrote,[35] "Actually, naval officers say, the PC has everything a 1905 destroyer had, barring torpedo tubes and a few knots of extra speed. . . ." This was not an exact comparison, but it conveyed the feeling many persons had about PCs.

PCs Justify Their Description and Design

PCs were sturdy and seaworthy. Design calculations predicted that PCs could roll 110 degrees and still right themselves. Many men who sailed them claimed that they came close to proving the calculations. PCs proved their seaworthiness in routine and in extreme operations. True to the Navy's description of their design, the Navy did produce PCs in large numbers, and the ships did carry the fight to enemy submarines. Not planned for or built into their "single purpose" design, however, were the varied and unexpected functions that area commanders assigned to them. Nor did their designers anticipate the various combat roles PCs played during and after World War II. PCs not only hunted and sank U-boats, they also stalked and destroyed Japanese submarines. As World War II progressed, the larger escort ships, such as PCEs, DEs, PFs, and DDs, slid down launching ways in greater numbers. They went to sea and joined the veteran PCs in herding convoys and prowling the oceans probing for submarines. When these larger ships took charge of the trans-ocean convoy work, the Navy released many PCs from these duties and assigned them to other important jobs. Chapters six, seven, eight, and nine contain some accounts of these activities.

Sailors who served on PCs griped about but took pride in their ships and believed that their ships would get them back safely from the sea. Most ships did that despite enemy torpedoes, shells, bullets, and bombs, and pounding seas, hurricanes, williwaws, and typhoons. PCs performed many combat roles under unusual and unexpected circumstances. They did this well and proved the wisdom and ingenuity of their design.

Figure 2-1. PC 461. Most PCs were of the 461 Class. U. S. Navy Photograph.

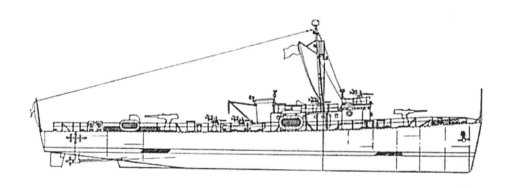

Figure 2-2. Profile Drawing of a PC.

Figure 2-3. PC 543. Many PCs mounted a 40-mm gun aft instead of a 3"-50.

Figure 2-4. PC 1264 on 25 April 1944. View of the flying bridge showing one 20-mm machine gun. This ship was commissioned with a black crew except for leading rates and officers. U. S. Naval Historical Center Photograph.

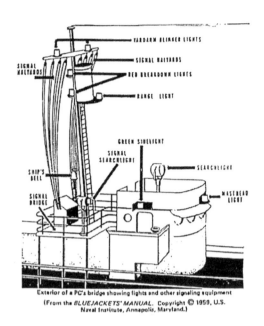

Exterior of a PC's bridge showing lights and other signaling equipment
(From the *BLUEJACKETS' MANUAL*. Copyright © 1959, U.S.
Naval Institute, Annapolis, Maryland.)

Figure 2-5. Sketch of the flying bridge of a PC showing lights and other signal equipment. The drawing is from *The Bluejackets' Manual*, U. S. Naval Institute, Annapolis, MD, 1959.

Figure 2-6. View of the bridge showing the wheel, binnacle, annunciator, overhead hand grips, voice tube, and other items on PC 820.
Photograph courtesy of George Fletcher and John Tombaugh.

Figure 2-7. Lt. George Fletcher, Commanding Officer, PC 820, sighting with a pelorus on the port wing of the bridge. Photograph courtesy of George Fletcher and John Tombaugh.

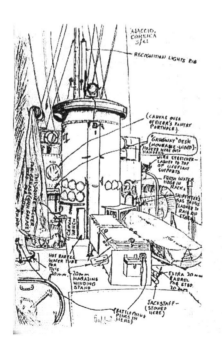

Figure 2-8. View of the stack and items aft of it. Drawing, about 1942, courtesy of Bob Baldwin.

Figure 2-9. View aft from the crow's nest of PC 779 underway. It shows two covered 20-mm guns, the 40-mm gun tub with helmets hung in place, the K-guns and their loading davits, two racks of depth charges, canvas-covered entrances to the engine room (forward of the 40-mm gun) and mess hall, and other details. Photograph courtesy of Arthur Fisher.

Figure 2-10. Stern View of PC 546 showing a camouflage pattern, ashcan depth charges in racks, stern light on flagstaff, and other details. National Archives photograph 80-G-K-13277, about 1942.

Figure 2-11. LT B. J. Belmore, Captain of PC 550 sitting at the desk in his stateroom. Photograph courtesy of B. J. Belmore.

Figure 2-12. Engine Room on PC 1191. The photograph was taken between the HOR engines looking aft. Under the gauge board in the center is a fire extinguisher. Photograph courtesy of Robert W. Daly, Sr..

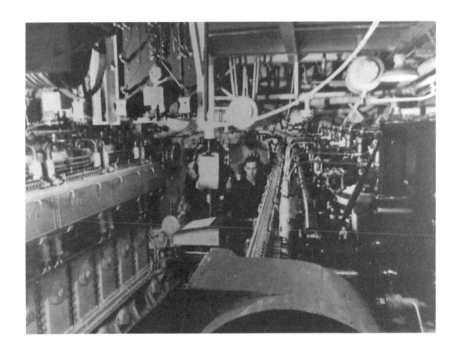

Figure 2-13. View of the engine room on PC 820 with HOR double-acting diesel engines. Photograph courtesy of George Fletcher and John Tombaugh.

Figure 2-14. View of the throttle station of an HOR engine on PC 793. Photograph from the author's collection.

Figure 2-15. PC 793 in dry dock in Adak, Alaska showing one shaft and screw. Photograph from the author's collection.

Figure 2-16. View looking aft in the mess hall showing the entrance ladder and other details. Drawing by Bob Baldwin in 1943 on PC 1181.

Figure 2-17. Crew members serving and eating chow in the mess hall of PC 548, circa 1942. Photograph from Real War Photos.

Figure 2-18. PC 820 in dry dock, about 1943, Adak, Alaska. Note the sleek prow, sound stack well back from the bow, mousetraps in raised position, crow's nest, and radar dome. Photograph courtesy of George Fletcher and John Tombaugh.

CHAPTER 3

The Construction of PCs

Sixteen Shipyards Built PCs

For five years, workers in sixteen shipyards around the United States labored to turn out PCs. Night and day, seven days a week, the shipyards glared red with welding torches and rattled with the roar of hammers and forges. The odors of ground metal and melting steel filled the air as men and women raced against time and the Nazi submarine offensive in the Atlantic Ocean to forge PCs. Appendix C contains a list of those shipyards that built PCs. Appendix D contains lists of ships that each shipyard built and includes their dates of keel laying, christening, launching, commissioning, and disposal.

On average, the target was for workers to build each PC in about six months, and they succeeded. At two shipyards, however, they bettered the construction targets by large margins. For example, workers at the Defoe Shipbuilding Company in Bay City, Michigan built PC 549 in three months and one day, and the staff at the Commercial Iron Works in Portland, Oregon finished PC 814 in three months and two days.[36] When the shipyard finished this ship on 19 April 1945 and the navy commissioned it on 5 June 1945, the Navy completed the construction program that it had started in 1939. Though the highest number PC commissioned during World War II was PC 1603, the PC 814 was the last of the World War II PCs the Navy commissioned.

Shipyard workers (called yard birds by sailors) welded PCs together on the Atlantic, Gulf, and Pacific coasts. Also, they built them two thousand miles from the oceans and eight hundred feet above sea level on the Great Lakes and other inland waters in Michigan, Wisconsin, and Tennessee. Other states in which workers built PCs during World War II were, in alphabetical order, Connecticut, Delaware, Florida, Indiana, Massachusetts, New Jersey, New York, Oregon, Pennsylvania, and Texas. Men and women labored in the shipyards night and day through blistering, humid, summer days and frigid, below-zero, winter nights. Ships that workers constructed inland floated or steamed on their own power to the Gulf of Mexico and then into the Atlantic Ocean. For many of these oceangoing ships, the fresh water of the Great Lakes and the muddy Mississippi River were the first waters to wash their keels.

The Birthplace of PCs

The World War II program of construction of the steel-hulled PCs started at the Defoe Shipbuilding Company in Bay City, Michigan. See Figure 3-1. In the summer of 1939 Harry J. Defoe, shown in Figure 3-2, who had started the shipyard[37] in 1905, signed a contract with the Navy for a little more than one million dollars.[38] With this money he completed PC 451 in August 1940 at a cost of $530,000.[39] It had high-forecastle, broken-deck lines and two Diesel engines for propulsion. Figures 3-3, 3-4, 3-5, and 3-6 show views of PC 451 under various stages of construction.

Soon after it placed that order, the Navy gave Defoe another award to build PC 452. This ship had a flush-deck design and had two experimental steam engines for propulsion. This flush-deck design became the hull configuration that the Navy adopted for all other PCs. All later PCs, despite who built them, had the flush-deck design. The picture of PC 551 in Figure P-5 shows an early model of a flush-deck ship. Figure 3-7 of PC 1603, the highest numbered PC, shows the latest model.

Because the Defoe Shipbuilding Company in Bay City,

Michigan built the first steel-hulled PCs, it is considered the birthplace of World War II PCs. Not only did Defoe build the first two World War II type PCs, but constructed more PCs during the war than did any of the other fifteen shipyards.

Though Defoe received contracts for seventy-three more PCs, the navy canceled seventeen of them in 1943. By the end of the war, Defoe had built fifty-eight PCs. Some of them displayed signs that the local people had paid for them with War Bond purchases. For example, Figure 3-8 shows PC 1141, for which the people of Wyandotte, Michigan paid.

PC 452 — USS Teakettle

With PC 452, the Navy learned that steam engines did not lend themselves to operation in small ships like PCs. The PC 452 was a failure, and the Navy canceled the experiment with steam engines. Because of the erratic operation of the steam plant in PC 452, the ship earned the nickname, "The Flying Teakettle." John W. (Jack) Hazard, the skipper of PC 452 said, ". . . when the PC 452 joined a convoy, the convoy was supposed to protect them!" Hazard wrote a story about the ship for the New Yorker Magazine.[40] In 1951, the 20th Century Fox Film Corporation made a movie from Hazard's story. It is titled "You're In The Navy Now" and stars Gary Cooper, Ray Collins, Jane Greer, Eddie Albert, Jack Webb, Lee Marvin, Harry Von Zell, and Charles Bronson. Hollywood used the designation for the secret project "Project XP11204," shot scenes on board PC 1168, and showed views of her when underway. This film is the only moving picture record of a PC known to the author.

Defoe Built PCs Upside Down

Harry Defoe deserves much of the credit for developing the methods of construction of PCs used by his and other shipyards. He adopted and introduced into PC construction the "upside down" or "rollover" technique by which welders worked "down hand" instead of up over their heads. Normally welders took a few years to become competent "overhead" welders. They only needed a few months to learn to weld "down hand." This saved time in training shipyard workers and in construction of the ships. With this method, workers assembled the main deck first on a hinged platform. Then they completed welding the hull upside down onto the deck of the ship.

Shipyards fabricated the hulls of PCs from 5/16 inch welded steel plate. Crews joked that this thin hull was, "Just thick enough to keep out the water and small fish." They also said it protected the ship from tin fish — torpedoes. "Her hull's so thin a tin fish can go right through without exploding," a Gunner's Mate said to comfort a young Seaman. PC 558 disproved that theory, though, off Anzio in May 1944. A Nazi U-boat rammed a torpedo into her guts and sent her down with the loss of many hands.[41]

This "upside down" procedure also let workers weld and lay piping and wiring down rather than overhead. After the hull took shape, the keel came last. Workers then lowered one half of the hinged platform, secured two large wheels to the hull, and rolled it upright. Figures 3-9, 3-10, 3-11, and 3-12 illustrate the procedure. The hull of the PC then started moving along an assembly line, and with the help of cranes the builders installed interior components, engines, and machinery. Later, workers added sound gear, galley fixtures, superstructure, ready lockers, rigging, weapons, and other equipment. Steel workers prefabricated many of those components in places like Gary, Indiana and shipped them by rail to the shipyards. Workers lowered them in place using cranes and welded them to the deck of the ship.

At the end of the assembly line, the ship moved to a launching platform from which workers launched the PC by sliding it sideways into the water. During the peak period of activities at Defoe, along with completing a destroyer escort (DE) every three weeks, the shipyard also finished a PC every week. In many cases, workers at the shipyards needed a little more than a month from the start of construction to the launching of a PC hull.

PCs Started With a Splash

A PC launching ceremony was not the most ornate or the flashiest affair the Navy conducted. Typically the Navy allowed only $25 for the ceremony that included costs for a modest amount of bunting, a public address system, and one bottle of champagne.[42] When launched, many PCs slid off their ways sideways with the squeal of metal on wood, the sweet aroma of champagne that dripped from their bows, and the stench of hot wood and burning grease. They tossed tons of spray skyward as they struck the water with a roar as shown in Figure 3-13 for the launching of the first PC. When they hit the water, the ships heeled sixty or more degrees. Men aboard during the launching grasped handholds and rode the ships like bucking broncos like those men in Figure 3-14.

Sixty-Degree Rolls Became Routine

At sea, this rolling motion to sixty or more degrees from vertical became routine to the crews who later sailed the ships. Design figures allowed for the ships to roll 110 degrees with the deck slanting inward twenty degrees past vertical. Calculations predicted that they would right themselves from that orientation.[43] Many PCs taxed the credentials of the designers with rolls that drove the little ships close to their beam ends. Some PC clinometers were graduated to 47 degrees, and often their arrows pegged against their detents. The ships endured the North Atlantic winter gales, Pacific typhoons, Aleutian williwaws, and Caribbean hurricanes. They also rode the mountainous waves and frigid blasts of winds off the Bering Sea that cascaded fifty foot waves onto the ships. Not one PC capsized. Their designers were correct and made accurate calculations, and the builders of PCs did their work with competence.

The Navy Lauded PC Construction

An item in the Bay City News dated August 8, 1942 illustrated the competence of the builders of PCs. The article described a visit to the Defoe Shipyard Company by Rear Admiral Alexander H. Van Kuren, Chief of the Navy Bureau of Ships. After he inspected the facility, the admiral said, "The Defoe product [PCs] is proving very satisfactory to operating forces of the fleet. We want all we can get of this type of craft in the quickest time possible."

Construction Was Not Always Complete

Because of the need for emergency production of PCs and Admiral Van Kuren's observation that the Navy wanted all the PCs it could get and in the shortest time possible, shipyards ground them out. They worked so fast that sometimes completed PCs stacked up in shipyards awaiting engines or other equipment.

The navy forced many PCs to sea improperly equipped or barely completed. Sailors not only manned, sailed, and fought their ships, they often even finished their construction while underway. Some ships had defective machinery, inadequate welds in bulkheads, or other problems. In one case of a PC overseas, the starboard Diesel engine began overheating. The engineers could not diagnose the problem. Then, during an inspection of the interior of the crankcase a Motor Machinist's Mate discovered, partially clogging the oil line filter and reducing oil flow to the cylinders, a pair of silk, lady's panties. The engineers displayed them in the engine room and often debated how they got in the engine.

Though at times deficiencies crept in, they did not keep the ships from going to sea. This problem of ships being incomplete in all respects was not one of oversight by the Navy or negligence by the shipyards and workers. It was because the Navy had to meet condensed rigid schedules for integrating hulls, machinery, armament, training and assigning of crews, commissioning of vessels, and rapid deployment of the ships to the fleet.

PCs Were Not Clones

The ship type, typical of most PCs, was PC 461 class as

shown in Figure 2-1. This class used hull numbers 461-1569, with the exceptions shown in Appendix A. Other classes of PCs include those listed in Appendix A. Modifications in PCs varied among those built at different shipyards and at the same yard over time. These modifications, however, did not affect the basic structure of the hull, superstructure, and machinery. Some of these changes included:

     1. a 3"-50 gun forward and a Bofors 40-mm gun aft instead of two 3"-50 guns

     2. 3"-23 guns instead of 3"-50 guns

     3. two 40-mm guns instead of one or two 3" guns

     4. hedgehogs, mousetraps, or mortars on the bow

     5. one, two, or four depth charge K-guns aft

     6. a 16 foot wherry with an outboard motor,

     7. other kinds of ship's boats,

     8. .30 or .50 caliber machine guns instead of or in addition to 20-mm machine guns,

     9. fewer than five 20-mm guns,

     10. twin 20-mm guns, and

     11. no radar or different models of radar atop the mast.

Photographs in this book of different PCs show most of these modifications.

The PC Construction Program

     Throughout the war the Navy identified, for construction, the hull numbers for 1,142 PCs.[44] As the shipbuilding and PC building program progressed, the United States Government canceled, converted, reclassified, and transferred some of these hull numbers. The Navy used some of these numbers for SC, PCE, and PCS type ships. The result was that the Navy built 361 as PC type ships. Of these ships, the Navy commissioned 319 as PCs at an average cost of $1,600,000 each.[45] Other estimates for the cost of a PC hull and fittings, minus engines and ordnance, range between $620,000 and $650,000.[46] Table 3-1 contains a list of man-hours proposed at the Defoe Shipyard for the construction of the second group of ten PCs on 26 January 1946.[47] This order was after World War II,[48] but it provides guidelines to the man hours needed to build a PC during World War II. The total average number of man-hours for the ten PCs is 117,326 per ship.

Table 3-1. Proposed Man-Hours for Ten PCs in 1946

ITEM	MAN-HOURS
Drafting	3,500
Model	—
Molds	1,500
Patterns	—
Yard Development	—
Supervision	44,760
Inspection	4,500
TOTAL HOURS	54,260
Direct labor by ship number after the first ten ships	
11	119,000
12	118,000
13	115,000
14	114,000
15	113,000
16	110,000
17	109,000
18	108,000
19	107,000
20	106,000

TOTAL DIRECT LABOR FOR TEN SHIPS	1,119,000
TOTAL DIRECT LABOR PER SHIP (AVERAGE)	111,900
TOTAL LABOR FOR TEN SHIPS	1,173,260
TOTAL LABOR PER SHIP (AVERAGE)	117,326

The Navy converted twenty-four PC hull numbers and commissioned them as patrol motor gunboats (PGM), and it converted eighteen of them into minesweepers (AM). Other ships were converted to control vessels (PCCs). Later, some of the converted ships were reconverted back to PCs. The United States also transferred some ships to allied nations during and after World War II. The details about the numbers of ships built, commissioned, and converted, taken from CDR Mann, are shown in Table 3-2. The numbers of ships built that are quoted by other sources are given in Appendix E. Figure 3-15 shows the number of PCs commissioned by year and month.

Table 3-2. PC Construction Program

CATEGORIES	NUMBER OF PCs
PC hull numbers originally identified	1142
PC hull numbers canceled or converted	781
Ships built on PC hulls	361
PC hulls commissioned as PCs	319
Ships converted from PC to PGM and commissioned as PGM	24
Ships converted from PC to AM and commissioned as AM	18
AMs reconverted to PCs then to PCCs	2
Ships converted from PC to PCC but commissioned as PC	32
AMs reconverted to PCs	16
Ships commissioned as PCs but converted to auxiliaries	3

PCs transferred to Allied nations during World War II	45
PCs transferred to Allied nations after World War II	110

Some PCs Became Motor Gunboats

In December 1943 when the Navy began converting some PCs into PGMs, during their construction, PC 1548 was the first ship the Navy changed. It became PGM 9. These converted ships retained most of the PC configuration inside but differed from PCs topside. PGMs had an open bridge made of armor plate. Armor plate, 3/4 inch thick, also covered the sides of the hull over the fuel tanks and the engine room, from above the main deck to two feet below the water line. The Navy removed the sonar, depth charge racks, K-guns, and mousetraps from the PGMs. The 3"-50 gun, six 20-mm guns, and one twin 40-mm gun were protected by steel splinter shields. Some of these ships also mounted a .50 cal. machine gun, a 60-mm mortar, and a rocket launcher aft. Figure 3-16 shows the former PC 1568 as PGM 32. Those PC hulls that the Navy converted to patrol motor gunboats (PGM) are shown in Table 3-3.

Table 3-3. PC Hull Numbers that Became Patrol Gun Boats (PGMs)

PC NUMBER	PGM NUMBER
PC 805	10
PC 806	11
PC 1088, PC 1089, PC 1090, PC 1091	12-15
PC 1148	16
1189	17
1255	18
1548	9

1550-59	19-28
1565-68	29-32
TOTAL	**24**

Some PCs Became Minesweepers (AMs)

Early in 1942 the Navy also needed minesweepers, so it converted eighteen PC hulls and commissioned them as Minesweepers (AM). Trawl gear and other mine sweeping equipment replaced the depth charge racks on the sterns of the ships. These converted vessels were poorly designed for mine sweeping, especially for storing aboard and towing trawl gear and paravanes. Another limiting factor was that the narrow hull of a PC near its stern did not provide adequate operating space to handle the sweep gear. These Minesweepers did limited service, and by 1944 the Navy converted them back to their original designation as PCs. Those ships numbered AM 82 through AM 95 used 1,700 HP Cooper Bessemer Diesel engines, and the others used 1,400 HP Alco Diesels. Neither of these engines powered the ships adequately for typical PC duties. Table 3-4 shows those sixteen PCs that the Navy converted to Minesweepers and then back to PCs and the two that it converted to PCs and then to patrol control ships, PCCs.

Table 3-4. PCs Converted to Mine Sweepers (AMs).

PC Number	AM Number	AM Name
1586	82	*Adroit*
1587	83	*Advent*
1588	84	*Annoy*
1589	85	*Conflict*

1590	86	*Constant*
1591	87	*Daring*
1592	88	*Dash*
1593	89	*Despite*
1594	90	*Direct*
1595	91	*Dynamic*
1596	92	*Effective*
1597	93	*Engage*
1598	94	*Excel*
1599	95	*Exploit*
1600	96	*Fidelity*
1601	97	*Fierce*
1602	98	*Firm*
1603	99	*Force*
TOTAL	**18**	

Some PCs Became Control Craft (PCCs)

Thirty-two PCs that the Navy commissioned as PCs became patrol control craft (PCC) and two that they commissioned as AMs became PCs and then PCCs for use in amphibious invasions. Because the PCCs carried additional communications equipment, they had to have larger crews, including eight Radiomen, two extra Signalmen, one extra Quartermaster, and two communication officers. To accommodate the larger crews they had more berths built in than did the standard PCs. The 20-mm gun on the flying bridge was removed to add room for signal equipment and more personnel. Near the end of the war the Navy replaced some single 20-mm guns on the PCCs with twin 20-mm guns.

Of these ships, sixteen reverted to PCs. During the conversions from PC to PCC and back to PC the ships retained their original PC hull numbers. These ships are listed in Table 3-5.

Table 3-5. Ships Commissioned as PCs and Converted to PCCs

PC Number	Disposition
462	Remained as a PCC. Sent to Maritime Commission.
463	Remained as a PCC. Sunk as a target.
469	Remained as a PCC. Sunk as a target.
549	Remained as a PCC. Sent to Maritime Commission.
555	Remained as a PCC. Sold.
563	Remained as a PCC. Sold.
578	Remained as a PCC. Sold.
582	Reconverted to a PC. Sent to Venezuela.
589	Reconverted to a PC. Sold.
598	Remained as a PCC. Sold.
802	Reconverted to a PC. Sent to Korea.
803	Remained as a PCC. Sent to Maritime Commission.
804	Remained as a PCC. Sent to Maritime Commission.
807	Remained as a PCC. Sent to Maritime Commission.
1079	Reconverted to a PC. Stricken.
1080	Remained as a PCC. Sold.

1081	Reconverted to a PC. Sold.
1125	Reconverted to a PC. Sold.
1126	Remained as a PCC. Destroyed.
1127	Remained as a PCC. Sent to Maritime Commission.
1136	Reconverted to a PC. Sold.
1137	Reconverted to a PC. Sold.
1168	Sent to China. Reconverted to a PC.
1169	Reconverted to a PC. Sent to China.
1177	Reconverted to a PC. Disposed of.
1178	Reconverted to a PC. Disposed of.
1180	Reconverted to a PC. Disposed of.
1230	Reconverted to a PC. Sold.
1231	Reconverted to a PC. Sold.
1244	Reconverted to a PC. Sold.
1251	Reconverted to a PC. Sold.
1260	Reconverted to a PC. Sold.
1599[49]	Remained as a PCC. Sent to Maritime Commission.
1601	Remained as a PCC. Sent to Maritime Commission
TOTAL	**34**

Some PCs Went to Allied Countries

In addition to the PCs used by the United States Navy, allies of the United States welcomed forty-five PCs into their navies during World War II under the Lend-Lease and other Programs as listed in Table 3-6.

Table 3-6. PCs Transferred to Other Countries During WWII

COUNTRY	NUMBER OF SHIPS
Brazil	8
France	33
Greece	1
Netherlands	1
Norway	1
Uruguay	1
TOTAL	**45**

After World War II the United States gave or sold 110 of the World War II PCs to other countries as shown in Table 3-7.

Table 3-7. PCs Transferred to Other Countries After WWII

COUNTRY	NUMBER OF SHIPS
Indochina then Cambodia	3
Chile	1
China	23
Cuba	1
Dominican Republic	3
France	4
Greece	6
Indonesia	5
Korea	7
Mexico	10

Philippines	9
Portugal	6
Spain	1
Taiwan	5
Thailand	8
Venezuela*	12
Indochina then Vietnam	6
TOTAL	**110**

* Friedman includes PC 1251 for 13 ships. Mann lists this ship as "sold" on 5/18/61.

Summary

When Nazi submarines struck the East Coast during 1941 and threatened England's existence, the United States Navy needed escort ships to guard convoys of merchant ships. To get them in a hurry, the government opted for small ships that shipyards could build quickly. Some of these ships were PCs. Owners of and workers at sixteen shipyards throughout the country recognized the importance of getting these ships to sea. They plunged in and labored around the clock to produce them. Through initiative, industrial knowhow, imagination, and hard work they ground out PCs on and ahead of schedules. Designers and workers had made these ships sturdy, reliable, and seaworthy so that they did their jobs with success. Though not large vessels, they comprised a sizeable fleet of ships that spanned the world's oceans and helped defeat the Axis forces.

Figure 3-1. The Defoe Shipbuilding Company, about 1940. Photograph Courtesy of the Institute for Great Lakes Research, Bowling Green State University.

Figure 3-2. Harry Defoe is on the left (striped tie). On the far right is Glen MacDonald, Editor, Bay City Times. The other men are probably from the Post Newspaper. Photograph Courtesy of the Institute for Great Lakes Research, Bowling Green State University. Identification of persons was by courtesy of Wm. Defoe in a private communication.

Figure 3-3. PC 451 under construction at the Defoe Boat and Motor Works, 15 February 1940. Photograph Courtesy of the Institute for Great Lakes Research, Bowling Green State University.

Figure 3-4. PC 451 under construction at the Defoe Boat and Motor Works, 9 May 1940. Photograph courtesy of the Institute for Great Lakes Research,Bowling Green State University.

Figure 3-5. PC 451 near completion at the Defoe Boat and Motor Works, 1940. Photograph courtesy of the Institute for Great Lakes Research, Bowling Green State University.

Figure 3-6. Shipboard bow view of PC 451 near completion at the Defoe Boat and Motor Works, May 23, 1940. Photograph, Negative 14, Courtesy of the Institute for Great Lakes Research, Bowling Green State University.

Figure 3-7. PC 1603, built by the Penn-Jersey Corporation, Camden, NJ originally as USS *Force* (AM 99). She was commissioned on 16 June 1943, the last PC commissioned during World War II. A Japanese suicide plane damaged the ship, and it was destroyed in October 1945. Note the mousetraps in firing position, and no weather cloths on the flying bridge. US Navy Photograph N - 142878 dated 6/13/44.

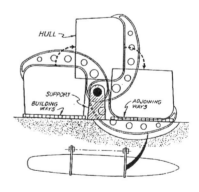

Figure 3-8. PC 1141 on the Ways at the Defoe Shipbuilding Co. on June 1943. The plaque on the bow reads, "This Fighting Ship Sponsored and Made Possible by War Bond Purchases of the People of Wyandotte, Michigan." Photograph from Real War Photos.

Figure 3-9. Sketch showing the rollover technique introduced by Harry Defoe. Drawing made by and courtesy of Robert Baldwin.

Figure 3-10. Destroyer Escort (DE 702) upside down with rollers in place at the Defoe Shipbuilding Company. Photograph courtesy of the Institute for Great Lakes Research, Bowling Green State University.

Figure 3-11. DE 702 during the rollover at the Defoe Shipbuilding Company. Photograph Courtesy of the Institute for Great Lakes Research, Bowling Green State University.

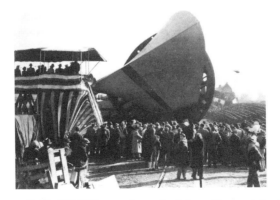

Figure 3-12. DE 702 near the end of the rollover at the Defoe Shipbuilding Company. Photograph Courtesy of the Institute for Great Lakes Research, Bowling Green State University.

Figure 3-13. Sideways launching of PC 451 on 23 May 1940 at the Defoe Boat and Motor Works. Photograph Courtesy of the Institute for Great Lakes Research, Bowling Green State University.

Figure 3-14. Sideways launching of PC 1174 on 22 July 2943 at the Latham D. Smith Shipyards, Sturgeon Bay, Wisconsin. Photograph courtesy of W. L. Nimick and the Institute for Great Lakes Research, Bowling Green State University.

PCs COMMISSIONED

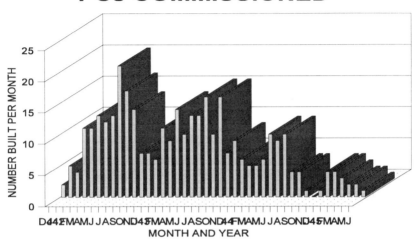

Figure 3-15. Construction of PCs by month from December 1941 through June 1945.

Figure 3-16. PGM 32 converted from the hull number for PC 1568 shown outfitting in New Orleans early in 1945. Photograph courtesy of Brainard J. Belmore.

CHAPTER 4

PC Crews and Their Training

Reservists and Ninety Day Wonders

Most of the enlisted men and commissioned officers who served on PCs were Naval Reservists. They were new to the Navy and had little or no sea duty. Many, however, had been through various training schools and activities, and some had been aboard training ships for a few days. A few of the leading rated men of the commissioning crews were regular Navy men, or Reservists with previous sea duty. Appendix F contains a list of the various rates of enlisted men aboard a PC. These leading rated men served as on-the-job instructors and "sea lawyers" for the rest of the crew, both enlisted men and officers.

Overall, the young lower rated and non rated men gladly accepted the help of these experienced sailors to learn more about their jobs. They also learned from the "old salts" that there are three ways to do things; "the right way, the wrong way, and the Navy way."

Even many officers, the famous "ninety-day wonders," were fresh from civilian jobs or college studies unrelated to naval issues and had much to learn. Most of them knew their limitations as naval officers and understood that they lacked seagoing knowledge. They were happy to get whatever assistance they could from the senior enlisted men to learn and to do their jobs. These "wonders" learned fast and became competent sailors and able leaders.

Many regular Navy men, when assigned to a PC, showed disappointment or resentment when the Navy did not assign them to a capital ship. Some regulars feared that duty on a PC would take them away from combat and would diminish their naval career prospects. After they got to know their small ship, its informality, the excellent prospects for promotion, and the chance to make close friends they felt better about their assignment. Then later, after putting some blue water under its keel, they respected the ship's design, seaworthiness, and functionality. Once they sailed her through heavy seas and battled storms that sailors on larger ships feared, they developed confidence in their ship. Many of them found plenty of combat action and at closer range to the enemy than if they had been on larger ships. These men took pride in their duty as subchasers as shown in Figure 4-1. They developed a team spirit that did not always exist on larger ships.

The Donald Duck Navy

Most of the men and officers, Reservists and regulars, on PCs served with pride in what they called the "Donald Duck Navy." The origin of that epithet "Donald Duck Navy" is obscure. An early use of the symbol of Donald Duck on a PC was by Jim Dickie, a Signalman on PC 564, which the Navy later named USS *Chadron*. He painted the "Fighting Donald Duck," shown in Figure 4-2, on the starboard wing of the bridge.[50] Similarly the Storekeeper on PC 546 painted on his ship a Donald Duck as a sailor in the crow's nest. Figure 4-3 shows this symbol and various insignia sported by other ships.[51]

Though PC sailors gloried in calling themselves Donald Duck sailors, they took offense when big ship sailors referred to them that way. They sensed that other sailors used the expression as one of ridicule. They felt the same way about people calling their ships, boats, though they used that term themselves. It was the classic Navy response of a sailor. "Don't call my friggin boat no friggin boat."

Early ASW Training

Crews for the new PCs needed the usual training in how to operate, maintain, and fight a Navy ship, but the primary, initial, intended mission of PCs was to hunt and sink German submarines. For this mission the Reserve crews needed specific training in antisubmarine warfare (ASW). With the rapid and steady buildup of the United States Navy, sailors flooded into and overtaxed the existing naval training stations and schools. This was especially true of ASW training stations. These facilities included the Atlantic Fleet Sound School at New London, Connecticut (later moved to Key West in September 1940) and the West Coast Sound School at San Diego, California. Men also trained at Quonset, Bermuda, Guantanamo, Coco Solo, Trinidad, and Recife. No other schools were available primarily for training subchaser crews.

Many enlisted men and officers who were already manning other ships at sea on escort and convoy duty did not have specific ASW training. They guarded convoys and hunted submarines with limited knowledge of the tactics needed to find and attack submarines. To inform them how to hunt and kill U-boats, the Navy relied upon distribution to its ships of its monthly publication titled the "Anti-submarine Warfare Bulletin." In practice, many sound operators reacted to false echoes, and their ships attacked different kinds of sea life. To help lessen these false alarms, the Bulletin even included articles on the locations and habits of cetaceans and crustaceans.[52]

The Submarine Chaser Manual

More specific information on and training in ASW tactics, than sailors could learn from the Bulletin, had to be given to men in the fleet and especially to submarine chaser crews. Some men who were with the fleet, the Navy recycled through New London or San Diego for refresher training. However, those facilities could not handle the large number of men that the Navy was assigning to newly constructed ships such as PCs.

To train these men the Navy needed a large, specialized, dedicated facility. So, in 1942 the Navy organized a rapid training program in ASW and prepared a "restricted" textbook to accompany the program. The Navy titled the textbook, *The Submarine Chaser Manual*[53] and, on 1 September 1942, issued it to ships and to commissioned officers ashore. Secretary of the Navy Frank Knox wrote in the Manual, identifying its purpose to the readers, "Your duty is to relentlessly hunt out and destroy enemy U-boats." He added, "You have excellent vessels, well equipped to accomplish this task."

The Table of Contents of the manual included the topics:

1. Ships' organization
2. Engineering
3. Gunnery
4. Sound
5. Attack doctrine and tactics
6. Escort Patrol Ship handling
7. Maintenance
8. Qualifications of the Naval Officer
9. The Laws of the Navy.

The Submarine Chaser Training Center Opened

Besides writing *The Submarine Chaser Manual,* naval leaders established a new training base for those sailors who would man the new subchaser fleet. In Miami, Florida, a locale up to that time reserved for wealthy men's yachts and sport fishing boats, the Navy selected a new site for an ASW training center. This activity would supplement the other antisubmarine warfare and sound schools in New London, San Diego, and elsewhere.

The Navy set up and commissioned this new facility in Miami, Florida on 26 March 1942.[54] They named it the Submarine Chaser Training Center (SCTC). The main building is shown in Figure 4-4. Sometime later, the center even adopted, unofficially, the Donald Duck insignia on its letterheads as shown in Figure 4-5. Here at SCTC, the Navy proposed to train men and officers for duty aboard submarine chasers.

Eugene McDaniel Became the Commanding Officer

For commanding officer of SCTC, the Navy selected then Lt. Eugene Field McDaniel, USN, Annapolis, 1927.[55] See Figure 4-6. Thin, ascetic, with glasses, he, ". . . looks like a professor but fights like a pirate. . . .," A journalist[56] wrote about SCTC's prospective commanding officer. McDaniel had just come ashore after a rough wintertime tour of North Atlantic escort duty aboard the destroyer USS *Livermore*. When informed of his selection as CO of this new center, he grumbled to Washington that he would rather be at sea. He knew, though, from first-hand encounters with U-boats, the importance of the job the Navy asked him to do, so he acquiesced. He understood the danger and had seen the fury of the Nazi submarine onslaught and did not want to waste time getting trained crews to sea to sink U-boats. In his blunt and direct manner he announced to the Navy brass in Washington, "If I'm the man for the job then let's get on with it." Navy brass, though taken aback by his demand, agreed with him.

McDaniel stormed into Miami in March 1942, and, without a "By your leave," threw out a civilian merchant's produce that lay stored on Pier Two. This site was the one the Navy had assigned for the school. The pier was his. There's a war on, he reminded the irate merchant.

Next, he shipped back three of six officers that the Navy had assigned to him. He demanded that Washington take them back, do not send any more, and let him choose his own staff and instructors. Only the most skilled and devoted men would do, he decided. Bureau of Personnel (BUPERS) staffers complied with his order. After he convinced himself that he had cleared the decks with the civilians and the Navy command, the brash Lieutenant accepted his assignment. On 8 April 1942, he assumed command of SCTC with an initial class of fifty trainees. That was a black day for Adolph Hitler, German Admiral Karl Dönitz, thousands of U-boat sailors, and Japan as well.

The Bullet-Riddled Lifeboat

McDaniel later obtained the ranks of Lieutenant Commander, Commander, and subsequently that of Captain. His zeal and devotion to duty, development of a rapid and thorough training program, and hatred of Nazis U-boat Skippers became legendary. A ship he was on in the Atlantic had rushed to the rescue of a sunken British ship. Lookouts spotted a lifeboat from the ship adrift. It was riddled with bullet holes, splattered with blood, and crammed with dead sailors. This vivid image outraged him and seared itself on his memory. He burned with the desire to destroy the men who had machine-gunned those helpless merchant sailors. On the SCTC grounds, he displayed a lifeboat drilled through with bullet holes and splotched with blood stains. See Figure 4-7. For this exhibit he earned the nickname, "Old Blood and Guts," but trainees at SCTC always viewed the boat with respect. McDaniel used the lifeboat to suggest what the Nazi U-boat Captains had done and would do to crews of ships they torpedoed. His goal was to inspire aggressiveness in the men at SCTC about the "Nazi Beasts" who they were to destroy.

Hotel Barracks on Biscayne Boulevard

PC sailors who attended SCTC remembered the bloodstained lifeboat and CDR McDaniel's impassioning welcoming speech. Nevertheless, they also remembered and exchanged stories of their living quarters in the hotels along Biscayne Boulevard in Miami. The Navy quartered sailors in hotels including three of the largest hotels, the McAllister, Alcazar, and Everglades. Figures 4-8, 4-9, and 4-10 show those three hotels. The Navy had stripped the hotel lobbies and guest rooms of the hotels of what had made them attractive peacetime resorts. The lobbies were barren except for a gangway watch area, a desk for the Officer-in-charge, and a coffee percolator on a hot plate. Rooms that once had plush carpets, fancy furniture, and artistic wall decorations now had bare walls and floors, double-deck bunks, and lockers for the sailors' gear and personal effects.

Sailors Filled Miami

Soon, students and instructors poured into the center. SCTC expanded and occupied most of the Miami Yacht Basin, two commercial piers, eleven hotels, a restaurant, a showroom, and a school. The tramp of marching feet and voices raised in songs echoed from the tall Royal Palm trees and the scented jasmine bushes along Biscayne Boulevard. Days and evenings, men hustled with their units from hotel barracks to classes, the mess hall, and the recreation center. Miami and Miami Beach buzzed with sailors in blazing white uniforms and sparkling blue dungarees. Activity was constant night and day seven days a week.

SCTC sailors loved Miami for liberty. Enlisted men decked out in snappy, crisp, whites and officers in sharp-creased whites or khakis, rushed from the hotels to the center of the city, Miami Beach, Coral Gables, and other locales. They found all the entertainment, female friends, and beer and liquor they could handle. Miami was a great liberty town. It was especially wonderful for those sailors who had spent time at the Small Craft or Mine Craft Training Centers in Norfolk, Virginia. Not only was the town of Norfolk ugly and loaded with dingy bars, tattoo shops, greasy-spoon restaurants, and cathouses, but the people snubbed, ignored, or ran hitchhiking sailors off the roads with their cars. Residents even displayed signs that read, "Sailors and Dogs Keep Off the Grass." In the Miami area, local people welcomed the trainees, and after leaving SCTC, the sailors recalled the fun-filled liberties in that magic city.

Miami Went Cosmopolitan

When the Navy began to transfer ships to Allied Nations, it included submarine chasers. This meant that men from those other countries had to have ASW training, and their Navies sent many of them to SCTC. Sailors from Brazil, the Dominican Republic, France, Norway, Peru, Russia, Uruguay, and Venezuela swarmed into Miami. This influx of foreign sailors gave the city of Miami a cosmopolitan aura. Red tassels on French sailors' hats bobbed as they paraded along Biscayne Boulevard. Soviet sailors strutted aggressively to and from classes and in the city and flashed their shiny "pig sticker" short swords. Their uniforms were so resplendent and epaulets so decorative that many U. S. and other Allied sailors and officers saluted them, thinking they were senior commissioned officers. Blond Norwegians and swarthy South Americans mingled with Dodger fans from Brooklyn, farmers from Iowa, and sun worshipers from California in classes, training sessions, and chow lines at the huge mess hall.

Meals at SCTC

Despite their culinary preferences, these sailors from across the United States and foreign nations learned to like the chow at SCTC. Mess Cooks in the huge warehouse-like structure at the end of Biscayne Boulevard tossed heaping blobs of solid nourishing food on compartmented metal trays of thousands of sailors three times each day. Dessert came last on the chow line and mess cooks plopped it on top of everything else. In the hot Miami weather, when dessert was ice cream, sailors gulped it first before it melted and oozed over salad, steaks, potatoes, and beans. With their loaded trays, they searched out seats on benches at the long tables. Often they asked their neighbors at the tables to "Pass the salt," in half a dozen different languages or by sign language. Figure 4-11 shows a view of the mess hall.

Recreation at SCTC

After meals, the men could march to the recreation area. Ping pong, billiard, and pool tables occupied center stage there, and exhibitions of skill with rackets and cue sticks ran daily. Regulations did not allow gambling and betting, but sailors are resourceful people. Monthly pay changed hands often though money never appeared at the tables.

Many other men idled around resting from the daily routine, wrote letters home, read magazines, or swapped scuttlebutt with buddies. An hour later their leaders marched them back to their training activities.

A Tough Curriculum

Though men and officers attended classes, SCTC was not a school. It was a training center. Its purpose was to give a quick and thorough indoctrination and hands-on practice to subchaser sailors and officers on how to protect convoys and sink submarines. McDaniel and the instructors provided motivation and knowledge of procedures and tactics to operate an efficient and effective subchaser. Training had to be thorough, and men and officers had to understand their missions and learn how to carry them out with complete success. They could accept nothing less than complete success because hunting U-boats was a matter of survival — life and death. Finding and destroying, or at least keeping U-boats at bay, meant survival of ships, merchant crews, soldiers, and even the crews of the subchasers. The men who left SCTC knew they would be in a war on raging seas with no forgiveness and with a relentless enemy who gave no quarter. Failure of subchaser crews to hunt out and kill U-boats meant death to Allied sailors and soldiers and possibly for themselves.

Most attendees at SCTC spent sixty days crammed close in rooms and training areas that reeked of tropic perspiration and rumbled with the noise from adjoining rooms and machinery. Figure 4-12 shows a class room for officers. On weekends and other special days men went to sea on small ships, including PC 483, PC 566, PC 1171, and PC 1193 to practice their book learning and training exercises. Instructors kept the trainees busy every moment learning and practicing seamanship, gunnery, and depth charge; mousetrap; and hedgehog attacks. For most of the men those days at sea were their first encounters with life aboard a Navy ship, and for some it was their first time on an ocean. On lookout duty, they stared intently through binoculars scanning the sea and dreaming of Nazi U-boats.

At General Quarters drills they manned the guns visualizing German bombers zooming toward them. Then at the close of the day, they stood at the rails of the ship and waved back at people, especially the pretty ladies, who gathered on Venetian Way to welcome them back to Miami.

The *Submarine Chaser Manual* used by officers at the training center stated, "The battle of the Atlantic is guerilla warfare at sea, a war of attrition using hit and run tactics, with the result dependent upon whether submarines or Submarine Chasers win most of the 'rounds.' Be ready when your chance comes." Lt. McDaniel insisted that his charges would be ready when their chance came.

To prepare those young, Reserve, junior officers for all aspects and duties of shipboard life and for submarine hunting, McDaniel made the curriculum at SCTC broad and complete. It covered the topics:

1. Ship's organization
2. Engineering
3. Gunnery
4. Sound gear techniques
5. Attack doctrine and tactics
6. Escort - Patrol - Ship Handling
7. Ship maintenance
8. Qualifications of the Naval Officer, by John Paul Jones, and,
9. The Laws of the Navy, by Captain Hopwood, R. N.

"Whenever I find the men have fifteen minutes to spare, I add another course," McDaniel decreed. The men and officers responded to the excitement of their mission and the enthusiasm of McDaniel. They reveled in the burden that the instructors at SCTC piled on them. A typical week for officers loaded them with the following schedule:

1. Twenty hours of ASW instruction,
2. Three hours of medical knowledge,
3. Eight hours of seamanship and ship handling on board a

Training Center YP,
4. Seven hours of communication, radar, and navigation,
5. All Saturday at sea for gunnery drills,
6. All Sunday at sea for gunnery, communication, or command procedures, and
7. Three written examinations.

Another week they devoted to all aspects of ships' and personal weapons. This activity involved firing weapons with live ammunition. Then the student officers embarked on a three-day cruise on training ships. On board the SCTC subchasers they performed all the functions of the enlisted men. These included chow-down in the mess hall and swinging up into a cramped upper bunk in a crowded compartment. McDaniel insisted that these new Reserve officers, unfamiliar with Navy life, be aware of how the enlisted men who would serve under them lived aboard ship.

Instructors lectured to enlisted men and officers every day and gave examinations every week. They lectured to and gave hands-on training to the enlisted men. Sailors learned seamanship, damage control, gunnery, boat handling, and sound gear techniques. Of equal importance, the men learned how to pump shells and bullets from their weapons. They also rolled depth charges from racks, fired depth charges from K and Y guns, and launched rocket bombs from hedgehogs and mousetraps. The demonstrations, drills, practice, and examinations weeded out those trainees not capable or sufficiently motivated, in McDaniel's opinion, to hunt Nazi U-boats. He sent them packing so the Navy could assign them elsewhere. McDaniel wanted only capable devoted U-boat killers.

The Instructors Knew Their Business

Another important feature of the training center was that McDaniel insisted that the instructors at the center be current in their knowledge gained from recent sea duty, especially antisubmarine warfare experience. At times, McDaniel even yanked a student from class to become an instructor because that person had more recent experience aboard ship than the current instructor in that or another class.

Instructors assigned to the center not only taught what they had learned but always sought new ideas, techniques, and tactics. Some new ASW tactics they developed at SCTC became standard procedures in the fleet. In addition, because they spent considerable time at sea on the small ships, the instructors and even the students improved on and originated ship handling procedures. For example, Lt. O. F. Williamson, an SCTC instructor on a PC and later commanding officer of PC 1196, invented what became known as the Williamson turn.[57] That maneuver became a standard technique for reversing a ship's direction along its own track, and it applies to ships of all sizes and types.

Instructors Were Multilingual

Because of the foreign sailors at the center, McDaniel recruited instructors, from all duty stations in the Navy, who could speak the languages of those foreign sailors. Once assigned to SCTC, if these instructors were not antisubmarine personnel, they soon learned the elements of ASW through intensive indoctrination at SCTC. They soon became competent in their specialties and succeeded in passing their knowledge to the foreign sailors. Before long, the tongues of fourteen different countries echoed in the class rooms and training areas at SCTC. During the period 1942-1943, McDaniel's training center graduated 360 officers and 1,374 enlisted men from fourteen foreign navies.

Fifty Thousand Trainees

Though the Navy had designed SCTC for a complement of 6,000 men and 150 officer trainees at any one time, by 1944 the classes held as many as 9,000 enlisted men and 2,500 officers. By 1 January 1944, the U. S. Navy had passed 10,396 of its officers and

37,574 of its enlisted men through SCTC. Eventually more than 50,000 officers and enlisted men from the United States and Allied nations completed antisubmarine warfare training at the Submarine Chaser Training Center. In particular also, SCTC instructors had trained crews for many different subchasers and at least 213 PCs.[58]

Many Crews Trained Together

Personnel Officers at SCTC selected pre-commissioning nucleus crews for specific ships. The men in these crews trained together at SCTC then went, as units, to various commands, training facilities, and receiving stations for further training. When they did, many of them sewed on their uniforms the red, white, blue, gold, and black Donald Duck patch that designated them as graduates of SCTC. Figure 4-13 shows the patch. While in Miami, Florida this patch was "out of uniform" and not worn by the men, but it was often acceptable elsewhere.

This additional training the men received at other stations sharpened their skills while they awaited for the completion of the subchasers of which they would become "plank owners." Upon reporting aboard their ships, they were tight-knit units of friends, had excellent training to operate their ships and fight submarines, and displayed high morale and team spirit.

Training Continued at Stations and Aboard Ship

Training of crews for PCs and other subchasers was not limited to that at SCTC. The other sound schools also put men through their paces. Receiving stations continued the training while men awaited their ships. The sailors fought shipboard fires and shored up damaged bulkheads in simulated ship interiors. They fired machine guns at targets towed by air planes, pulled on oars in lifeboats, and plunged into icy water to learn water survival techniques. They also learned many other things that would help them to sink submarines and survive aboard ship or if they lost their ship.

Finally, when the crews went aboard their ships, the ships did shakedown cruises. Often, these cruises included time at a sound school, such as the one in San Diego on the west coast or at SCTC on the east coast. There, the ships hunted and ran attack problems on submerged U. S. Navy submarines and fired guns at towed targets.

After they completed their shakedown cruises, the crews settled into their own training routines and schedules. This effort continued without letup during the war. Officers and Soundmen read ASW bulletins and spent time on ASW attack trainers ashore. Most of the continuing training was done, however, by drills aboard ship. Day and night under all conditions of weather and sea state and despite how tired the men were, claxons blared and bells rang. Boatswains bellowed, and ships' Captains glared at their stop watches and complained. Faster, faster, they demanded that their crews respond to emergencies, especially battle stations (General Quarters, GQ). Training aboard ship was relentless.

Just after coming from the midwatch, men slumped into their sacks, closed their eyes, and sighed. Sleep at last. "Fire. Fire. All hands. Fire in the engine room," voices yelled. Eyes snapped open. Out of their bunks, the men rolled. Twenty-five foot seas pounded over the bow. Winds of Beaufort Scale Force 6 tore freezing spindrift from wave tops. Men huddled in the bridge or lugged hoses and fire extinguishers below decks.

"Man overboard. Man overboard," the speaker blared. Grasping lifelines, men struggled along the decks, soaked and shivering, and tossed life preservers to the "victim.".

Sailors settled at benches in the mess hall and reached for the bowls of chow. "General Quarters. Man your battle stations," the squawk box blared. Food dropped to the tables and men raced up the ladder. This drill, of all of them, excited the men the most. They sprinted along passageways, slid down ladders, and hauled themselves up to guns as shown in Figure 4-14. Speed was essential. The Skippers drilled this idea into the men. They knew that well-trained submariners could clear the bridge, slam hatches closed, and dive their boat to periscope depth in thirty seconds. To be able to attack the submarine instead of dodging its torpedoes, a PC crew had to get to battle stations in about twenty-five seconds.

On one PC a new shiny Ensign reported aboard with no experience beyond his college lectures. The Captain assigned him as Gunnery Officer. Because the ship would sail the next day, the Captain decided to indoctrinate the Ensign by running drills at dockside. All went well until General Quarters. "Set depth charges on shallow," the Captain ordered. Instead of simulating the settings, the Ensign jammed his wrench on the charges and twisted to "shallow." He got three of them set before the Gunner's Mate yanked the wrench away and hauled all the men away from the depth charge rack release levers. If someone had rolled a depth charge, it could have torn the ship apart and blown the dock to splinters.

Training at SCTC and Elsewhere Was a Success

Enlisted men and commissioned officers who trained at SCTC and other training activities in the United States went to their various submarine chaser ships, including many PCs.

At sea, guarding convoys and stalking submarines, they proved that the philosophy, leadership, and training they got at these training stations, and especially at SCTC, led to successes in combat with Nazi U-boats. Those ships, including the PCs, were responsible for and successful at keeping enemy submarines at bay while escorting convoys along the east coast of the United States and across the Atlantic Ocean. In addition, they sank U-boats and helped demolish German Admiral Dönitz's Operation Paukenschlag and contributed to saving England from defeat by Germany and her Axis partners.

These accomplishments were the ones intended for PCs by their designers, but PCs had even more successes. PC sailors, and others, who went on to fight the war in Europe and in the Pacific against Japan also trained at SCTC and other facilities in the United States and had similar victories against Japanese submarines. PCs became one of the most active of the Navy's smaller men-of-war. Much of their success at defeating enemy submarines and doing many other combat and support missions were because of the training the crews received at the various training activities, aboard their ships, and especially at the Small Craft Training Center.

Despite isolated incidents, such as that of the Ensign and the depth charges, most men and officers came aboard PCs with sufficient training. They got it at Midshipman Schools, Officer Candidate Schools, SCTC, sound schools, damage control schools, gunnery classes and drills, time at sea on small training craft, "A," "B," and "C" schools for training in their ratings, and at receiving stations. Though most of the men were Reservists, they strode aboard their ships ready to sail and fight their PCs. What they did not know they learned fast because the Navy needed them at sea. They went to sea, and they did their jobs with ability and honor. Their performances were a tribute to the men and officers who manned PCs and to the Commanding Officers, administrators, and instructors at the facilities where they had learned their jobs, especially at the Submarine Chaser Training Center in Miami, Florida.

Figure 4-1. "I'm Nasty Naturally . . . I'm a Sub-chaser !!!" Drawing courtesy of Bill Buffington.

Figure 4-2. Jim Dickie, Signalman on PC 564 (USS *Chadron*) and His "Fighting Donald Duck Insignia." Drawing and photograph courtesy of Bill Buffington.

Figure 4-3. Insignia Used on PCs 546, 565, 1225, and 1242. Drawing and insignia courtesy of Bill Buffington and George Amaral.

Figure 4-4. U. S. Navy Submarine Chaser Training Center, Miami, Florida. Photograph courtesy of the Bay County Historical Society.

Figure 4-5. Letterhead used at the Small Craft Training Center. Courtesy of James McMahon.

Figure 4-6. LCDR Eugene Field McDaniel, Commanding Officer, SCTC, Miami, Florida. National Archives and Records Administration photograph 80-G-16044.

Figure 4-7. Bullet-riddled life boat on the grounds of SCTC. Official Navy photograph courtesy of the Bay County Historical Society.

Figure 4-8. McAllister Hotel in Miami, Florida used as a barracks for enlisted men at SCTC. c. 1942. Photograph courtesy of the Bay County Historical Society.

Figure 4-9. Hotel Alcazar, Miami, Florida used as barracks for enlisted men at SCTC. c. 1942. Photograph courtesy of the Bay County Historical Society.

Figure 4-10. Everglades Hotel, Miami, Florida used as barracks for enlisted men at SCTC. c. 1942. Photograph courtesy of the Bay County Historical Society.

Figure 4-11. Exclusive restaurant used as a mess hall for enlisted men at SCTC in Miami, Florida. Photograph courtesy of the Bay County Historical Society.

Figure 4-12. Class room at SCTC, Miami, Florida.
Photograph courtesy of the Bay County Historical Society.

Figure 4-13. Donald Duck PC Navy Patch that some enlisted men wore on their uniforms after leaving SCTC. Photograph courtesy of Jim McMahon.

Figure 4-14. Gun drill on the 3"-50 on Coast Guard PC 556, on 8 October 1942. The photograph shows the gun, flying bridge, mast, and crow's nest. Trainer is Seaman 2/C Andrew J. McAnally, Pointer is SM3/C Theodore Cholewinski, Sightsetter is Jack Friedman. Photograph 80-G-K-864, National Archives.

CHAPTER 5

Life Aboard a PC

Sailors Were Proud of Their Ships

"Boy, ain't she a beauty," a two-hash-marked Gunner's Mate exclaimed to his Seaman shipmate while they watched their PC steam into the Brooklyn Navy Yard in 1943.[59] His companion was not as enthusiastic as the gunner, but like most other sailors, after serving aboard a PC, he learned to appreciate and even love his ship. Those "Donald Duck Navy" sailors admired their craft and were proud to be PC sailors.

Big ship sailors teased them though, with remarks about how small and fragile appearing a PC was. Once, a PC tied up against a battleship in a South Pacific anchorage. A bemused sailor on the battleship leaned over the rail. He squinted down at the PC, shook his head, and shouted to a couple of PC sailors, "Hey. Do you guys stay on that thing at night?"

Even destroyer escorts (DEs) hulked over PCs. A feud started between the crews of a DE and a PC that had moored against the DE in Seattle. A sailor on the DE called to men on the PC, "Catch this." He leaned over his ship's rail and spat across the deck of the PC. It splashed into the water outboard of the PC. Laughter burst from his shipmates. The sailors on the deck of the PC stormed to the gangway that sloped up to the larger ship and "prepared to board."

The Executive Officer of the PC yelled, "Knock it off. Back

to work." Grumbling and flashing threatening signals up to the DE crew members, the men eased away from the gangway. After that incident, ships' companies of those two ships could not meet ashore without bloodied noses and blackened eyes unless the shore patrol hovered nearby.

The Complement of a PC

The number of men on a PC varied among ships, but a typical complement was sixty enlisted men and five commissioned officers. Most petty officers were third or second class with a few first class and one or two Chief Petty Officers. Most ships started with at least a Chief Motor Machinist Mate.

The five officers on a PC most often carried General Line designators, and all of them stood OOD watches. Among them they shared the usual responsibilities. These included Captain, Executive Officer, First Lieutenant or Damage Control Officer, Gunnery Officer, Navigation Officer, Engineering Officer, and Supply Officer. The Skipper was also the Medical Officer and Chaplain. The most junior officer usually also got collateral duties such as Morale Officer and any other task that the Captain felt was necessary.

Everyone Did More Than One Job

Despite their rates or ranks the enlisted men and the commissioned officers soon became Jacks-of-all-trades in operating, maintaining, and fighting their vessels. Usually a crew had only three of each rate, one for each of an underway three-section Watch Quarter and Station Bill. If any one man got sick, injured, or worse, other men had to and could fill his billet. Despite the bars on their collars, officers could do each other's duties. Whatever the symbols or number of chevrons on the arms of their uniforms, most enlisted men could stand other ratings' watches. Often they could maintain and repair equipment other than that associated with their specialties. Some enlisted men, especially Chief Quartermasters, acted as Junior

Officer of the Deck (JOOD) not only in port but even when underway.

The largest segment of the rates was the engineering rates because typically four men stood underway watches in the engine room. That accounted for twelve men plus a Chief Motor Machinist Mate who did not stand watches in the engine room. Underway, an engine room watch needed at least two Third, Second, or First Class Motor Machinist Mates as throttle men, and at least one fireman for messenger, gauge reader, and handyman. An Electrician's Mate, to oversee problems in the generator room, sometimes stood watch or else was on call and found in his sack most of the time. All three or four men in the engine room learned to do each of the other mens' duties, including those of the Electrician's Mates, and they frequently did them.

The Men Knew Each Other

Most crews of PCs had trained together at the Submarine Chaser Training Center in Miami, Florida or elsewhere. After months living, messing, marching back and forth to classes, and training aboard other ships as a group, they got to know each other. They learned to work together, recognize each other's strengths and weaknesses, and build friendships and understandings. Those features made them close-knit units, each man of which thought his crew was better than any of the others. That spirit stayed with them and grew stronger after they went aboard their ship. Even to the end of the war, the men on PCs were contented and happy crews like the crew shown in Figure 5-1.

Pets Also Served on PCs

Along with approximately sixty enlisted men and five officers, often a pet dog or other animal helped crew a PC. See Figure 5-2 of Salty, First Class Watch Dog, who sailed on PC 1125 for two and a half years. Many pets' names appeared on Watch, Quarter, and

Station Bills, and the pets stood watches with some crew members who took care of them. They even had life preservers assigned to them for emergencies. Sailors loved their pets and treated them with care, affection, and concern. They were pets but also a link to the civilian world the men had recently left and to which they longed to return. To the men, their pet was a member of the crew, and they extended their loyalty to the pet as they did to each other. Some animals even got an "official" discharge certificate at the end of the war, like the one in Figure 5-3.

One incident shows how the men cared for their pets. While PC 1213 conducted speed trials, with senior officer observers on shore checking the ship's actions, a voice on the squawk box blared, "Man Overboard!" Heeling over, the PC wheeled around and circled back on its course.

"What the hell are you doing?" the stunned observers on shore radioed to the ship.

"We're going back to pick up Salty Mose," the radioman on the PC responded. Finding their pet dog in the choppy sea, six sailors dove in after him. They hauled him aboard and rushed him to sick bay. After Salty revived, the ship continued with its maneuvers.[60]

The Pre-Commissioning Crew

Like with most ships, before the navy commissioned a PC, a skeleton crew of a dozen or so senior petty officers and a couple of commissioned officers went aboard the ship. They set up essential gear and paper work and prepared the Watch, Quarter, and Station Bill. The time that the crew had spent together at SCTC and other stations gave these leading rated men and officers the opportunity to learn each man's abilities and idiosyncrasies. They knew how to fit the men into the most efficient duty and emergency billets, and they gave their recommendations to the prospective Commanding Officer who made the final decisions. While doing that task, the skeleton crew also checked out the gear in their departments and made it ready for when the rest of the crew would come aboard.

The Crew Went Aboard

A few weeks after the pre-commissioning skeleton crew started activities aboard ship, the rest of the crew departed their last station. They assembled at the ship they would board and ". . . shouldered their seabags, mattresses, and hammocks and strode across a gangplank . . ." to their new home.

The first duties aboard ship for the men consisted of selecting a bunk, usually with senior rated men getting first choices. Then they stowed their personal gear from a sea bag into a locker half the size of the sea bag. Men arranged their bunks with a mattress cover (fart sack) slipped over the mattress, two cream-colored woolen blankets stowed at the foot of the bunk, and a pillow at the head end. The hammocks they got in Boot Camp they draped over the made-up bunk to help keep it clean. On many PCs the First Lieutenant or Damage Control Officer confiscated the hammocks to contribute them to damage control shoring material. After the sailors arranged their bunks, Division Officers ordered them to trice them in the up position using the two chains attached to them near the head and foot ends. This procedure was to make it easier for men in the compartment to move around. It also kept men from sleeping (sacking out) during hours off watch when they should be working.

Every Man Had to Learn the Ship

The next item of duty was to learn the compartments and where everything was on the ship. On a PC, that effort did not take long. She only had two decks below and one deck above the main deck, not like a battleship or carrier with many more decks. The various rated men, and those striking for rates, then learned the details of the spaces in which they would work and stand watches.

For the radar operator that meant he would study the bulkheads inside a four-by-four-foot compartment that contained only a radar console and a chair. His job did not end there, however, and, like other men, he also learned the details and operations of many other parts of the ship.

The radio shack was an open space across from the chart table and held the radio gear, a chair bolted to the deck in front of the radio, and a typewriter. During watch, the Radioman screened incoming "fox schedule" traffic with one ear pressed against a headset. When his ship's call preceded the messages, he typed groups of five letters that the Communications Officer decoded later.

The Soundmen stepped down a few rungs of a ladder to the lowest compartment near the keel to examine their sound stack. Then they climbed back up to the bridge to try out the dials and ear phones of their listening post. Their space was hardly large enough for more than two persons.

A Yeoman worked in an "office" open to view and with no more than a small desk, typewriter, file cabinet, and chair. It was one pace from the bridge, two paces from the chart desk, radio, and ladder to below-decks, and three steps to the ward room. It was the "Times Square" area of the ship with constant heavy traffic. Here the Yeoman typed up, filed, and kept the ship's records and all the ship's paper work. The crew usually knew what the ship's business was because anyone could peer over the Yeoman's shoulder while passing by. It was the favorite spot from which to get the latest scuttlebutt.

Signalmen, in the open on the flying bridge, clipped snaps on flags in the flag bag and hoisted the "bunting" on lanyards to the yardarms. They too learned the functions of other topside parts of the ship and often swapped jobs with Quartermasters.

Motor Machinist Mates and snipes labored in the largest and most complicated spaces. The main engine room held two propulsion Diesel engines, two superchargers, a centrifuge, various pumps, two reduction gears, two shaft couplings, an air compressor, and two air tanks. The auxiliary room housed an evaporator, two auxiliary Diesel engines, two generators, an electrical panel, and associated apparatus.

Besides all that machinery, the engineers were responsible for the piping systems throughout the ship. An order from the Engineering Officer required that the engineering gang had to trace out and draw sketches of the tanks and pipe lines aboard the ship. This included fresh water, sea water, oil, fuel, and steam lines with joints and valves and where the pipes passed through bulkheads. Teams of two men each for days scrambled, crawled, and squeezed through large and small spaces and into the bilges from the peak tank to the lazaret. They grasped a flashlight in one hand and a pencil and a grimy notebook in the other on which they sketched the lines and valves. The life of the ship and the lives of the crew could depend on the engineers' knowledge of how to control the vital fluids of the ship during emergencies.

This knowledge had other advantages. While on continuous convoy and patrol duty in the North Pacific, the Skipper of one PC imposed strict fresh water rationing. Men and officers could wash their hands and teeth only twice a day. After a week at sea the grimy, odorous, bearded men noticed that the Captain appeared fresh shaven each day and was not as redolent as the rest of the crew. An Officer's Steward told some sailors that the Skipper, despite his edict, took a shower each day with fresh water. Irate at this discovery, a few engineers planned retribution. They searched out the water lines to the Captain's quarters. Armed with wrenches and hacksaws, they diverted the hot water supply to the Captain's shower and replaced it with the condensate line from a heater in the crew's compartment. This rusty water would burst into steam if someone released it. Next day they huddled in the companionway near the Captain's stateroom, listening.

"YOW! GODDAM," the Skipper roared as a surge of scalding, rust filled, condensate blasted his naked frame. Exploding with laughter, the engineers raced down the passageway. A few hours later they reworked the plumbing to its original form. The Captain did not complain about his shower, but he never showered at sea again.

Officers' Routine

Officers on PCs did what those on larger ships did. They ran their divisions, looked after the men, scribbled endless paper work, and fretted over the list of Registered Publications. All that work was done, however, with much less routine and formality than that on big ships, and the officers shared much of each other's work.

Not Much Spit and Polish on a PC

Because most of the men and officers had come recently from civilian life, some reluctantly, they did not practice the spit and polish and formalities of the regular Navy. Life aboard a PC was informal. Figure 5-4 shows a typical in-port Quarterdeck Watch on a PC. One can compare the work uniform and relaxed attitude of the man on watch with the formal Quarterdeck Watch on a big ship. There, enlisted men and an officer wore dress uniforms, a Boatswain piped visitors aboard, and messengers ran errands. Even ashore, PC sailors wore their uniforms and acted informally. Figure 5-5 shows a Shore Patrolman from a PC and some of his shipmates on an island in the South Pacific.

For Captain's inspections on PCs, the enlisted men wore undress blues or whites with white hats, or earlier in the war, blue "flat" hats. Officers wore service dress blues or khakis. Inspections were not frequent, but according to regulations and tradition, Captains did hold inspections. As usual, the ship's company fell in with some Boatswain bellowing orders, checking uniforms, and threatening men who had deficiencies.

Except during inspections, the uniform of the day for the enlisted men was mostly dungarees, chambray shirts, and black watch caps or white hats. In warmer climes and to add a little levity to daily activities, on occasion, some men wore even more casual attire as shown in Figure 5-6. Frequently the men wore Marine issue, brown, high-topped boots. Officers usually wore khakis or greens with white, blue, khaki, or green hat covers. The varieties of uniforms for officers are shown in Figure 5-7.

Rarely did officers expect or receive hand salutes from the enlisted men, though the men usually used "sir" in exchange of orders and commands. After months and years aboard ship together through raging seas, withering heat, bloody wounds, and death, enlisted men and commissioned officers bonded with each other like the two in Figure 5-8. Often they maintained friendships that lasted long after the war.

Hygiene and Laundry

Fresh water was always scarce, so conservation of fresh water at sea required that the crew would limit their washing to hands and teeth before meals. Especially restricted were fresh water showers. Men could use salt water, but without a fresh water rinse it left a man with a sticky, scaly feeling. Many men in the warm climate of the South Pacific flushed off their sweaty bodies topside during rain squalls. Those sailors in northern waters, however, lived with their dirt and sweat until they reached port.

Doing laundry in port was not much of a problem, where the crew could use hot fresh water. Most ships had a washing machine bolted to the deck in the head. Sometimes the men contributed the money to buy a machine. In other ships the shipyard or some civic organization donated the machines. The washers helped in port but rarely at sea where fresh water was not available, and the pitching and rolling of the ship made operation of the machine impossible. At sea the men cleaned their clothes by hand in buckets with cold salt water as seen in Figure 5-9. With sheath knives, they scraped chips from bars of brown saltwater soap into buckets and scrubbed their clothes by hand.

The popular way to wring grime from dungaree trousers and chambray shirts was to tie them to a heaving line, toss them overboard, and tie the running end of the line to a depth charge rack at the stern. This technique worked well at one-third speed or even two-third speed but was a problem at higher speeds.

"All ahead standard," the OOD would command and men would leap up, race to the fantail, and heave on the lines before the ship speeded up. If they were late, it took three men to drag in a set of dungarees only to find a bundle of blue cloth shreds at the end of the line. For an occasional sailor with unhygienic habits, the crew sometimes recommended this washing technique for him also as shown in the cartoon in Figure 5-10.

Living Quarters

Seamen and other "deck apes" lived in the forecastle, the forward compartment just aft of the peak tank and head. The forecastle is traditionally where the enlisted men sleep on any ship. It is that part of the ship that rises and falls the farthest in rough water. Except the enlisted men's head it is the roughest riding part of a ship, especially on a PC.

Other rated men berthed in the compartment aft of the seamen. The next section of the ship aft of that one, which rode better in rough seas, was reserved for the Chief Petty Officers. The few CPOs aboard shared a compartment that had only two bunks. When more men achieved a CPO rating they still bunked with the rest of the crew. The section at the center of gravity or floatation of the ship, where it pitched and rolled the least, was officers' country. There, the officers shared two compartments, separated by a head. Each compartment held two bunks.

Befitting their watch station in the bowels of the ship, engineers berthed in a lower compartment. It was near the water line, and at sea the swish of the hull gliding through the water helped lull men to sleep. All twelve of the engineers lived in a space twelve feet long, fifteen feet wide, and seven feet high. A ship's ladder descended through the forward center part taking up some space. In the compartment were twelve fold-up bunks, twelve lockers of a few cubic feet each, foul weather gear for twelve men, lumber and mattresses for shoring ruptures in the hull. Often it also housed a couple of guitars or maybe even a bass fiddle. See Figure 5-11.

The Social Center

The enlisted men's social life centered on the mess hall and its galley. On such a small ship, the mess hall was the only area large enough to hold more than a few men at a time. Men gathered there when off watch and not working or sleeping. It was a place to talk about mail from home, swap pictures of girl friends, and ask buddies, "What are you going to do after the war?" Also, except the Yeoman's office, the mess hall was the best place to catch up on scuttlebutt. Here, traditionally, one learned what the ship's orders were before the Skipper knew them.

In the mess hall, jammed together on benches bolted to the deck, thirty enlisted men gathered for chow at each of five mess tables. They bellowed friendly obscenities as they carved steaks, forked powdered eggs, or spooned that infamous breakfast, chipped corned beef on toast (shit on a shingle). These five long tables, with their attached benches, filled most of the space in the compartment. Fiddle boards hung from the edges of the tables, and at sea the mess cooks raised them for almost every meal. Without the fiddle boards dishes, pots, pans, knives, forks, food, coffee, and anything loose would disappear off the table and crash on the deck with each roll of the ship. That was if weather and sea state allowed for the cooks to serve a meal. Often, when the weather was bad, the crew ate only sandwiches, saltine crackers, and coffee diluted with sea spray (and the crew suspected also, saltpeter). Many men could not even tolerate that light menu at sea in bad weather.

Open Galleys

Overall, meals on PCs were tasty, healthful, and substantial. That is except Sunday night chow when standard fare was baloney (horse cock) and (head) cheese. Officers in the wardroom, with more gentility than the enlisted men displayed, called the Sunday menu cold cuts. Frequently also, the ships had "open galleys" so that anyone any time could fix a meal or get snacks. The only times the cooks closed the galleys were when they prepared chow, cleaned their gear, prepared for inspection, or took personal time.

On one ship that personal time included doing the Cook's

laundry — in the coffee urn. The crew soon put a stop to that practice. Five sailors hovered over the cook as he scrubbed the urn — twice — and sweated about the threat by the men to "deep-six" all his clothing.

In the galley, men prepared their own night rations in port or at sea. Common practice was to drop a slab of butter on the grill and toss in two slices of bread and a chunk of meat. On some ships that meat may have been a T-bone steak "borrowed" from the officers' mess supplies in the reefer behind the galley. The hungry sailor would then saunter back to his watch station fortified by that sandwich for the long dreary mid-watch.

The Crews Loved Movies

When sea state allowed, men and officers booed Hollywood heroes and whistled at leggy actresses in the movies shown in the mess hall. Even at sea in rough weather, the men clutched the table edges and swayed with the motion of the ship to watch movies. By tradition the crew always reserved a seat front and center for the Skipper whether or not he attended. Starting the film always awaited his appearance or his regrets sent by an Officer's Steward.

With maybe three movies aboard on a three-week cruise, all hands learned the lines of the actors and actresses in each film. They knew when to leave and return to the mess hall timed with the appearance of curvaceous Betty Grable or sexy Rita Hayworth. Every man aboard ship longed to have Rita Hayworth or Betty Grable aboard, even for a few minutes. Most men also wanted June Allyson to be waiting for them when they got home. W. C. Fields in "My Little Chickadee" and Tallulah Bankhead in "Lifeboat" always caused laughter. They booed Tarzan as a bad guy and cheered for Abbott and Costello. The sounds of the big bands of Tommy Dorsey and Glenn Miller playing "In the Mood," "Begin the Beguine," or "Jersey Bounce" always made the men melancholy for their girls back home.

The Men Liked Poker Too

Between the evening meal and the movie and again after the movie, cards skittered across and chips rattled on the mess tables. A kind of segregation existed at the tables. One table would have a dime limit game, at another table a quarter limit, and at another table the men played poker for open stakes. The Navy did not allow gambling for money, but plenty of chips and match sticks traded hands. And they were not free. Many men won and lost their monthly pay in poker games.

Sick Bay

Men attended Sick Call on a PC wherever they could find "Doc," the Pharmacist's Mate. His Sick Bay, however, was in the mess hall where he fed APC pills to CAT fever patients, held periodic short-arm inspections, and patched the injured and wounded. No matter what a man's ailment, Doc always had a supply of APC pills. They cured more ills than snake oil. He kept his other medicines in a medical kit welded to the forward bulkhead. It was a metal box with either solid doors or doors made of screens with one-inch spaces. On its latch hung a lock to protect the items inside, especially the bottle of medicinal whiskey. Only the Captain had the key to the lock.

One day, "Pills" or "Doc," the Pharmacist's Mate on one PC reported to the Skipper that the whiskey bottle was empty.

"Evaporated or spilled. Loose cap I suppose," the Captain declared and replaced the liquor with all hands speculating on how it disappeared because the Skipper did not drink.

A week later only a few drops of the brown liquid sloshed around the bottom of the bottle. This time the Skipper glared at the Pharmacist. Red-faced, the Captain refilled the bottle and screwed a seal on the cap that required a pipe wrench to open it. The whiskey never "evaporated" again.

Later, the thief, who was an engineer, told some of his friends how he got the whiskey. He had fashioned a two-foot long sheet metal trough that was narrow enough to fit through the openings in the screen door. After inserting it through an opening, he used two pairs of long nosed pliers, one to hold and tilt the bottle and the other to unscrew the cap. The contents drained down the trough and into a canteen he had swiped from the gunnery department's landing party equipment.

Ship's Store on a PC

Along with all else that happened in the mess hall, on regular schedules, the Storekeeper opened the ship's store, a metal cabinet bolted to the starboard bulkhead. From the store, men bought a pack of cigarettes for a dime or a bar of candy (pogy-bait) for a nickel. Both items were popular, because PC sailors, like those on other Navy ships, could not seem to survive without their sweets, coffee (Joe), and cigarettes.

At night, at sea, the smoking lamp was out topside because the prying eyes of enemy submariners could see the glow of a match or cigarette for miles. After a long night without a smoke, when daylight broke, the OOD would announce, "The smoking lamp is lit." Most hands would quickly dig into a pocket for a pack of Camels, Lucky Strikes, or Chesterfields. They would snap open a black, matte-textured, Zippo lighter and lean into a two-inch high flame to light up a butt.

Religious Services on a PC

On Sundays, by naval tradition and Navy Regulations, the Captain of the ship offered religious services. In good weather the men met topside, usually aft away from activity on the bridge. Otherwise, church was in the mess hall. Men did not attend religious services as much as they did the poker games or movies. At times the Captain had a small congregation, hardly large enough to justify using the mess hall. Nevertheless, the Skipper always offered service.

One young sailor on a PC noticed the lack of attendance at

services and how small the group looked in the mess hall. In jest he announced over the squawk box one Sunday morning, "Now hear this. The Captain will hold church services in the lazaret at 0900."[61] That bit of humor, involving the smallest and least used compartment on the ship, did not amuse the Captain. He added a Captain's mast to that young man's schedule. Church services were important, though, for many men, especially as contact with raging seas or the enemy increased.

A Day in Port

"Now hear this. Reveille. Reveille." The words rattled around the compartments and echoed topside at 0500 to start a day in port. Men rolled out of their sacks. They grumbled, belched, scratched themselves, and griped about life, the Navy, and officers. With a towel over a shoulder and soap dish in hand, a man ambled forward to the head in his white skivvies and marine boots to wash, shave, and shake off the cobwebs of sleep.

"Sweepers man your brooms. Clean sweep down fore and aft," the Boatswain growled over the squawk box. Deck apes drew their gear, and all hands turned to for cleaning ship. Men scrubbed their compartments and the decks. Below decks, the snipes started polishing, oiling, and wiping down deck plates and machinery. The Yeoman rolled a sheet of paper into his typewriter. Ship's Cooks and mess cooks swept the night's debris from mess tables and set out the platters and bowls of chow. Officer's Stewards ambled aft to draw food for the officers. About the spaces, Gunners Mates, Radiomen, and other rated men readied their compartments for the day.

Officers turned out, washed up, and pulled on their khakis ready for breakfast. After their meal, coffee, and a smoke they held muster of the men in their divisions, inspected ship's spaces, or caught up on paper work. The Skipper checked all messages and awaited reports from his officers.

At 0630 the first mess call sounded. Hungry sailors off watch raced to the galley for first call. They were anxious to learn what new trick the cook had learned to camouflage the gummy texture and fetid odor of powdered eggs. Despite the faults they found with breakfast, they always found the coffee just right, hot enough to scald a man's throat and thick enough to float a flag grommet. After chow, the crew turned to on work, and at 0800 the duty section changed watches.[62]

Wherever the men might be topside at sunrise, when the bugle or voice-order blared, all hands snapped to attention. They saluted aft as colors sounded and the flag fluttered up the flagstaff.

Men fell in for quarters only when the Skipper had to impress some local senior officer or just for practice. Most times Division Officers performed quarters and muster by an informal visit to working spaces, getting reports from leading rated men, or just looking around. On a PC, counting heads and recognizing that a man was missing was easy.

In port, all hands not on watch turned to every day except Sunday. Deck apes followed the old naval tradition of, "If it moves, salute it. If it doesn't, paint it." They scraped and chipped paint, wire-brushed the metal, and swabbed on fresh coats of red-lead or lemon-yellow zinc-chrome. Seamen then swabbed blobs of gray paint over the exposed and treated holidays.

Bright colored signal flags flapped and crackled from halyards that draped from the yardarms as signalmen aired their bunting and repaired halyards. Mattresses and blankets lined the rails as men took advantage of sunshine to air their bedding. Gunners' Mates scoured gun barrels and checked ammunition lockers and depth charges. They smeared grease and oil on the ship's weapons. The Shipfitter hauled out his wrenches and hammers and lit off the acetylene torches to repair damage done to the ship on its last trip. Officers read messages and directives. They scribbled their reports and passed them to the Yeoman who rattled the keys of his typewriter recording the ship's business and issuing correspondence. Paperwork. Always, officers did paperwork, even in combat.

Sweat dripped from the snipes' foreheads as they crawled along on their knees oiling and polishing the diamond-stud patterned deck plates of the engine room. Below the plates, arms and legs soaked in bilge water, motor machs grunted and strained repairing leaking pipe couplings. In clean pressed dungarees, the Chief sat at the log desk in the forward part of the engine room. He sipped hot coffee and passed judgment on the progress of repairs and maintenance. After the men finished the work and the engine room gleamed like a hospital operating room, the Engineering Officer climbed down the ladder under the hatch. He strutted around, nodded, and whispered to the Chief. Then he climbed back up for a whiff of fresh sea breeze to expunge the stench of Diesel fuel and lube oil from his nostrils.

"All hands standby to receive stores," the Boatswain blared over the squawk box. Replenishment of consumable supplies was an all-hands evolution with men forming chains like fire bucket brigades to pass food, spare parts, and other items aboard. With his long tape the Oil King doused in the ship's tanks to measure oil, fuel, and water levels and request topping off the tanks. On a small ship, storage space was scarce so replenishment of supplies and fuel happened at most ports of call.

Best of all, though, was the sound that echoed from the speaker, "Mail call. Mail call." Bodies tumbled from sacks, appeared like magic from hiding places, and raced toward the quarterdeck faster than they ever went to General Quarters or Abandon Ship. Mail call was the highlight of every return to port, especially while overseas. Mail from parents, friends, wives, and girl friends was the only direct contact with the peaceful world they had left for the surging ocean and enemy actions. Lucky men with a fistful of letters would huddle behind an ammunition ready-locker or settle in their bunks. Though anxious to tear open the envelopes, they prolonged the task to raise their expectations and to make the experience last longer. Sad-eyed sailors without mail would slink away like lepers, embarrassed before their shipmates that the folks back home had ignored them. Worse than no mail was the occasional "Dear John" letter from a girl friend who had found another man at home. Then, there was the letter from the Officer's Steward's girl that read, "You've been gone a long time. I go out twice a week — always with other sailors only, of course." He knew his romance was in trouble.

During daylight hours men and officers worked at ship's maintenance, charts, forms, correspondence, and drills. Always the men ran through drills such as Fire, Man Overboard, or General Quarters (GQ). In combat areas, condition-three or even condition-two might be set with men stationed at one-third or one-half of the ship's weapons while lookouts scanned the horizon and the sky. Often GQ sounded at sunrise and sunset. When planes came in, men ripped covers from guns, slammed ammunition into them, and pounded shells at the enemy.

"Knock off from work" and "liberty parties away" came at 1600 hours if the ship was in a friendly port and the Captain did not expect enemy action. Men hustled to the head to shave, shine, pull on their bell bottoms, and square away their white hats to make liberty. They would capture more memories to relive during the dreary days at sea. If there was no town to visit, liberty at some overseas base might have been in dungarees or khakis and limited to a few cans of 3.2 beer, a ball game, or a movie. Figure 5-12 shows sailors on Esperito Santos waiting for their beer party in Duffy's Tavern.

Then, the evening mess closed the day. For the duty section left aboard, card games, washing clothes, writing letters, and movies kept the men busy. At 2100 hours the smoking lamp went out, and "silence about the decks" sounded. Then liberty parties returned, and envious mates joined them in the head to hear their tall tales of raucous life ashore and their feminine conquests.

Technically that was the way it was, but on a PC the Skipper and other officers relaxed formalities. Not every day was a work day. After a special effort by the crew in some activity, the Captain might give the men a day off. He might announce swimming, and men, wearing their navy blue, woolen, itchy swim trunks, would climb to the flying bridge and dive overboard. See Figure 5-13. Often, a couple of men posted themselves fore and aft on the ship with rifles to discourage curious sharks.

The crews on PCs cooperated with each other and with the officers. They rarely took advantage of the relaxed conditions and did not need much supervision. Officers enjoyed their reduced need for constant guidance of and checking on the enlisted men. They spent more time on important ship's functions, censoring the enlisted mens' outgoing mail, or on their own personal matters.

A Day at Sea

In many ways the routine at sea was similar to that in port, especially sunrise and sunset GQ. "Now hear this. Now hear this," the Boatswain's voice howled from the ship's speakers. "Stand by for dock trials. Set the Special Sea Detail." Those words shifted a sailor's world from dockside to the open ocean. PC sailors, like most other sailors, struggled with the mixed emotions of sea duty. The thrill of the unknown, the wonderment of new sights and lands, and the possibility of heroic episodes urged them on. These ideas clashed with those of discomfort, uncertainty of what lay ahead, and fear of the unknown. In the end, though, youth and its quest of adventure and sense of invincibility won, and the men went to sea with a feeling of urgency and excitement. Despite the eagerness of the men, the rumble of the Diesels and blasts of black smoke from the exhausts, churned the stomachs of some of them with the anticipation of seasickness.

"Take in all lines," the Captain at the conn ordered. "Left ten degrees rudder. Starboard back one-third." The ship eased away from the dock. A few more commands and she was breasting the swells at the harbor's mouth and headed out to sea. Then, the "Old Man" gave the conn to the officer on watch.

At sea, usually the crew stood watches of four hours on duty and eight hours off duty. The first watch, the dreaded mid-watch, ran from 0000-0400. The morning watch was from 0400-0800. This was followed by the day watches of 0800-1200 and 1200-1600. Then there were two dog-watches of 1600-1800 and 1800-2000 so that all hands could eat the evening meal at a reasonable time. Dog-watches also rotated the watches so that men would not have to stand the same duty hours on consecutive days. Men envied those on the dog watches, because those watches were only two hours long. The evening watch ran from 2000-2400 when the mid-watch started again.

All officers except the Captain, and sometimes the Executive Officer, stood underway Officer of the Deck (OOD) watches. They learned some routine of watch standing in Officer Candidate School (OCS) where they became "ninety-day wonders." The rest they got from time at the Submarine Chaser Training Center (SCTC), on-the-job training from other officers, and tactful advice from a few senior rated men who had previous sea duty. The enlisted men learned their seamanship and specialties the same way as did the officers. Though many had come aboard with rates they had earned in Navy training schools, they were still "Boots" without sea legs. And one thing a man needed aboard a PC was sea legs.

When underway, men in the engine room lived four hours at a time amid the high frequency high decibel whine of superchargers and roar of engines. Immersed in the noise they communicated with hand signals and body language. After watch, they could not hear normally for hours. Not known at the time, this was a "temporary threshold shift" (TTS) of their inner ear mechanisms. For some men this developed into a permanent hearing loss later in life.

Station Keeping in Convoys

The young officers accepted grave responsibilities for ships and their crews and were enthusiastic and anxious to do well. Station keeping in a convoy at night in a storm was a tricky and dangerous activity. Less experienced OODs, anxious at these times, wove and stumbled back and forth between the radar shack and the bridge where they rang up orders to the engine room for changes in speed to maintain the ship's position in the convoy. Most changes were not by the standard speeds but in small numbers of revolutions per minute (rpm or turns). "Ten rpm up," the speaker on the phone would relay to the throttlemen who advanced the throttles and stared at the tachometers. Engineers explained to the officers that they could not adjust engine speeds at increments less than five revolutions per minute. In their excitement, zeal, and fear of collision, often the OODs forgot this fact.

One PC, pinging for Japanese submarines on the port flank of a lumbering eight-knot convoy, battled through fifteen foot seas off her port bow. Wave tops broke against the portholes of the bridge as the officer and men peered out into the blackness during the mid-watch. They saw no ships and relied on radar to keep station. "Up ten rpm," the OOD yelled. He ran to the radar console, groaned, then struggled back to the bridge. "Down five," he ordered. Back to the radar. Return to the bridge. "Up five rpm." Back to the radar. Race to the bridge. More small changes in speed. And on and on.

In the engine room, in one hour, the snipes logged fifty of these "Bells" and ran the throttles up and down each time. Then they heard, "Up three." They shrugged, logged the bell, and looked at the throttles. Then they heard, "Down two."

"What the hell?" Tisch, the First Class Motor Machinist, groaned. "Log them in but leave the throttles alone." Three more hours droned away. The engineers responded with many five and ten rpm changes but also filled pages of log sheets with orders for three or fewer changes in rpm without touching the throttles.

After the next watch relieved the men in the engine room, Tisch groped through the passageway past officers' country to his compartment. The OOD's head popped from his stateroom. "Tisch," he yelled.

The engineer froze. He was sure that the Ensign would read him out and put him on report for endangering the ship by not trying to change speeds. He gulped. "Yes sir?"

"Well done on those throttles. We stayed right on station the whole watch." He smiled and disappeared back into his stateroom.

Drills At Sea

At sea just after the crew had settled into the routine of four hours on and eight hours off watch the klaxon blared. "General Quarters," screamed a voice from the squawk boxes. Men lunged from their racks, dropped knives and forks, yanked on their foul weather gear, and tumbled over each other to their battle stations. "This is a drill. This is a drill," the speakers informed them. And so it started. Drills and drills. Always the crew ran drills to train for accidents or battle. None of the men shirked, because they understood that their lives depended on fast responses to emergencies.

Life on a PC Was Not Easy

Duty on a PC was rugged. Most men claimed that PCs rode rougher than any other ship afloat. Two sailors wrote,[63] "It [a PC] rides like a roller-coaster with a flat wheel . . . ." The authors added, "If she's not pitching, she's rolling . . . if she's not rolling, she's shaking . . . and if she's not shaking — then she's tied up in port." Men on a PC fished a British seaman out of the Atlantic after he was adrift in a life raft for seven days. He said about his ride to a safe haven on the PC, "I say, but I'll be dogged if I don't believe it was smoother on the raft."[64]

Seasickness was as common on a PC as was the longing to return home. It affected almost everyone at some time or other. Many men heard their stomachs rumble and felt dizzy at dock trials even before they had cast off the mooring lines. Some sailors gradually got used to the ships' motions but not all. A few hardy men never had to run to the leeward rail or grab for a bucket. On the other hand, some men seemed always to be in agony, even on smooth water. All of them, though, did their duty despite how sick they became.

"Compared with a PC, riding a destroyer in rough seas was like sitting in a stuffed chair in your living room," an old salt on a PC told the author. Some men who suffered chronic seasickness on a PC received transfers to the beach or to larger ships. Among them were former big ship sailors who could not take the rough life aboard a PC. Crew members were young men. Anyone over about thirty-five found life aboard too difficult.

Pitching and Rolling

"We were pitching and rolling a little . . . . Then all at once it hit. Boom! The whole ship shuddered. . . . I was sure we were all goners. . . . we were hit again . . . I was thrown across the deck . . . . I learned from him [the Quartermaster] that we weren't being torpedoed . . . PCs just normally ride that way," Grundman wrote of his early days on a PC.[65]

Men exiting hatches onto the weather deck, struggling through passageways, or climbing ladders timed their steps to coincide with the pitch or roll of the ship. They hurried ahead a few steps then grabbed something nearby and hung on until the ship leveled. Then they slogged ahead again and grabbed another handhold. A few steps at a time, with timed pauses not to get smashed against a bulkhead or washed overboard, they clawed their way from one place to another. Builders had welded hand rails and eye bolts to the overhead inside the bridge to help the helmsman and other men keep their feet in rough seas. See Figure 2-6. In especially rough seas the helmsman might tie a line around his waist. He would then secure the ends through the hand rails or eye bolts in the overhead to keep himself erect and leave two hands for the wheel.

In heavy weather, when a man stumbled down the mess hall ladder and threw back the canvas hatch curtain, salt water sprayed down the ladder and doused nearby sailors. Inside a PC, the bulkheads, especially those below the water line, always dripped water. Moisture seemed trapped in them. They sweated like the men. Because of this constant dampness, some men said that as much fungus grew on PC sailors as on the bulkheads.

After a few weeks at sea in rough water and weather, during which time they never took off their dungarees for sleeping, and when the crew had fresh water only to wash hands and teeth twice daily, the engineers began to stink like real sailors. Coming from topside in the fresh, cold, sea wind and descending the ladder into the compartment felt like getting smashed in the face with a dead decaying fish. The deck apes stayed clear of that compartment as much as they could.

When one of them had to come in to wake an engineer for watch he would try to hold his breath and would rush in and out. The snipes always felt revolted by the odor but got accustomed to it. It was simply something with which they had to live. When a man from the black gang got a chance to wash and change clothes, it felt as good as going on liberty.

Over all parts of the ship, especially the mess hall, hung the odor of cooked food, soggy wool clothing, sweat, oil, and vomit. As the ship rolled and pitched, butcher knives, meat cleavers, and other galley gear flew through the air. They clattered against bulkheads or smashed against men's heads and bodies. Cook helper Joe Cooper, on PC 477, said, "The ship would roll so bad I would take the lid off the pot and the stuff would fly out. A hunk of meat would fly all over the table . . . ."[66]

Like a world class belly dancer, a PC had all the moves — and then some. PCs pitched like no other ship. Up a wave they would climb, soar over the crest with half their keel staring at sky. James F. Kennedy depicted this action in one of his paintings shown in Figure 5-14. The ship would hang on the crest of the wave, shudder all over, twist, strain, and groan. Then she would pitch over as though some giant hand had yanked its bow down. The screws would blast foam in all directions as they broke through the surface and raced until the governors responded to slow the engines. Men hung on the throttles in the engine room and hauled back on them to help the governors. That was a tricky and dangerous task while sliding on the oiled deck plates and bashing against the hot engine housing. Throughout the ship, men clutched any hand hold, flexed their knees, and hung on. Racing down the wave, the ship would plunge her prow — BLAM — into the sea and bury like a submarine on Emergency Dive.

This action was especially dangerous in fresh water, which has less buoyancy than salt water, as men on PC 1213 discovered during a storm on Lake Huron in 1946. Thomas Nolan wrote, ". . . when the ship's bow dove in, it just kept going down!"[67]

Ever so slowly the ship would dig up from the sea raising her bow like a trembling whale. Solid water would boil over the forecastle right up to the portholes in the bridge. Up she would soar with green water cascading down the superstructure and sweeping along the decks. Over again the ship would go and on and on for hours or days or weeks. Weary men grumbled, "We ought to get 50 percent flight pay and 50 percent submarine pay."

Even when men could sack out, it was not easy. It was the up and down motion that made it difficult to sleep or even rest. As the ship slid down a wave, a man would rise weightless. As the ship climbed up from the trough, the man would flatten into his bunk with a g-force like in a sharp-turning airplane. This motion was rough on sleep but also on a man's back and kidneys. Men would rub their backs and say, "Damn. We ought to wear motorcycle belts on these ships."

Running Deep

On some convoy runs the waves were so high that the men could not see over them or could men on other ships see the PC. From the troughs, the waves were higher than the mast on the PC. "We thought you guys went down a dozen times," men from other ships would say when they met the PC crew in port. Other ships in convoys sometimes reported a periscope sighting that turned out to be the top of the mast of a PC. Its superstructure and hull were lost between the towering waves and deep troughs.

PC 486 was escorting an American submarine that was returning from a war patrol, to Pearl Harbor.[68] The sea was rough with waves towering over the mast of the PC, which was often lost to view from men on the submarine. As the two vessels soared above the waves together, the Skipper on the submarine signaled to the PC, "We have an extra periscope on board. You're welcome to use it." The two ships disappeared from each other's views. A few minutes later they rose on the crest of waves into each other's views. Back flashed the reply from the Skipper of the PC, "Thank you, but we are below periscope depth."

Tossed Like Peanuts

High winds tore words from speakers' mouths and whipped spindrift from waves and crashed it against the ships. It soaked the men topside and slammed them against the hard metal bulkheads. Seamen rigged lifelines along the ships' decks for men to grasp as they stumbled along the wet slick surface. Often, though, men could not venture out on deck even with the lifelines, because towering waves marched across the ocean, beat and pounded ships and men, and swept men over the side.

Ernie Pyle, on board a transport, watched the invasion force proceed toward Galena, Sicily in July 1943. Mistral winds tore at the sea and buffeted the PCs and other small ships. He wrote, "The little subchasers [PCs] and infantry-carrying assault craft (LCIs) would disappear completely in the wave-troughs as we watched them. The next moment they would be carried so high they seemed to leap clear out of the water."

At Palermo, Italy, Christmas morning 1944, a duty Signalman on the beach watched in awe as PC 1246 tossed and pitched on the horizon.[69] "That crew's being thrown around like peanuts," he mumbled. "They'll be lucky to get coffee and sandwiches," he said and thought of the Christmas dinner with which he would gorge himself. The small ship rose on a swell. He glued his eyes on the ship's signal halyards expecting a distress signal to soar up to the PC's yardarm any minute. Then the ship disappeared as it fell into the trough of a huge swell. A few minutes later the PC thrust up from the sea, and up the yards of the PC flashed a preparatory signal. "Here it comes," the man on shore said. The ship sank from sight again. Minutes later it wallowed up a wave with its bow sweeping free of the sea, throwing spray like a waterfall. A signal flew from its yardarm. The Signalman on shore studied the colored flags snapping in the gale. He blinked, checked again, then shook his head in wonder. The flags on PC 1246 read, "Merry Christmas."

Despite cruel weather or enemy action, Christmas was always festive on a PC with home style seven course dinners served. If the cooks could not serve it at sea on Christmas Day, they served it for the crew at the next chance.

PCs took terrible beatings and often had to drop out of convoys and head into or run with the seas just to keep from broaching and sinking. At those times the weather was so bad that submarines could not attack anyway, so the convoys did not need the PCs. Other times a PC would "snuggle up" in the lee of a big merchant ship to let the bigger ship protect it from the wind and seas.

Edward P. Stafford, a Skipper of an SC accompanying a PC in heavy weather, wrote, "The PC directly ahead stood up so straight on her fantail that we could see her 3-inch/50 main battery just forward of her high pilothouse." On some PCs pounding waves wrenched those three-inch guns askew as shown in Figure 5-15. Some times the waves even popped two-inch diameter bolts holding the gun to the deck. This pounding would go on not only for hours but for days and weeks until it debilitated the men. The physical stress of combating the ships' motions exhausted the men not only physically but psychologically. Often they were so seasick or fatigued they were almost ready to give up and let the ship go under. Somehow, though, they always rallied. Despite their fatigue they hung on and did their jobs. Duty, courage, and self preservation always fought back.

Flying Objects

The other ship's motion that crews hated and feared even more than pitching was rolling. As bad as the pitching motion was, at least sailors could stay in their racks. It was the rolling that kept them flat on their stomachs with arms wrapped around the edges of the bunk, tricing chains, stanchions, or anything handy. The ship would roll from one side to the other, climb over a wave crest, and plunge down into the trough. Down to the bottom it would sink. Then, rolling sluggishly onto its beam, it would stagger up the next wave on its side. The pounding, twisting, and tons of water that swept aboard wrenched topside gear. Stanchions, ready lockers, even ship's boats ripped from the decks and plunged overboard. Everything unfastened on the ship, including the crew, slid or tumbled across the decks. Even items that the crew had fastened down or clamped in receptacles would tear free and become part of the moving insides of the ship. In heavy seas with short wavelengths, the ship would snap roll violently. Then, those loose objects became deadly missiles. Sliding heavy objects, rolling twenty pound cans of food, flying knives, forks, cleavers, and other gear injured many men.

How Far Would it Roll

In the engine room, the snipes had to duck from missiles that were screw drivers, wrenches, and hammers. Also, the engineers had to fight the bilge water rising over the deck plates at the end of each long roll. All this, however, was secondary to the fear that the ship would capsize. If it rolled past its design limit it might never return to vertical. Though designed for a 110-degree roll, that calculation did not allow for shifting of the center of gravity of the ship. If crew members and heavy objects broke free and slid to one side of the ship or fluids sloshed to one side of partly empty tanks during a roll it would change the center of gravity. These changes could prevent the ship from righting itself. Always, the engineers nursed the engines, tended them with care, and listened for strange sounds or unfamiliar rhythms. They knew well the capricious nature of machinery and constantly lived with the fear that the engines might stop. In heavy seas a PC could capsize if it lost way and wallowed over and down the steep sides of a large wave.

Always Busy and Crowded

Unlike on a submarine where men shared bunks, hot bunked, a PC had a rack for each crew member. But the men could not always use them. When not on watch during the day, maintenance and repair required the men to do ship's work. Men had no time to catch up on sleep they had lost during rough weather or when in combat.

Because of the cramped quarters and violent motions of the ship, even in moderate seas, the men got in each other's way and made problems for watch-standers. This condition was especially bad on those PCCs or control ships. Often they carried extra officers and communication men. Such a ship, designed for about sixty-five men and officers might have sailed with one hundred crew members.

The Struggle With Boredom

Despite sea state, stifling tropic air, North Atlantic gales, Caribbean hurricanes, Pacific typhoons, or frigid Aleutian williwaws, PCs sailed, and their crews endured. As with most sailors of all navies of all time, a PC sailor's chief burden at sea was boredom. With monotonous regularity for days on patrol, in convoys, or during training they stood four- and eight-hour watches, except the two-hour dog watches. Day after day they did ship's work, ate meals, raced through drills, gulped gallons of coffee, filled log books, puffed cigarettes, operated their ship, and longed for news of home.

On patrol or in convoys, the Soundman on the bridge, huddled over his gear listening for echoes from the Pings of the sound that his gear thrust into the sea. After each Ping, he twisted the dial five degrees and launched another sound pulse. Always, even in sleep, everyone kept an ear tuned to the constant Ping . . . Ping . . . Ping of the sound gear awaiting a return echo from a stalking submarine. Lookouts strained their eyes, days on end, for enemy aircraft. Radar operators glared at their screens examining every blip of sea clutter for an enemy ship. Many days at sea were dull with monotonous routine numbing sailors' minds and dimming their alertness.

When contacts did happen, though, GQ blared, and men leaped to their feet and raced to their battle stations. They dogged hatches shut and yanked covers from and manned the weapons. Excitement and fear flushed boredom aside. With the bitter taste of danger, the men flung themselves into the tasks for which they had trained. They closed with the enemy and proved that their ships and they were equal to the job for which they had gone to sea.

Figure 5-1. Officers and crew of PC 1131 at Olongapo, Subic Bay, Luzon, Philippine Islands, April 1946. Photograph courtesy of Richard Janelli.

Figure 5-2. "Salty," Watchdog 1/C. He spent two and a half years on PC 1125 in the South Pacific. Many pet dogs had the names Salty, Saltie, or Salti. Photograph courtesy of Wilfred Tlusty.

NAVPERS 661 (Rev.)

Certificate of Discharge

Under Honorable Conditions

UNITED STATES NAVAL SERVICE

This is to certify that ___ TRIXY, Muubs ___

K-9-793 ___ Chief Mascot ___, United States Naval Reserve

has this day been discharged from ___ the U.S.S. PC-793 ___
and the U. S. Naval Service, under honorable conditions.

Dated this ___ 24th ___ day of ___ February ___, 1945, at 0800

Character of discharge ___ Dependency ___

Ralph Daniel Benefiel, RM2c

Ralph D. Benfiel - RM2c ___ U.S.N.R.

Reason for discharge ___ Dependency ___
Authority for discharge (if for reason other than expiration of enlistment) ___ ALNAV 6-46 ___
is ___ not ___ recommended for reenlistment.
Enlisted as ___ 1st Class Mascot 13 Dec. 1944 Attu, Alaska ___ for D.O.W.
Born on ___ at ATTU, ALASKA
Qualifications ___ TRICKS
Ratings held ___ 1st Class Mascot, and Chief Mascot
Certificates ___ None
Service schools completed ___ None
Special duties for which qualified ___ Sitting Up
Service (vessels and stations served on) ___ PC-793

Rating at discharge ___ Chief Mascot ___ (Permanent) Service No. ___ K-9-793
Final average ___ 4.0 ___ Marital status ___ Married

___ U.S.N.,
and Executive Officer.

DESCRIPTIVE LIST

Height ___ ft. 15 ___ in. Weight ___ 25 ___ lb. Eyes ___ Brown
Hair ___ White, Brown, Black ___ Complexion ___ Ruddy ___ Personal marks, etc. ___

I hereby certify that I have examined the man herein named and find that he:
Is ___ (physically qualified for reenlistment.
Does ___ require treatment or hospitalization.
I CERTIFY that this is the actual print of the right index finger of the man herein named

___ U.S.N.,
and Medical Officer.

Monthly rate of pay when discharged ___
I hereby certify that the man herein named has been furnished travel allowance at the rate of ___
cents per mile from ___ to ___ and paid
$ ___ in full to date of discharge.
Total net service for pay purposes ___ years ___ months ___ days

___ U.S.N.,
and Disbursing Officer.

Figure 5-3. Certificate of Discharge for "Trixy," a pet dog who served on PC 793 almost two years. Courtesy of Ralph Benefiel.

Figure 5-4. Quarterdeck Watch on PC 793 in early 1945. The sailor is William O'Connor, Shipfitter 2/C. Photograph from the author's collection.

Figure 5-5. Shore Patrol, Walter H. Haag, GM3/C and shipmates from PC 478 on Naha Jima, 1945. Photograph courtesy of Walter H. Haag.

Figure 5-6. Sailors on PC 619 relaxing a few days before D-day in Plymouth, England. Left to right: John Kostyk, Ernie Meserole, and the twins Robert and Harold Magil. Photograph by Jules Monek and courtesy of Ray Goin.

Figure 5-7. Change of command ceremony on PC 779 at Adak, Aleutian Islands, winter 1944. The variety of uniforms worn by officers included blue, khaki, and green with four different hat types. Photograph courtesy of John Tombaugh.

Figure 5-8. An officer and an enlisted man share a quiet moment on PC 789. Photograph courtesy of Webb Nimick.

Figure 5-9. Armando Turaichi, Seaman 3/C on PC 1207 in 1944 at the Naval Section Base, San Juan, Puerto Rico, takes time out to wash his clothes. Photograph courtesy of James J. McMahon, Jr.

Figure 5-10. WW II Hillbilly. Drawing courtesy of William Buffington.

Figure 5-11. "Swing Trio" on PC 1603. How the bass viol got on board and where the owner stowed it is still a mystery. Photograph courtesy of Albert W. Young.

Figure 5-12. Sailors from the Fifth Fleet waiting at the beer garden named Duffy's Tavern on Esperito Santos. Photograph courtesy of Harold Raymond.

Figure 5-13. A PC swimming party off the coast of Southern France. Photograph courtesy of Mrs. Latimer B. Hyde.

Figure 5-14. Black and white copy of James F. Kennedy's painting of PC 574. Painting courtesy of James F. Kennedy.

Figure 5-15. View of the forecastle of PC 555 showing the starboard mousetrap rails ripped from their mounting and the 3"-50 gun knocked out of line by waves during a typhoon. Photograph courtesy of Edward R. Emanuel.

CHAPTER 6

PC Exploits — General

Many Missions for PCs

The ". . . famous and most efficient 173-foot PCs . . ."[70] operated in all theaters of war. Though the Navy conceived PCs, to respond to the U-boat threat until the Navy built larger ships, commanders, around the world, found other uses for them. Not only did PCs hunt and sink U-boats along the east coast of the United States, they hunted submarines across the Atlantic Ocean and into the Mediterranean Sea. Then they stalked and destroyed Japanese submarines in the Pacific Ocean. As PCs displayed their capabilities, Navy leaders developed many other missions for PCs as new and unexpected needs of combat appeared during the war.

The Navy used four forms of ships based on the PC hull as discussed in Chapter 3. One type was the standard PC. A second version was the AM or mine sweeper. The third variant was the PGM or motor gunboat. A fourth modification was the PCC that the Navy used as control ships during amphibious campaigns. The historian Samuel Eliot Morison wrote, "Experience had proved that a ship-to-shore movement involving several hundred landing craft of many different types required a well-trained control group as traffic policemen . . . ."[71] Many of these "policemen" were patrol craft and submarine chasers, particularly PCs. In the Pacific campaign they included the modified versions of PCs, the PCCs.

Some missions the Navy assigned to PCs required them to

have sea keeping abilities and endurance up to and beyond the limits built into their design. Overall, they showed their excellent sea keeping characteristics and survived all varieties of storms. Despite their limited range for transoceanic voyages, they plowed across the Atlantic and scurried along with the fleet across the broad Pacific refueling and replenishing at sea when necessary. For example, Figure 6-1 shows PC 477 fueling at sea in May 1942.

PCs steamed in coastal patrols near shorelines and were among the largest vessels that worked near shore. At invasion beaches, PCs entered waters of only a few fathoms depth as they spearheaded amphibious invasions. They guided and led landing craft to invasion beaches and were the largest vessels deployed in front of the landing craft. Some PCs even went in before the first wave of troops to scout the beaches and search for channels for the LCIs and LSTs that landed the troops.

Far from land, they sailed across the Atlantic and Pacific Oceans. On these occasions they were among the smallest escorts that herded convoys across gale-swept oceans.[72] In frigid weather and under tropic skies they hunted and destroyed submarines. PCs also sailed and fought on the deep sea with task forces of capital ships, and they guarded convoys in the Mediterranean Sea.

Ice encrusted their halyards and guns in the North Atlantic and along the Aleutian Island chain. See Figure 6-2 that shows PC 1209, along the East Coast of the United States, covered with ice. Tropical heat off Africa and in the South Pacific baked their crews and blistered their paint. Where the Navy needed PCs, they went. When the Navy needed a job done, they did it. PCs performed well and justified their design and construction and the training given to their crews.

Errors and Omissions About PCs

Elliott, in his book about escort ships,[73] overlooked the varied roles PCs played. He wrote, "These [PCs] were useful for inshore work, but were not seaworthy enough, or of great enough endurance, to undertake effectively the longer screening duties." He added, "The PC class was designed as a coastal escort and submarine chaser . . . and it is understandable that we do not find them appearing in mid-ocean escort duties." Silverstone[74] wrote, "The steel-hulled class (PC) were useful as patrol vessels but of little value as convoy escorts, being too slow and weakly armed." Elliott and Silverstone were wrong when they wrote their books. They were not aware of the facts about the jobs PCs did or the capabilities of the ships and their crews.

Elliott was correct, however, when he wrote the following words. ". . . PCs . . . made a very significant contribution to the USN's war effort, both on the Atlantic seaboard and in the Caribbean (where we find them hunting in groups), and in the wider Pacific." He continued with the words, ". . . they [PCs] performed bravely and efficiently, and played a new part as navigation and control ships, leading the waves of landing craft into the beaches once the leapfrog assaults back across the Pacific began." This generosity by Elliott does not amend for his omissions of the functions of PCs in the invasions in the Mediterranean Sea and Normandy. Also, it does not atone for his remarks about PCs not being seaworthy and that they did not appear as mid-ocean escorts. They were rough riders, but they were seaworthy. This feature is shown in Figure 6-3 of PC 554 as she breasted heavy seas in an Atlantic convoy during 1943.

PCs and their crews suffered similar omissions, oversights, and errors by other authors during and after World War II. Many writers about World War II naval operations that involved PCs did not even ask PC sailors what they did or how they endured. They did not read the original reports or ships' logs of patrols, convoys, transoceanic activities, and amphibious landings in which many PCs participated. Writers of official Navy publications made similar mistakes about where PCs served and the duties they accomplished. Even the United States Navy, only five years after World War II, failed to recognize and acknowledge the work done by PCs far from harbors and coastlines during that war. The 1950 edition of *The Bluejackets' Manual*[75] mislead recruits, from their first days in the

Navy. It contains the statement, "The PCE was designed for general escort, whereas the PC normally stays near harbors or works with coastal convoys."

Many accounts of battles and invasions in which PCs participated do not even list them among the ships engaged. Furthermore, writers rarely mentioned the damage that PCs inflicted on Axis armed forces. Also, the Navy all but ignored the PCs that the enemy damaged or sank, and it did not memorialize the PC sailors who enemy weapons had maimed or killed.

PCs Were Among the First Ships on the Job

While the Navy waited for PCEs, PFs, and DEs to slide down launching ways to assume the job of escorting convoys across the oceans, PCs were pounding into the seas and attacking U-boats. Off the Atlantic seaboard and across the Atlantic Ocean they scoured the depths pinging for U-boats. Rolling and tossing depth charges from stern racks and "K" and "Y" guns, they struck at and killed submarines. See Figure 6-4. Sinking submarines was only part of the effectiveness of PCs as convoy escorts. Even without attacking submarines they did their job. Their appearance around convoys in threatening numbers kept U-boats away or prevented them from closing to attack positions with the ships in the convoys. As convoy escorts, with or without making attacks on submarines, PCs probably saved many Allied ships and sailors' lives.

Depth Charge Attacks

Because of their small size, thin hulls, and the slow speed at which they deployed depth charges (no more than fifteen knots), the impacts of the explosions from their depth charges, particularly when set at shallow depths, devastated PCs. The explosions damaged PCs almost as much as they did a submarine. With charges exploding at fifty or one hundred feet below the surface, a PC's stern heaved up from the water. Deck plates in the engine room twisted and tore loose. Pipes burst and sprayed water and oil about the spaces. Radar consoles lost images. Compasses whirled. Electrical circuits tripped. Shock waves tore through men's feet and knees knocking the sailors to the deck. Pain lanced through their ankles and legs. Every shallow depth charge attack was a traumatic experience for a PC and its crew. Despite this self-inflicted damage, their Captains never hesitated; they attacked. Figure 6-5 shows a deep set depth charge attack made by PC 478 on a submarine, in the South Pacific in 1944, that tailed the ship. A Navy plane sank the submarine a few days later. For comparison of the effect on the PC, Figure 6-6 shows the explosion of a shallow set depth charge behind a PC.

Crews Manned the Guns and Rescued Men

Across the Atlantic Ocean, in the English Channel, in the Mediterranean, across the Bering Sea, and around the Pacific they sailed and fought. They swept for and killed submarines and enemy ships and aircraft. With their machine guns, PC sailors blasted German, Italian, and Japanese aircraft from the skies. On the open deck and flying bridge, men strapped themselves in 20-mm machine guns and stood unshielded as in Figure 6-7. On the 3"-50 and the 40-mm guns they fed ammunition and fired the guns while exposed to enemy fire like the men in Figure 6-8 and Figure 6-9. They pounded enemy beaches with shells and bullets. Risking being sunk, the crews cleared mine fields by blowing up mines with their ships' guns or rifles. Despite lurking submarines that could have torpedoed them, PCs stopped dead in the water to haul aboard bleeding drowning sailors from sunken ships and soldiers and marines from foundering landing craft. They plucked downed Allied airmen from the sea. On picket and patrol duty, PCs ran ASW screen for larger ships. Though not always in direct contact with enemy craft, they guarded ships that delivered war supplies and troops to ports and invasion sites around the world as shown in Figure 10. Wherever American and Allied forces went to war, PCs were there doing their part.

Return From the Sea

Often, PCs were at sea for weeks without rest. At these times they exceeded their endurance and range capabilities, and other ships replenished them at sea. Now and then they got lucky when a new ship arrived in their group with mail aboard for them. Sailors then rigged lines and hauled sacks of mail from one ship to the other treating the packages like newborn babies.

Weary from standing long watches, tense from battling U-boats or kamikazes, exhausted from fighting waves and winds, PC sailors nursed their battered craft into safe harbors. See Figure 6-11. After short rests and hard labor to repair and replenish their ships, they went out to sea again.

Enemy Kills

PCs not only participated in many actions and battles, they also added to the toll of enemy losses of men, supplies, aircraft, boats, and ships. For example, among the confirmed Axis vessels sunk by PCs are those shown in Table 6-1. Some aircraft shot down by PCs are given in Table 6-2. Besides sinking these ships and downing the air planes, PCs inflicted damage on many other enemy submarines, surface ships, and aircraft. Some vessels they damaged so badly other Navy ships sank them later.

Table 6-1. Enemy Ships Sunk by PCs

PC Number	Axis Ship and Type	Date	Location
L'Indiscret (W-32), PC 474, with USS *Fowler*(DE 222)	German Submarine U-869	3/45	Casablanca Africa
PC 477	Japanese midget submarine	12/8/42	Guadalcanal

PC 487	Japanese submarine I-24	6/10/43	Kiska, Aleutian Islands
PC 545	Italian torpedo boat	2/18/44	Anzio, Italy
PC 558 and PC 626	Two German midget submarines	5/9/44	Anzio, Italy
PC 565	German submarine U-521	6/2/43	Delaware, USA
PC 619	German submarine U-986	4/17/44	Land's End, England
PC 624	German submarine U-375	7/30/43	Sicilian Strait
PC 627	Italian torpedo boat	2/22/44	Anzio, Italy
PC 627	Italian MAS Mosquito boat	5/14/44	Anzio, Italy
PC 1123	Two Japanese suicide boats	5/5/45	Polillo Island, Philippines
PC 1129	Two Japanese suicide boats	1/31/45	Nasugbu, Philippines
PC 1135 and USS *Manlove*	Japanese submarine I-32	5/24/44	Central Pacific
TOTAL	**15**		

Table 6-2. PCs That Shot Down Aircraft

Number	Axis Aircraft Type	Date	Location
PC 477 and PC 479	Two Japanese planes	12/31/43	New Britain
ex PC 542 French, *Tirailleur*	Two German planes	1944	Mediterranean
PC 543	German two engine bomber and German single engine fighter	7/10/43	Off Sicily
PC 555	Japanese torpedo plane	7/21/44	En route to Guam
PC 559	German two engine bomber	6/6/44	Tiber River, Italy
PC 617	German Junker 188 bomber	6/10/44	Baie De La Seine, France
PC 619	German Heinkel bomber	6/10/44	Baie De La Seine, France
PC 623	Three Japanese planes	1945	Pacific
PC 1119	Five Japanese planes	2/45	Off Corregidor, Philippines
PC 1125	Japanese torpedo plane	7/21/44	En route to Guam
PC 1128	Japanese plane	12/15/44	Mindoro, Philippines
PC 1133	Two Japanese planes	44, 45	South Pacific
PC 1134	Two Japanese planes	1944	Leyte, Philippines
Total	24		

Too Many Stories to Tell

Some PCs were hero ships. Others were pluggers. All, though, did the jobs assigned to them, and most often they did more. Many PCs and their crews earned battle stars and citations for actions in battles and invasions. See Appendix G. None of them, however, received the honors they deserved for the months of monotonous patrols or the weeks at sea in convoys.

In Chapters 7, 8, and 9, I record some adventures of PCs and their crews in the three theaters of war during World War II. The story is neither a continuous nor a complete account. I took the accounts recorded in those chapters from various sources. They included official records, ships' logs, government documents, interviews and correspondence with former PC sailors, and written histories. In many accounts I used the words of the men who lived through the episodes.

The events and ships I mention in the following chapters I selected for two reasons. First because they were of significance to the war and second because they illustrate the variety of activities and the range of exploits in which PCs were involved. Each case, though, represented the actions of all PCs.

I did not list all those PCs that took part, and I did not tell all the stories of those PCs I did list. The lack of inclusion of some ships or the omission of the full stories of others does not imply that those ships or incidents were less important than others. The reason is that a book is limited in size, and cannot mention all exploits. Because of the large number of PCs, it was not possible to include the stories of all of them or list all the activities of those ships selected. Many tales of PCs and their crews, therefore, are still to be told.

Figure 6-1. PC 477 fueling at sea from USS *Long Island*, CVE-1 on 22 May 1942. Photograph from Real War Photos.

Figure 6-2. Lt. Russell L. Harris, Skipper of PC 1209 on the left and LT Allen, Executive Officer, stand on the ship's ice-laden signal bridge while on patrol in January 1945 off Connecticut, USA. Photograph courtesy of Franklin Smith.

Figure 6-3. PC 554 on convoy duty in the Atlantic in 1943.
Photograph courtesy of Harry R. Ayres, Jr.

Figure 6-4. Depth charge fired from a "Y" gun aboard a submarine chaser (PC) patrolling the Atlantic coast in 1942. Photograph 80-G-40330 of the National Archives.

Figure 6-5. PC 478 unleashing deep set depth charges on a submarine in the South Pacific in 1944. Photograph courtesy of Walter Haag.

Figure 6-6. Shallow set depth charge exploding behind a PC. Official U. S. Navy Photograph.

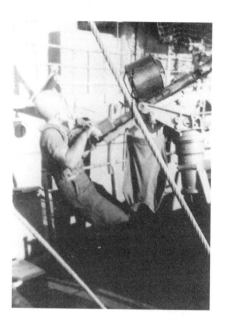

Figure 6-7. Sailor on a PC strapped into the shoulder harness of a 20-mm Oerlikon machine gun. Photograph from Real War Photos.

Figure 6-8. Sailors manning 3"-50 gun on a PC. Photograph courtesy of the Bay County Historical Society.

Figure 6-9. The crew of PC 1198 manning the 40-mm gun during General Quarters while on patrol from Port of Spain, Trinidad in 1945. Photograph courtesy of Harold R. Walker.

Figure 6-10. Aboard PC 1122 during attack on Sanspor, Dutch New Guinea, 29 July, 1944. Photograph from Real War Photos.

Figure 6-11. PC 818 tying up in one of the Aleutian Islands. Note the Special Sea Detail manning the rail wearing foul weather gear, the engines at "all stop," bow lines on the dock, fenders over the side, the steaming colors dropping from the mast, and the Officer's Steward at the flagstaff raising the ensign the moment the first line went on the dock. Photograph courtesy of John Tombaugh.

CHAPTER 7

PC Exploits — American Theater of War

PCs Helped Win the Battle of the Atlantic

After newly constructed ships began to enter the battle of the Atlantic, convoys had the faster, better armed, and ASW-equipped PCs as escorts. These escorts scurried around in the van, on the flanks, and astern of the convoys, pinging for submarines. Figure 7-1 shows PC 818 leaving port to guard a convoy. Often the PCs peeled off from their sweeps at the sound of a contact, raced to the target, and harassed and stung U-boats with depth charges and mousetrap bombs. Even if they did not sink the enemy submarines, they kept the U-boats from attacking the merchant ships.

PCs Damaged U-boats

As part of an escort for a convoy off the North Carolina coast, PC 462 steamed its zigzag pattern.[76] She accompanied the prewar PC 68, destroyers *McCormick* and *Ellis*, British trawlers HMS *Cape Warwick* and *Coventry City*, and Coast Guard cutter *Dione*. On 22 May 1942, about noon, an echo from the sound stack on PC 462 rang through the ship. The PC and *Dione* charged toward the contact and attacked with a barrage of eighteen depth charges. Oil and bubbles swarmed to the surface, but the escorts, wary of such tricks by U-boat Skippers, searched for three more hours. They never made contact again though, and finally they raced back to their convoy. On the PC and *Dione*, men knew that even if they had not sunk the U-boat they had damaged it and had saved the convoy from an attack.

On 13 July 1942, the PC 458, working with US Army aircraft off the east coast of Panama, damaged U-153 with a depth charge attack. That action kept the U-boat from attacking local convoys.

PC 462 Saved USS *Spry*

A few days later, July 15, 1942, the PC 462, PC 463, and PC 480 patrolled the mine fields off Hatteras. An order from their commander detached PC 463 to chase a reported submarine nearby. At the same time PC 462 peeled off from the patrol to rescue another PC that had run out of fuel.[77] The destroyer, *Spry*, was escorting toward Hatteras, two wounded merchant ships, *Mowinckle* and *Chilore*, from a convoy that a submarine had attacked. The two ships limped toward the harbor unaware of the mine fields they approached. PC 462, having refueled the other PC, headed back. Her Captain saw the merchant ships lumbering toward the mine field and ordered the ship to flank speed. The stern of the PC dug in, and the ship lunged toward the merchant men. Blinker lights flashed. The radio crackled with warnings to the ships about the mines. Too late. Flashes lit the night, and columns of water burst up from the sides of the two freighters. PC 462 raced to the remaining ship, the *Spry*, just in time to halt the destroyer's plunge into the mine field and lead her to safety.

The Decline of the U-boat

Having learned from experience, the Navy made improvements in convoy and ASW tactics. Also, they introduced hunter-killer groups of aircraft working with surface vessels. With these changes, the United States Navy began to demolish the U-boat campaign along the East Coast of the United States and in the Caribbean. By November 1942, Dönitz had conceded the superiority of American naval and air forces in the submarine war off the

American coast and in the Caribbean. The hunter-killer groups and admiral Andrews' fleet of escorts, including PC 496, PC 549, PC 550, PC 553, PC 554, PC 555, PC 557, PC 602, and PC 1228, had decimated the U-boat fleet. The Nazis could not sustain their losses, many of which were their ranking U-boat aces and crews.

1943 – The Battle Continued

Attacks on submarines by PCs waned, but PCs and their crews still had plenty to do and continued their convoy duties. On New Year's Day, 1943, for example, convoy KG123 rounded Cape Maisi on its final leg to Guantanamo, Cuba. PC 1122, Lt. j. g. Joseph Peck commanding, swept the port flank of the group of ships pinging for U-boats. At 0500 hours a blast lit the sky. SS *James M. Sprunt*, loaded with tanks and ammunition, "dissipated into the sky then rained down on the convoy."[78]

Peck ordered General Quarters and started the hunt for the U-boat. The sound gear picked up an echo, and a destroyer joined the PC. Together they searched for the submarine but never found a firm enough contact to attack. Later they learned it was the U-185 that had sunk *Sprunt* and a tanker and had escaped.

In its original intended role, after commissioning at the Philadelphia Navy Yard in September 1942, the PC 577 zigzagged in choppy seas off the starboard side of convoy #1 from Trinidad to Bahia, Brazil. She, along with another PC, a Canadian Corvette, and Destroyer USS *Goff*, ran screen for the convoy. Without warning, at 2340 on 8 January 1943, red flames ignited the quiet black night. An exploding German torpedo had ripped open the hull of the tanker, *Broad Arrow*, which was on the port side of the convoy.[79] Within minutes, with the convoy illuminated by the flames, the U-boat blasted another tin fish into a second vessel, *Birmingham City*. Ninety minutes later, the U-boat Kapitan fired torpedoes into the ships, *Collingsworth* and *Minotaur*. Taken on the *Minotaur*'s port bow, the torpedo destroyed her integrity. She plunged to the bottom in four minutes with a cargo of 4,100 tons of coal and her crew.

The sea swarmed with burning oil, debris, and wounded and dying men. With three of his four escorts to protect the embattled convoy, the Escort Commander in *Goff* ordered PC 577 to lag the convoy. Donald M. Kerr, Lt., USNR (a former instructor at SCTC) in command of the PC got orders to drop behind, keep the U-boat down, and then pick up survivors. The PC spun around, raced astern, and spent hours tossing depth charges and harassing the submarine. Lt. Kerr kept the submarine on the defensive so the wounded convoy could escape further loss. Then his ship became a target and had to dodge two of the U-boat's torpedoes. Finally, as the sun peeked over the horizon on 9 January 1943, the crew of PC 577 began plucking 152 bleeding, dazed, exhausted survivors from the sea.

PC 576 Rescued Three Men on a Raft

While on convoy duty in the South Atlantic during January 1943, Seaman Earl Carpenter on PC 576 spotted an object on the horizon.[80] The Captain of the PC got permission from the convoy commander to peel off and investigate the sighting. When they closed on the target, they discovered a raft with two Dutch seamen and one US Navy Armed Guardsman aboard. Sailors on the PC lifted the three men aboard their ship and tended to their needs. Earle Thompson, a PC sailor, wrote about the dazed and debilitated survivors, "They were only skin and bones, as they had spent eighty-three days on the raft."

Nazi Milch Cows Appeared

Sinking of merchant vessels along the eastern seaboard almost stopped, and a lull set in that deceived the United States Navy into thinking that the coastal U-boat campaign had ended. This reprieve was short-lived, however when a U-boat sank a merchant ship off Jacksonville, Florida in April 1943. Soon after, men on ships sighted ten U-boats and two supply submarines 400 miles east of Bermuda.

These supply boats or "Milch Cows" were the German Type

XIV with more than a 12,000 mile range and 423-ton fuel capacity.[81] Also, the Germans used Type IX (Variant d1) submarines for replenishment of fuel and Type VII (Variant F) for resupply of torpedoes to the attack submarines. U-boats previously had to make the 3,000 to 4,000 mile and ten to fifteen day transit from America to the Bay of Biscay, France to resupply. This time off-station effectively reduced the U-boat fleet in U. S. waters. Dönitz had more boats at this time, but when he also introduced the tactic of using the supply submarines he could keep the Wolf Pack boats on station longer. These tactics kept convoys alert and PCs busy along the eastern seaboard. Again, though, the ASW campaign succeeded. By mid-1943 U-boat losses exceeded the tonnage of ships that they sank. The gap between victories and losses accelerated to the end of the war[82] as shown in Figure 7-2.

1943 – Q-Ships and PCs

During World War I, the Navy had deployed 180 decoy or Q-ships. They sank twelve and damaged sixty U-boats for a modest success. Though the Q-ship concept seemed outmoded by 1942, the U. S. Navy was desperate to stem the U-boat onslaught along the Atlantic seaboard and reincarnated the Q-ship idea. It fitted out six such ships. Only one, the *Atik*, saw a U-boat, which sank the Q-ship.

Two PCs worked in concert with a Q-ship in the Atlantic Ocean to try to trap gullible U-boat commanders.[83] PC 617 and PC 618, wearing the two-tone blue colors of the fleet, escorted USS *Big Horn*, a Q-ship. The Navy had selected the tanker SS *Gulf Dawn* and converted her to a decoy ship. They renamed her USS *Big Horn*, AO-45. Under command of Captain J. A. Gainard, the Navy disguised *Big Horn* as a fleet oiler. She contained thousands of sealed, empty, oil drums for buoyancy, and workers had compartmentalized her for watertight integrity. She carried thirteen officers and 157 enlisted men. Trap doors on deck, concealed six 4"-50 guns, and *Big Horn* also mounted a seventh similar gun on the stern. For ASW attack, a double hedgehog launcher perched on the bow. Various machine guns and six K-guns, to throw depth charges, completed her armament.

Operating out of Trinidad alone on two trips she had no luck with U-boats. The navy then assigned the two PCs as decoy escorts for *Big Horn* with the group under command of CDR Louis C. Farley, USNR, the new Captain of the Q-ship. The plan was for *Big Horn*, while in a convoy, to run up a breakdown signal and drop out of the convoy. She would then straggle behind the other ships with the PCs lurking just over the horizon on her beams.

On 3 May 1943, using a similar tactic and after detecting a submarine, *Big Horn* and the PCs went to GQ and charged to the attack. The PCs closed on the submarine and launched mousetrap bombs and rolled depth charges on the U-boat. Despite the explosions and concussions, the attack was without success. During two more cruises, *Big Horn* and the PCs attacked submarines but with the same negative results. Once while PC 617 tracked a contact the sonar failed due to an electrical short in the sound dome. The PC aborted the attack. On another cruise during December 1943 the radar operator on the PC detected a surface contact at 2500 yards. The OOD rang GQ. Men scrambled to their battle stations, yanked covers from the guns, and set the depth charges and mousetraps.[84] The Skipper of the PC ordered his gun crew to fire three star shells. The men on the 3"-50 rammed out three shells that arced up, exploded, and lit the darkness. "It's a sub," a lookout yelled, and the ship plunged toward the target as it crash-dived. Soon the Soundman made contact and reeled off the ranges and bearing to the U-boat, which was now under the surface. After maneuvering the PC into an attack position for what should have been a sure kill, the Captain fired the mousetraps. All eyes stared at the rockets on the forecastle that sat silently. All of them failed to lift off. Again, an electrical short had stymied an attack, and a lucky U-boat crew had survived.

The Q-ship ruse did not result in sinking any U-boats, but it made U-boat Skippers wary of trying to pick off real stragglers. This result probably saved ships and lives, but despite that fact the Navy abandoned the Q-ship project.

1943 – Back to the Convoys

Sprinting around a convoy on 15 May 1943, the PC 552 lashed her sound waves into the depths.[85] An echo bounced from a submarine, and the PC swung into action. At 2300 she closed on the contact, and her mousetrap bombs swept up into the dark sky, splashed, and sank. The Captain of the PC stared at his stop watch, as the charges plummeted down, counting seconds to determine the depth if one exploded. When the bombs reached a depth of 240 feet, he heard a muffled explosion. The water was deeper than forty fathoms, so the blast meant he had hit something above the bottom.

"It could have been a submarine. More likely just a fish," the Captain said, but he ordered the ship spun around to stay with the contact. Seven minutes later another explosion ripped the ocean and knocked out lights on the PC.

"That 'fish' we attacked had a swastika on its side," one sailor suggested to the Captain of the PC.

1943 – A Sure Kill

PC 565, Lt. W. T. Flynn commanding, escorted a convoy to Cuba off Virginia on 2 June 1943. About 85 miles southeast of the Five-Fathom Bank Lightship, the Soundman aboard the PC heard an echo. "Contact," he yelled.

General Quarters blared throughout the ship. The crew raced to battle stations and slammed and dogged hatches. Heeling over, the ship spun toward the contact and thundered ahead at flank speed. Closing the gap, and changing course according to the Soundman's bearings of the contact, Flynn ordered the ship to standard speed. The little subchaser slowed to attack speed, and as the ship crossed ahead of the contact, Flynn ordered the crew to roll depth charges.

Seconds later, in the depths, U-521 shuddered. Her hull split as the depth charges exploded. The sea flowed down through her main hatch. Her diving planes jammed. The U-boat plunged down. Her Captain shouted to the crew to blow ballast. The sea foamed as compressed air drove out the ballast water. In a few seconds the buoyancy changed, and U-521 soared up and popped to the surface.

Shells streaked from the PC's 20-mm machine guns and blasted the submarine. Knowing that his boat was lost, and fearing the PC would capture it, the German Captain ordered his crew to open the sea cocks and abandon ship.

Before his crew could react to scuttle the boat and escape, water poured through the open hatch trapping the men inside. U-521 plunged toward the bottom. PC 565 raced back and laid another barrage of depth charges over the spot. Oil, air bubbles, debris, and human remains washed to the surface. Amid the rubble floated only one survivor, the commanding officer, Kapitänleutnant Klaus Bargsten.[86] Sailors on the PC fished Bargsten from the water. An "ace" who wore the Knight's Cross for having sunk 39,000 tons of Allied shipping, Bargsten did not regret the loss of his crew. Instead, he was humiliated that his boat had been destroyed by an American officer who only two years before had been a landlubber lawyer.

After the crew of the PC stowed the German Kapitan aboard, covered their weapons, and secured from General Quarters, PC 565 continued her journey. The crew set the watches and shifted back to their normal routine. Cooks called chow down, and the PC sailors hurried back to the mess hall as shown in Figure 7-3.

1944 – The Hunt Continued

Less than two weeks after commissioning, PC 1209 headed for SCTC for her shakedown cruise. At 1835 on 14 May 1944, the crew had settled into the routine of the dogwatch and the evening meal. Everything was normal. Suddenly, Ray Clifton, the Boatswain, screamed, "Two torpedoes astern, port side." The OOD ordered the helmsman to come hard left. General Quarters blared, and men raced to their stations. As the ship heeled around, two more torpedoes streaked by on the starboard side just missing the PC.

At the sound stack, the Soundman leaned forward and listened. Finally, he heard an echo. "Contact," he blared. The Captain took the conn, gave his orders, and the PC charged toward the enemy submarine. As the PC approached the spot determined by constant sound ranges and bearings, it slowed to attack speed. The Skipper ordered the men aft to roll the depth charges. A shallow pattern of charges sank from view. A few seconds later they exploded. The shock tore the surface of the ocean and pounded the PC. After the boiling sea subsided, the ship hunted for the contact but with no luck. The results of the attack were not conclusive. PC 1209 continued the search for a full day then secured from the operation.[87]

In the Caribbean off Point Manzanillo on 15 March 1944, PC 469 hounded and attacked U-518 for five hours and dropped many patterns of depth charges. Though men on the PC knew they had damaged the submarine with their depth charges, the U-boat had escaped. It happened that the German Kapitan had decided it was too dangerous in the area. He declared that "no traffic" was there for him to attack, and he hightailed it for home.[88]

1944 – The "Black Company" Ship's First Mission

In 1944 the Navy started an experimental program to place Negro crews aboard two ships. They were destroyer escort USS *Mason*, (DE 529) and patrol craft USS PC 1264. See Appendix H for the story behind and leading up to this experiment.

PC 1264 rolled depth charges while on her first convoy mission in July 1944. Running from New York to Guantanamo with a convoy and escorts including PC 1209 and PC 1212, an echo from her sound gear jarred the men on the bridge. The OOD shouted the order for General Quarters. Determined to prove their ability and justify their experimental status as a ship with a black crew, the men dashed to their battle stations. The sailors strapped on helmets and manned the guns and depth charge racks as the ship wheeled toward the target and slowed to fifteen knots. When the Captain gave the order, sailors at the stern yanked the levers, and the "ashcans" flopped into the ship's wake. Moments later, the shallow pattern of depth charges exploded. Shock waves pounded and shook the little ship.

For three hours PC 1264 hunted, rolled more depth charges, and fired mousetraps on the elusive contact. Having finally lost the contact, the PC sped back to the convoy. Though they did not sink the submarine, they had kept it from attacking the convoy and probably had saved American ships and lives. Settling back into routine, the crew on the PC continued their mission to Cuba.

Like most reservists in the Donald Duck Fleet, sailors on PC 1264 had never been far from their home towns before the war. Cuba seemed to them to be a strange and exotic land. On arrival in Guantanamo, Seaman George Alexander got set to pass a mooring line to a man on a dock. The black sailor yelled to the line handler, "Do you speak American?"

"No," the man replied. "But I do speak English."

Hurricanes Pounded PCs

Despite the decline in submarine activity, PCs still herded convoys between places like New York and Key West, Florida or Guantanamo, Cuba. During the hurricane season on these runs, PCs fought an enemy worse than U-boats. When they ran into these storms, 100 knot winds and thirty foot seas tossed the small ships like corks. Frothing green water cascaded over a ship's bow. It pounded against the bridge, swept in torrents along the deck, poured through the scuppers, and boiled aft over the fantail like a raging waterfall. Its weight and force stripped away lifelines as though they were spider webs. Tons of water tore ammunition lockers, stanchions, and life rafts loose and dashed them overboard.

PC 1217 had a trial with a hurricane off Florida on 13 September 1944. During this storm, with winds to 150 knots and seas as high as sixty feet, the Navy lost five vessels and 344 men dead or missing.[89] On PC 1217 water and wind bent, cracked, and carried away topside gear. Plates buckled. Water ran through the doors and ports of the pilot house. Six inches of water flooded the radio room, crew's berth, wardroom, mess hall, and galley. Seas poured through cracked seams and piled six feet of water in a magazine. Electricity failed. Fuel oil sloshed on the decks of compartments. Waves pounded life rafts, the wings of the bridge, lockers, and other topside gear beyond repair. Hydraulic couplings between the engines and the propellers spewed fluid. Twisting of the ship yanked the main engines out of line. Later, after the storm had passed, the ship had to carry five degrees of right rudder to hold a steady course.[90] Figure 7-4 and Figure 7-5 show some damage to the exterior of the ship.

A Hurricane Swept Three Men From a PC

At sea, even in moderate weather, the deck of a PC was usually awash. Spindrift sprayed onto the ships. Wave crests broke over the gunnels. Solid water flooded the decks as the ships dug up from the trough of a wave. At times when the ships rolled and caught a big wave, men held on for their lives. In hurricanes, even with life lines rigged on the decks, men got swept over the side.

While PC 564 helped escort a convoy along the east coast of the United States, it almost capsized in a hurricane off Cape Hatteras. Waves swamped the deck and flung three men overboard. One man, Seaman Richard Tull, disappeared. Swept away by one wave, the next surge of the sea tossed a second sailor, Chief Boatswain's Mate John Black, back aboard the ship where shipmates grabbed him. Figure 7-6 shows the third sailor, Radioman Daniel Riley, thrashing in the water and drifting away from the ship. Electrician's Mate Norman Scaffe, bent a line around his waist and dove over the side. He swam to and grasped the drowning man. Men on the PC hauled on the line and brought the two men back aboard. For his action, the Navy awarded Scaffe the Navy and Marine Corps Medal.[91]

A Last Time at Sea

Excited about his first submarine hunt, Matthew Jordan, Seaman 2/C, fresh out of Boot Camp, paced the deck of PC 1217 as a member of the crew. It was his first duty, his first ship, his first time at sea.[92] Off Cape Hatteras, out of New York, bound for Cuba, in midwinter of 1945, the seas began to kick up. The ship, with three other escorts herding a convoy south, started pitching and rolling as the wind whistled through the ship's rigging. Heavy dark clouds bulged against the horizon ahead. "Hurricane," the radio message read. They had been through this before, so all hands rigged the ship for what they knew was a trial to come. Spindrift whipped from wave tops. Seas pounded against the ship. Up, the PC soared over the waves, and then plunged into the troughs. Stanchions ripped loose, and ammunition ready lockers buckled under tons of foaming sea.

Jordan, ready for the mid-watch, stripped off his red night goggles and struggled through the starboard hatch to the deck. Clinging to lifelines, he lurched and waded aft through knee deep water streaming along the deck and out the scuppers. At his station by the 40-mm gun tub, he slipped his sound-powered phones over his ears and plugged the cable into the jack. He felt thrilled knowing that he was doing his duty to guard the convoy from enemy submarines.

Near the end of the midwatch, Gomez, Boatswain's Mate 1/C, burst into the chart house. "The starboard lifeline's stripped away from stem to stern," he shouted. "Anyone seen Jordan?" The men on watch stared at him and shook their heads. Over the squawk box, the Boatswain passed the word. All hands turned out and searched the ship. A few of them struggled aft to the 40-mm gun. There, they found the shredded end of the phone cable. A towering sea had plucked the sailor from his post and had swept him overboard. It was Matthew Jordan's first time at sea. It was his last time at sea.

1944 – U-boats and Buzz Bombs on the East Coast

The Germans again broke the underwater calm along the east coast of the United States. On 3 December 1944, the Canadian ship SS *Cornwallis* took a torpedo launched from U-1230. She sank with the loss of all but five of her crew.[93] Again, U-boats prowled the Eastern Sea Frontier. This time they employed the snorkel (Schnorkel) to give them freedom from having to surface often to recharge their air supply and batteries. They ran under water on their

Diesel engines making them more secretive in their attacks and more elusive targets to discover and flush to the surface. Fear of these U-boats increased. Captured German spies said that the U-boats carried Buzz Bombs they would fire at New York and other coastal cities.

1944 – Buoy Able Underway

A few days later, on 14 January, the Eastern Sea Frontier erupted into action. It recalled from a convoy the Coast Guard Cutter *Galatea* and PC 1264 and assigned them to an Anti-Buzz Bomb patrol. It ranged from Montauk Point, Long Island south to Cape Charles at the Chesapeake Bay.

Weeks afterward, while patrolling alone off New York near the sea buoy "Able," Lt. Purdon, the Skipper of PC 1264, decided to hold a drill. He ordered the Executive Officer on the flying bridge, "Man your battle stations! We're going to disable Able."

Manned and ready, the ship steamed at two thirds speed toward and echo-ranged from the massive chain and anchor that secured the buoy in twenty-two fathoms of water.

"Range two thousand. Bearing steady," the Soundman, James, reported. A few minutes later he said, "Range twelve hundred. Bearing steady."

"All engines ahead standard," the Captain ordered bringing the ship to attack speed. "Right ten degrees rudder," he added following attack doctrine.

"Target bearing left rapidly," James shouted.

Purdon froze. "Repeat," he bellowed.

"Bearing went left . . . disappearing." The Soundman confirmed again and added, "Doppler down."

"All engines ahead one third. Hard left rudder." This was no buoy anchor but a submarine that had been hiding against it waiting for a shot at a passing ship. The U-boat had spooked when the PC had come to attack speed and bore down on her.

"Set the mousetraps," Purdon ordered. He conned the ship into position and, with the ship's recorder, fired the rockets. Like lazy seagulls, the bombs soared ahead of the ship. They struck the water and plunged below the surface. Five seconds later, a tremendous explosion churned the water. The bombs had probably exploded by contact with the sea bottom Purdon thought. Nevertheless, men aft swore that, shortly after the detonations, a submarine conning tower broke the surface then sank below the waves.

After two more attacks an oil slick appeared on the surface. PC 1264 and PC 1149, with the Coast Guard Cutters *Thetis* and *Icarus*, hunted a bit longer. Then the PC quit the chase and resumed her patrol. Two weeks later, off Nova Scotia, other U-boat hunters sank the damaged U-866. No one could prove it, but most likely PC 1264 had damaged U-866 and had contributed to her end.

1944 – Götterdämmerung for U-boats

The sinking of U-866 was one episode in the closing chapter, the Götterdämmerung, of Dönitz's Untersee Krieg. Not only the U-boats, but trained German crews and experienced officers died at suicidal rates. The Allied forces, through the convoy system, mass construction of escorts, including hundreds of PCs, and rapid training of crews for them, had won the Battle of the Atlantic.

1944 – The Move to Europe

With the defeat of Operation Paukenschlag, the United States and its Allies shifted more of their naval attention toward Europe. Uppermost in the minds of strategic planners by 1944 was the need to drive the Nazis from western Europe and back to "The Fatherland." It appeared that the only way to defeat Hitler was to crush his army and Germany if necessary. In addition to putting Allied armies ashore in Italy and southern France, an invasion of the Continent from England was essential. The obvious route to France was across the English Channel.

To haul an army and its supplies from the British Isles to the coast of France and force them ashore against heavy defenses would require an enormous amphibious campaign. These included PCs for escort, picket, and beach control duties. The Navy began its plans and deployments to get the PCs to England, so PCs began the long trek across the ever stormy and treacherous wintertime north Atlantic. Many of them went as escorts for convoys of merchant ships. PCs had a maximum range of 3,000 miles at twelve knots under ideal conditions. Zigzagging on the flanks of convoys, chasing sonar contacts, rounding up stragglers, and battling the heavy seas and gale winds for up to a month at sea burned up their fuel, food, and other supplies. Often they had to replenish at sea. This procedure was a major ship-handling task for a small ship nestling against a much larger one in twenty foot seas and thirty knot winds. Nevertheless, their Reservist officers and sailors learned their tasks and got their ships supplied and across the Atlantic.

PC 564, PC 565, PC 567, PC 568, PC 617, PC 618, PC 619, PC 1232, PC 1233, PC 1252, PC 1261, PC 1262, four DEs, and two AMs, all under the command of USS *Moffett* (DD 362), escorted thirty-four barges from New York to Plymouth, England. They departed 24 March 1944 and zigzagged for twenty-six days across the Atlantic. Planners of the coming invasion of France wanted these oil barges, railroad car floats, and wooden scows. They would use them to ferry ammunition to the soldiers who would be grappling for their lives on the beachhead.[94] The organizers of the invasion forces knew also that they would need PCs for the invasion, so they added the twelve PCs to the convoy's screen. The journey was long, slow, and filled with hazardous and terrifying incidents. It reached England almost intact, however, and the two-hundred concrete caissons in the convoy became breakwaters at Normandy in what planners called Operation Mulberry.[95]

Throughout the rest of the war with Germany, PCs continued their convoy work along the east coast of the United States. They ran other chores too. Besides their standard duties as escorts, one PC even became the only PC Aircraft Carrier in the US Navy.[96] At Curacao on 6 February 1945, the Boatswain on PC 1213 shook his head in disbelief. He had to order the wherry removed to make room on the deck of the PC for a single-seater airplane. With the wings of the plane stowed along the sides of the aircraft's fuselage, PC 1213 delivered the plane in San Juan, Puerto Rico three days later.

The West Coast

Though the principal actions in the American Theater of War occurred on the Atlantic Coast, PCs and their crews trained along and guarded the Pacific shores of the United States. They did shakedown cruises between Seattle and San Diego, and held gunnery and ASW drills off San Clemente Island. Some PCs ran patrols off our major port cities to search for Japanese submarines.

PC 616 also cruised the Pacific coast, but her journey was under unusual circumstances.[97] Starting from Balboa, Panama Canal Zone, PC 616 rendezvoused with the Soviet submarine USSR L-15 out of San Francisco. From there, the PC escorted the submarine back to Balboa from where the Soviet boat departed for Cristobal, the eastern terminus of the canal, and on into the Atlantic Ocean. PC 616 followed along and spent the rest of her career guarding convoys in the Caribbean and along the Atlantic coast.

1945 – Off to the Pacific

As the European war progressed and the U-boat problem dwindled, strategists turned more attention toward the Pacific Ocean. Now the United States would shift many of its naval forces from the Atlantic Ocean to the Pacific Ocean. PCs had proved their worth in the Atlantic along the east coast and in Europe. Many of them had completed their jobs in the Atlantic, and commanders began to reassign them. The United States Navy recognized the importance of PCs to the island hopping campaign that had started in the Pacific. For this need, they signaled to many PCs to transit the Panama Canal. Having brought the fight to the Nazis, suffered their casualties, and taken a short rest, these PCs then sailed to the war in the Pacific.

Figure 7-1. Bow View of PC 818 leaving port for convoy duty in 1943. Photograph from the author's collection.

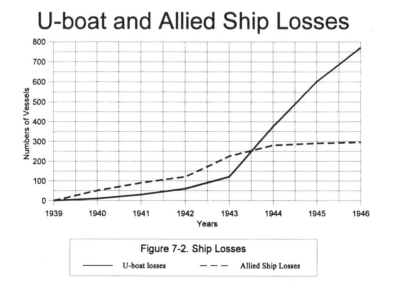

Figure 7-2. U-boat and Allied ship losses in the Atlantic Ocean from 1938 through 1945.

Figure 7-3. Crew of PC 565 at mess after they disposed of the Nazi submarine U-521 in ten minutes and captured the German Captain. It was obviously a calm day for the men to eat so leisurely. Photograph courtesy of Robert Baldwin.

Figure 7-4. PC 1217 in September 1944. Bow-on view shows damage sustained after eighteen hours battling a hurricane off the east coast of Florida. Official U.S. Navy photograph courtesy of Walter Mackey.

Figure 7-5. PC 1217 in September 1944. Starboard bow view shows damage sustained after eighteen hours battling a hurricane off the east coast of Florida. Official U.S. Navy photograph courtesy of Walter Mackey.

Figure 7-6. PC 564 in a hurricane off Cape Hatteras, 30 September 1943. The man overboard, Radioman Daniel Riley, was rescued in two hours. A shipmate was lost. Photograph courtesy of the Patrol Craft Sailors Association.

CHAPTER 8

PC Exploits — European, African, Middle Eastern Theater of War

PCs Arrived in Europe

After their successful deployment with the Eastern Sea Frontier as U-boat hunters and convoy escorts, the Navy assigned many PCs to convoys to England. On arrival there, the Navy used them in their accustomed ways but also found new assignments for them. They did air-sea rescue, patrolled the English Channel for German submarines and E-boats, and did a myriad of other duties. PCs also escorted landing craft between British ports as the Allies shifted vessels to confuse German Intelligence about the site of the coming invasion of Europe. While some of the PCs stayed in England, others sailed into the Mediterranean as escorts for merchant and troop ships for the African campaign. After arrival, they guarded convoys in the Mediterranean, ran patrols outside North African harbors, and did rescue and picket duty and other chores.

As Allied planners developed the tactics for the invasion of Africa and Southern Europe, they initiated the idea of using PCs as navigation and control vessels. In this role they would guide landing craft to the invasion beaches. The ships and their crews adapted to this new role and learned their new tasks even as they continued doing their original duties. PCs and their crews fought through most of the actions in the European, African, Middle Eastern Theater. In this theater of war they had victories and they suffered casualties, both in ships lost and men captured, missing, wounded, and killed. In this chapter, I use the guidelines outlined in Chapters 6 and 7 to illustrate some exploits of PCs that served in the Atlantic Ocean, the English Channel, and the Mediterranean Sea.

Actions in the Mediterranean

PCs sailed directly from the United States, or from England, through the Straits of Gibraltar to join the war in the Mediterranean. There, they took part in many operations and invasions. For example, after PC 542 arrived in Arzew, Algeria she participated in the invasions of Scoglihi, Brollo, and Salerno, Italy, and in Southern France. Another example of PC actions is shown in Figure 8-1 that depicts PC 543 in its originally intended role attacking a submarine that stalked a convoy the PC escorted. The figure is a black and white copy of a painting made by Bob Baldwin, a sailor on PC 543.

Another ship that helped storm the beaches of North Africa, Sicily, Salerno, Anzio, and southern France was PC 577. Later, the United States transferred her to the French Navy where she continued her fighting career.

Bombs at Bizerte and PC 546

Upon arrival in Tenes, Algeria from Bermuda early in 1943, the PC 546 ran patrols off the harbor. Also, she escorted convoys from Tenes to other ports and exploded floating mines with ship's gunfire.[98] While at Bizerte, Tunisia her crew fought their first engagement.

A German bomber appeared unexpectedly and roared toward the PC. Her gunners raced to their stations, manned their guns, and opened fire. Shells from the PC's weapons streaked up as bombs from the plane whistled down toward the ship. Geysers of water sprayed up as the bombs exploded nearby. Men on deck ducked as the plane darted over the port bow of the ship, almost crashing aboard. The bombs did only minor damage to the ship, and the plane escaped. This attack was the first of many fought by PC 546 and was typical of air attacks on many other ships in North African harbors.

Torpedo Sank the "People's Choice" PC 496

PC 496 was the "People's Choice," according to her crew.[99] Under command of Lt. James S. Dowdell, the ship left her convoy duty on the East Coast of the United States and joined the war in the Mediterranean. After their arrival at Beni Saf, Algeria, when they were not at sea patrolling for submarines, constant air raids by the Germans kept the crews at their battle stations. The men adapted to the air raids and decided to prepare themselves and their ship for a long war. However, the cruise of PC 496 did not last long.

On 4 June 1943 she entered a swept channel leading to the harbor of Bizerte, Tunisia in North Africa, escorting a group of landing craft. With eight miles to go, one hour after relieving the 0800-1200 watch, an underwater explosion ripped open the hull and the aft deck of the PC. Men toppled against bulkheads. Water flooded into the ship. Equipment tore loose and scudded across the decks. The Captain, whom the explosion had jolted while in his bunk, leaped up and dashed to the bridge as the ship heeled over. He stared at the ship's clinometer pointer that had already swung fifty degrees to port.[100] He could do nothing to save the ship.

Yeoman Carter Barber recalled,[101] "Suddenly there was a terrific explosion, and I made a mad dash for topside . . . ." The Captain ordered the crew to abandon ship. "The skipper was the last to leave, but it seemed as if we all left together as she went down in less than three minutes after we went over the side." Brown, a lookout on the bridge when the blast shook the ship, wrenched open the life jacket lockers and cut loose a ten-man raft. "Then I was in the water," he wrote. Barber struggled topside and stepped off the one foot of the ship's remaining freeboard, into the water. The sea gobbled PC 496 stern first in less than one minute.

Figure 8-2 is a black and white copy of a painting by Barber. It shows how PC 496 looked to him, from his position in the water, as she went under. Barber and many other shipmates received letters of commendation for their actions from James S. Dowdell, the Captain of the PC.

Such was the sudden fate of PC 496 and the five men who died of an underwater explosion.[102] When PC 496 sank, the crew thought the ship had struck a mine. Years later, records showed that a torpedo from an Italian submarine had destroyed her. Ironically, the Captain of the submarine, instead of being decorated, received a court-martial for mistaking the PC for a destroyer and wasting a valuable torpedo.[103]

The First Shot Fired at Gela

In the darkness just before dawn at Gela, Sicily on 9 July 1943, the PC 627 inched toward the enemy shore. She led her brood of LCVPs to the invasion beach.[104] Two searchlights on the shore suddenly flashed probing beams of light across the water. The lights lit up the swarm of little craft. The glare of the lights made the landing craft, that were loaded with vehicles and soldiers, easy targets for the enemy's guns.

Responding instantly, sailors on the PC rammed home a shell in the 3"-50 gun. Gabe Whitcomb, the pointer on the gun, squeezed the grip. The jolt of the gun shook him in his bucket seat, but he kept his eye glued to the sight ring ready to fire again. A glowing red eye of the hot end of the shell arced toward shore, slammed into the earth, and erupted in flame and smoke. One searchlight beam on the shore disappeared.

Whitcomb and the other gunners on PC 627 poured more rounds into the area on the shore where the other light still glowed and smashed it and its operators. By destroying the lights, the gunners on the PC had kept the shore batteries from pounding the LCVPs and had saved the equipment and the lives of the men aboard them. Lt. j. g. Stotzer credited PC 627 and Gabe Whitcomb with firing the first shot of the invasion of Gela.

PCs Fight at Sicily

The day following the invasion of Gela, SC 530 and PC 550 rushed to the rescue of men from *Sentinel* (AM 113) that a German dive bomber had sunk. Fighting heavy seas, the SC took off some sailors, and the PC rescued the remaining survivors. From a ship's company of 101, on *Sentinel*, ten men died and fifty-one suffered wounds.[105] The toll would have been higher if it had not been for SC 530 and PC 550.

Continuing her activities, PC 550 screened the amphibious command ship and guided landing craft that dropped troops behind the German lines in North Sicily. Then, for the invasion of Salerno, Italy, PC 550 escorted LSTs from Africa to the beaches.

Later, on 10 July 1943, the PC 546 helped guide landing craft to the beaches in the invasion of Licata, Sicily. Retiring from that task, and while standing off the beach, the ship dodged Nazi aerial bombs. Then, when PC 562 struck a mine off Sicily, PC 546 raced in and took aboard survivors from her sister ship.

PC 562 had steamed out of Port Empodocle, Sicily on 18 July 1943 through a mine field in company with PC 546.[106] Her Signalman blinked to the other PC to come alongside. Just then an exploding mine heaved up her fantail. A cloud of smoke and flame gushed out of the ship, and PC 562 began to sink. After the wounded and other crew members shifted to PC 546, ten volunteers stayed aboard to help save the ship. A Gunner's mate from PC 562 died of his wounds as PC 546 started towing the damaged ship to safety.

Other PCs in the Mediterranean that participated in the invasion of Gela, and the following campaign included PC 543, PC 591, PC 621, PC 624, and PC 625.

PC 543 Blasted Two German Planes

On 10 July 1943 the destroyer *Maddox* (DD 622), PC 543, and the British submarine H. M. S. *Safari* cruised just south of Sicily. Invasion planners had assigned the submarine as a beacon submarine for the landing at Gela, Sicily. With little warning, a German dive bomber loomed over the group and darted down toward the ships. One bomb dropped from the plane and burrowed into the depth charge magazine of *Maddox*. A blast ripped the destroyer, and smoke and flames shot up into the sky. The explosion tore open the destroyer, and she sank to the bottom. Figure 8-3 shows a rendition of the attack on *Maddox* drawn by Bob Baldwin, a sailor on PC 543.

Plowing through the boiling sea, that a strong mistral wind had churned to a froth, PC 543, Lt. M. W. "Silver" Silverstein in command, escorted the British submarine, *Safari*, from Gela to Malta.[107] At 2245, ten minutes after *Maddox* had gone down, PC 543 closed on the British submarine to screen her. Without warning, a twin-engine German bomber roared in at low level along the port beam of the PC. Men on the 40-mm and two of the 20-mm guns swung their weapons around and fired. Tracers lit the stream of shells that ripped into the German plane. Moments later the aircraft crew's parachutes blossomed below the aircraft, and the plane dove and plunged into the sea.

Only six minutes after the crew of PC 543 had recovered from the exhilaration of this deed, a single-engine fighter plane zoomed toward the PC. The 20-mm guns chattered, the 40-mm thumped, and the 3"-50 on the forecastle belched shells as all guns on PC 543 hammered at the German plane. This time too, smoke and flames blossomed from and trailed behind the plane. Seconds later, the pilot's parachute flared open, and, as he drifted down, the plane smashed into the sea. After the incident, the Captain of *Safari* said that his ship was only a spectator during the battle. He congratulated PC 543 on her excellent shooting.[108]

Torpedo Boat Attacks Beat off by PC 556

Along with *Niblack*, PC 556 screened two merchant vessels and two LSTs they were escorting from Gela to Syracuse, Sicily.[109] Near the harbor, just after the midwatch on 20 July 1943, under a bright moon on a flat sea, two explosions ripped the calm. Geysers of water flew up, one geyser 300 yard away and one only seventy-five yards ahead of PC 556. Anticipating a mine field, the OOD ordered the engines back one-third to stop the ship's headway.

Moments later, a lookout on the PC yelled, "Torpedo. Starboard bow." General Quarters rang, and the officer on the bridge ordered the ship ahead at full speed. The PC's crew of Coast Guardsmen rushed to their battle stations. Then, a second stream of bubbles from a torpedo swept from starboard past their stern. The helmsman swung the wheel hard right, and before the ship came around, the wake of a third torpedo crossed the port bow of the ship fifty yards ahead.

After scanning the area, men on PC 556 spotted two surface targets to the left of their position. The PC veered around and raced toward them. At closer range the Skipper ordered the ship to come right to bring its guns to bear on what appeared to be two Italian torpedo boats. The Captain ordered his crew to fire, and the guns on the PC pounded at the boats. Shells from the 20-mm and 40-mm guns on the PC raked the boats and exploded against their sides. Smoke billowed from them, and the badly mauled torpedo boats broke off and scurried away to the north under a curtain of heavy smoke.[110]

No Let Up in Air Raids

Air raids continued almost daily. On one occasion German bombs exploded ammunition on a freighter and sent shrapnel sizzling across PC 546, bloodying some of the crew. Fires and flares lit the night sky, and PC 546 and the ship they were tied against became prime targets. The Skipper of the PC readied the ship to clear the dock. Before the crew could cast off the lines, however, the aircraft droned in for another pass at the ships in the harbor. To escape from their mooring against the freighter the crew of the PC swung their fire axes and chopped the mooring lines.

The PC's engines roared, and the ship churned away from the flames and the ammunition on the freighter, that was cooking off from the heat. The PC's luck ran out, however, when her lookouts mistook a flight of German planes for American P51s. When the PC's gunners relaxed, the Germans swept in and unloaded their bombs. One near miss, only fifteen yards off the port bow of the PC, blew a hole in her hull and filled the storeroom with water. A damage control party raced to the compartment, plugged the hole to stop the flow of water, and saved the ship.

PC 624 Sank U-375

During the grim hours of the midwatch on 30 July 1943, water slid down the conning tower of U-375 as her black hulk surfaced in the Sicilian Straits. Just southeast of the Italian island of Pantelleria at 0230 hours, the submarine's commander had spotted a small convoy of landing craft. The convoy had departed Bizerte, Tunisia and was bound for Licata, Sicily.[111] After a couple of range and bearing checks the Kapitan maneuvered his boat into attack position and fired a torpedo. The weapon blasted from a forward tube, streaked toward the convoy, and just missed PC 624, one of the two escorts of the convoy. The Kapitan of the U-boat saw a beam of light blink toward him, and he realized that his boat was in danger. He ordered the boat to dive. The hatch slammed shut behind him, the last man down, as he dropped into the U-boat. He ordered his ship to dive down for what he thought would be the safer depths of the Mediterranean Sea.

On PC 624, which had been pinging for submarines while escorting that convoy of landing craft, the operator on the radar set had seen a blip at 0230. When he reported it the Captain of the PC, LCDR R. D. Lowther, USNR, challenged the unknown vessel. The target ignored the challenge.

Lowther decided to illuminate the target. On the PC the gun crew loaded a star shell in her 3"-50 gun. "Fire one," rang out. The shell soared up, burst, and lit the night. Men on the PC spotted a submarine on the surface racing away. Almost immediately PC 624 heeled over as it turned away from the convoy and sped toward the surfaced U-boat. At the time the star shell burned out the contact disappeared from radar. Then the Soundman heard an echo from the submerged submarine. PC 624 charged toward the U-boat. When she closed the range, the Captain slowed the ship and rolled a pattern of depth charges.

Explosions thumped in the waters around U-375. The underwater concussions drummed into the men on the PC, and the ship shuddered. Unable to leave the landing craft with only one escort, Lowther broke off the attack and returned his PC to its station with the convoy. On the way he reported that his ship had damaged an enemy submarine. Though commander Lowther and his crew did not know the results of their depth charge barrage, the Kapitan and his U-boat never returned from that patrol.[112] Later, LCDR Lowther and his crew learned that they had sent U-375 to the bottom.

Death Aboard PC 627

In the darkness of the night of 31 July 1943, a flight of up to fifty enemy bombers droned in over the hills around Palermo on the north coast of Sicily.[113] PC 627 was moored outboard of the *Strive*. When the planes drew near, flares dropped from the lead aircraft and lit the targets in the harbor. The planes flew over the harbor and let loose their bombs. One of the first bombs screeched down and exploded fifty yards from PC 627. Shrapnel whined and clattered about and ripped through the decks and bulkheads of the ship. Jagged metal missiles tore into and killed one man and seriously wounded two more men on the PC.

Fighter Bombers Attacked PC 546

During the Sicilian campaign, off San Stefano on 11 August 1943, a flight of Focke-Wulf 190 fighter bombers attacked a small-ship amphibious operation. They soared overhead and dropped their load of bombs. One Bomb headed for PC 546, Lt. Jack O'Meara in command. The missile plunged into the water just missing the ship, but it blew a hole in her hull and bloodied a couple of the crew. PC 546 received repairs, remained in the fight, and went on to earn three battle stars for action in the invasions of Sicily, Salerno, and Southern France.[114]

Attack on Anzio, Italy

After screening convoys and escorting small ships, the Navy gave PC 543 and PC 550 orders as invasion control vessels for the attacks on Anzio. Before the landing craft arrived at the invasion beach, PC 550 steamed in close to shore. There, it acted as a marker vessel for the minesweepers to clear channels and for the landing craft to bring their troops to the shore. Figure 8-4, drawn by Bob Baldwin, depicts PC 543 acting as a control ship for the landings at Anzio, Italy on 22 January 1944. In the background of the picture a British LCT(R) fires rockets onto the beach before the first wave of troops goes in.

PC 559 in Action

Four hours before minesweepers cleared the area, Lt. John R, Cain and his officers and crew maneuvered PC 559 into position off the beach at Salerno, Italy. They established a position from which to control the lowering of landing craft from amphibious ships. Despite near misses of shells from concentrated shore fire and bombs from heavy aerial attacks, PC 559 hung onto her position for eight hours during the invasion. As a guide and control ship for the landings on 8 and 9 September 1943, she guarded and led waves of assault craft to shore. Then she retired from the beach to take up antisubmarine patrol. Her perseverance under fire earned her a Navy Unit Commendation Medal.[115]

Nine months later, on 6 June 1944,[116] silver sparkles shimmered on the rippling water from the bright moon that hung over the mouth of the Tiber River, Italy. The silhouette of a German twin engine bomber swept across the moon at point blank range and closed on PC 559. Men at their guns on the PC followed the course of the plane as it bore down on them.

"Commence firing," the officer in charge of the 20-mm gun

station yelled. Goggins, Gunners Mate 1/C, leaned back against the 20-mm harness, swivelled around, sighted through the rings, and squeezed the trigger. His gun and the other guns on PC 559 chattered, shaking the gunners in their straps. The glow of tracers streaked toward the plane and struck one of its engines.

"The aircraft port engine inhaled tracers as fast as they arrived. No tracers were observed beyond the target," Latimer Hyde, the Captain of the PC, wrote. Eight seconds, and only 106 rounds of 20-mm shells, after the crew spotted the aircraft, it flamed and crashed. The Commander, 8th Amphibious Force commended the crew of PC 559 and commented on the "excellent fire discipline maintained by this ship."

Besides this action, PC 559 helped evacuate Tunis. Then for participation in three landings on Sicily and southern France she earned five battle stars and a Navy Unit Commendation Medal.

PCs Sank Torpedo and Mosquito Boats

On 18 February 1944 off Anzio PC 545 sank a motor torpedo boat, with gun fire, in a ten minute battle. PC 627 also got its chance and used its guns to finish off another torpedo boat during the night of 22 February 1944. A few months later, on 14 May 1944 near Anzio PC 627 encountered an Italian MAS mosquito boat, opened fire on it, and sent it to the bottom.[117]

PC 619 and *Swift* Destroyed a U-boat

PC 619 and *Swift* (AM 122) cruised three hundred miles off Land's End, England on 17 April 1944.[118] On the bridge of the PC, the men tensed as an echo bounced back from the "Ping" of the sound gear. It was a submarine. Officers shouted orders, the crew ran to general quarters, and the ship began maneuvering on the contact.

Below the surface, Kapitan Karl Kaiser recognized his danger and ordered U-986 to take evasive action. This boat was a 1,950-ton supply submarine or "milch cow" that had left France to bring supplies to German Wolf Pack U-boats.

The PC hung onto the dodging contact, and, when in attack position, gave the order to roll depth charges. A pattern dropped into the sea and sank from view. Moments later their explosions blew geysers of water into the air, and banged shock waves against the hull of the PC. The stalk of the U-boat continued. After six hours of hunting and four depth charge attacks, men on the PC and *Swift* gazed at a two-mile long oil slick that spread over the surface. U-986, her hull crushed, had plunged to the bottom with all hands.

Two Submarines Sunk by and the Loss of PC 558

On patrol off Italy on 9 May 1944, a lookout on PC 558 shouted, "Submarine wake off the starboard bow." All hands rushed to battle stations.[119] The Captain stared through his binoculars at a two-foot glass dome, awash with a wake trailing ten feet behind it, circling his ship. Gunners on the PC opened fire with the 20-mm and 40-mm guns. Shells walked across the water and pounded into the dome. Heeling in a quick turn, the PC steamed toward the contact. The Captain ordered the crew to roll depth charges. In the explosions that followed the shallow pattern, the target, a Nazi one-man submarine, disappeared and plunged to the bottom.[120] The PC spun around and came back to fish out of the water a German Oberleutnant who had manned the submarine. Later, the Captain of PC 558 repeated this action with the help of PC 626 and sank a second German one-man submarine.[121]

Revenge by the Nazi Navy was swift, however, when a German torpedo ripped through and sank PC 558 the same day with the loss of many of her crew.[122] Accompanying PC 558, when she sank, PC 1235 dodged three torpedoes herself. After the U-boat that had fired them retired from the area under pursuit, PC 1235 hurried back to where PC 558 went down. There, her crew plucked thirty survivors of PC 558 from the water.

PC Squadron One at Normandy

Besides their actions in the English Channel and in the Mediterranean, PCs also poured their gunfire into the beaches and herded landing craft ashore during the invasion of Northern France. Because of the many PCs in the D-day operations and the previous lack of coordination among them in other operations, the Navy organized them into PC Squadron One.[123] LCDR Ralph Stevens, a former Skipper of PC 1263, assumed command of the squadron. His command consisted of the eighteen PCs numbered PC 484, PC 552, PC 553, PC 564, PC 565, PC 567, PC 568, PC 617, PC 618, PC 619, PC 1176, PC 1225, PC 1232, PC 1233, PC 1252, PC 1261, PC 1262, and PC 1263.

These little craft had pounded through the North Atlantic gales and heavy seas escorting ships to England. After their crossing, they spent months on patrol off the British Isles, ran picket and rescue duty in the English Channel, and did many other chores. While doing all that, their crews also waited for the parts they would play in the big job of storming Hitler's Festung Europa. They knew they would be in the invasion, but their crews did not take part as control ships in the invasion rehearsals. It was not until late May 1945 that planners gave the PC sailors limited briefings on the duties they expected of them in the coming invasion of France.[124]

When the time came for the invasion, they got their assignments and learned their jobs in a hurry. The Navy assigned many of them to act as control ships for the landings. This required precise close to shore short range positioning. To help in this delicate navigation task, the Navy installed on them a British electronic navigational system called "QH" and known as the "Gee Box." This device on the PCs helped them guide their charges accurately, even through smoke screens, to their assigned assault positions.

When H-hour struck on 6 June 1944, the PCs of Squadron One were some of the first ships near the beaches. They went close to shore to take up their control positions well before the assault forces arrived. Figure 8-5 shows the view from the port side looking forward on a PC as it approached Omaha Beach on D-day. From their stations just off the beaches they led the landing craft to the shore and pounded German pillboxes with their guns. At Omaha Beach PC 552, PC 553, PC 567, and PC 568 controlled the landings on Beaches Fox Green, Easy Red, Dog Red, and Dog Green, respectively. PC 1176 and PC 1261 preceded the landing craft to the Red and Green beaches at Utah Beach. Along with them, PC 617 and PC 618 struggled all morning to help land tanks ashore. All these ships came under intense machine gun and 88-mm gun fire.

The battleship *Texas* hovered well away from shore and fired her big shells at German strong points including an antitank wall, but she needed close-in fire support. An LCT and a group of PCs got the job. Despite heavy enemy gun fire, LCT 464, PC 553, PC 567, and PC 568 defied the German gunners. They bored right up to the shoreline and battered Nazi pillboxes, other fortifications, and the antitank wall with their guns.

After the assault troops fought their way up from the shoreline, PCs got relief from their control work and were given many other jobs. For example, senior officers used PCs to put them ashore closer to their commands. As the invasion continued, PCs scurried around pulling from the water survivors of landing craft and other ships that German shells or mines had sunk.

During and after the landings the men on PCs even had the odious task of recovering GI corpses floating near the shore. "Then after their hours at the beaches, the ubiquitous PCs were rewarded with picket and patrol duties."[125]

After convoy duty between New York and Gitmo, PC 1263 helped screen a convoy to England. Later she escorted ships to the Normandy beachhead and patrolled off the beaches to protect the larger ships from U-boat attacks. While on patrol she raced to the rescue of *Meredith* (DD 726), which had taken a hit near the water line from a glide-bomb. Running their ship in close to the destroyer, the crew of PC 1263 hauled one hundred survivors of the damaged ship aboard their vessel.[126]

PC 1261 Was the First United States Navy Ship Sunk at Normandy

At Normandy, PC 1261 arrived at the transport anchorage at 0300 on D-day eleven miles off the Red Sector of Utah beach.[127] At 0430 the ship headed for the shore to act as a control ship for the landings. Near the six fathom mark, she sent in a few waves of landing craft. Her crew watched GIs stagger in the surf, wade ashore, dig in, crawl forward, charge, and drop on the beach, slaughtered by German gunfire. German gunners on shore also targeted the ships nearest the beach, including PC 1261, and they opened fire. Shells whistled overhead and exploded near the PC throwing up plumes of water and rocking the ship.

The Quartermaster on PC 1261 rushed into the charthouse and shouted, "We've been straddled by a shore battery." Lt. Barrett wiped sweat from his brow, leaned over the chart, and checked his position against a fathometer reading. The ship was on station and had to stay there. They could not maneuver.

Suddenly, with a crash, gear clattered onto the decks. The pilot house door flew open, and the ship heeled 50° to starboard. Glass shards, jagged metal, and other flying debris hurtled around the compartment. Blood ran down Barrett's face from a gash over his eye. "That's it," he yelled and threw down his pencil. He climbed out to the port wing of the bridge and gazed up at the sheared-off stub of a mast. Men huddled on the sloping deck wondering if they should abandon the ship. The Captain glanced around, evaluated the ship's condition, and ordered the Radioman, "Tell the Admiral we're sinking."

All hands plunged across the deck as the ship heeled to her starboard beam, and the clinometer arrow swung up and pegged against its detent. For a moment the ship hung on its side — then it rolled over. In six fathoms, she sank. Men trapped below deck drowned. Other men struggled and gasped for life in the 48° Fahrenheit water. They pulled themselves onto rafts or clambered onto the PC's overturned hull and shivered.

"Help Kelly. Help Kelly," a voice screamed from the water.

George Peterson, a Fireman 2/C, saw the floundering man and plunged in. He swam to Al Kelly, who had manned a telephone on the 40-mm gun. Peterson grasped the man and held him up until shipmates hauled the two of them aboard the capsized PC.

"... a five inch shore battery shell ... struck our engine room and broke the ship transversely ...," Lt. Barrett wrote later.

Twenty-one percent of the crew of PC 1261 died in the first few minutes. Among the dead was Lt. Ralph Noble. Al Kelly wrote about him, "They said he died from exhaustion because he went after so many guys."

Eventually the survivors of PC 1261 scrambled aboard empty landing craft that were returning from the beaches. From them, they watched their ship slip below the water with only her number, PC 1261, above the waves lapping at her sides.[128] Some of the crew, soaked and shivering, perched on the part of the hull peering out above water. From there they waved and cheered at GIs who were heading for the battle ashore. Many soldiers waved and cheered back at the stranded sailors. Barrett wrote of the reactions of the crew and the many episodes of heroism, "There was no whimpering, no self-pity — only concern about rescue and thinking about other shipmates."

PC 1261 is shown at her launching in Figure 8-6. The ship had controlled her sector and guided boatloads of GIs to Omaha Beach before she became the first United States Navy assault ship sunk during the invasion of France.

PC 1176 at Green Sector of Utah Beach

A sister ship to PC 1261, the PC 1176, controlled the Green Sector of Utah Beach.[129] Her crew gazed in horror at PC 1261 as the little ship staggered under German shell fire, rolled over, and slid below the waves taking many men with her. For five hours after PC 1261 sank, PC 1176 held down the job of control ship for both beaches until the commanders relieved her.

During her stay at Normandy, less than 2,000 yards from the beach, she dodged shells from German shore batteries, and her guns blazed away at German air attackers. Like other small ships, after withdrawing from the beaches, PC 1176 then spent days on patrols hunting for U-boats and surface vessel. Later she also helped in the blockade of the German held Channel Islands.

Other D-day Activities by PCs

On D-day, other small ships including PC 1225, PC 1262, PC 552, and PC 553, boiled through shallow water and German fire to escort landing barges to the beaches. They destroyed floating mines and pummeled German pillboxes with their guns. Often they rescued men from blasted landing craft and sinking vessels. In addition they did many unrehearsed chores to help make the invasion of northern France a success.

For example, PC 553, which is shown in Figure 8-7, acted as the Primary Control Vessel for Easy Red Beach. There she guided waves of DD tanks ashore and pounded a German pillbox into submission. Often she rolled from concussions of near-miss German 88-mm shells as she shuttled back and forth plucking survivors from the frigid water. When otherwise not busy she hosted Generals Wyman and C. J. Huebner, USA, to transport them near shore so they could observe the landings.[130] Col. James E. Kerr, USMC also got a ferry ride shoreward on PC 484 to observe the progress his Marines made against the German army.

After hours at the invasion beaches, the ubiquitous PCs, with their battle-weary crews, got another reward. Theater commanders assigned them to picket and patrol duty on the "Dixie Line" offshore. This Dixie Line was a ring of protective ships including cruisers, destroyers, destroyer escorts, and PCs, to protect the capital ships and transports from submarines and E-boats.

During the evening of D-day a group of German E-boats sortied against the ships anchored off the assault beaches. PC 617 spotted one of them racing in at high speed. The Commanding Officer of the PC gave the order for flank speed, and the PC charged directly at the E-boat. As the PC drew within range of her guns and swept into a turn to bring her guns to bear, her steering cable snapped. Unable to respond to her helm the PC chased its tail while the German E-boat dashed away.

Some PCs helped escort coal carriers from Newcastle to France to warm the population of Paris during the approaching winter. Then, with green crews on board, they patrolled the stormy English Channel for U-boats. PC 617 even escorted a convoy of small boats loaded with potatoes up the River Seine to the hungry civilians at Rouen.[131] Among the other many tasks they performed Bill Weidenheft remembered the strangest mission for PC 1262. He said, "We escorted a flotilla of French potato boats at five knots up the Seine to Paris." En route, German gunners fired at them, but they never hit any of them.[132]

PC 1232 — The Gray Ghost

The crew of PC 1232, which they dubbed the "Gray Ghost," labored for thirty-three days to save survivors of craft sunk at the Omaha and Utah beaches. Then she rescued men from *Meredith* and LST 496. For this action the Navy commended them and awarded the Commanding Officer a Bronze Star.[133] The ship did all this after having run convoys between New York and Cuba for six months. Returning to Bermuda after the invasion of France, PC 1232 served as an air-sea rescue craft.

Der Blaue Engel, PC 619, Captured a German Flyer

Four days after D-day at Normandy, in the Baie De La Seine, gunners on a ship from PC Squadron One, PC 619, blasted a German bomber from the sky. It happened in the dim sky of early morning when a Heinkel - HE 177 medium bomber darted toward the PC. The PC's gunners blasted away. Shells thudded into the aircraft, and the German plane tumbled from the sky. Of its crew of six aviators five died, and only one man bailed out. He floated under his parachute into the choppy water of the English Channel near the PC.

Philip Padelford, Captain of PC 619, conned the ship near the

German, dusted off his High School German, and yelled to the floating flier, "Kommen sie hier."

The German replied, "Ich kanne nicht."

Padelford told him, "Stehen sie darauf - wir kommen."

The German floated where he was, Padelford maneuvered the ship to him, and the crew hauled him on board.[134]

On the ship, the Captain ordered Ray Goin, a Seaman, to guard the flier, Hermann Goldenbaum, a waist gunner on the plane. Goin also used his High School German to talk to the prisoner and develop a friendship with him. Forty-six years later Goin researched the German's name, located his home in Germany, and visited him. The former adversaries became close friends, and the crew of PC 619 made Goldenbaum an honorary member of the ship's company of PC 619. When Goin presented Goldenbaum with James Kennedy's painting of PC 619, the former flier said, "Here's Der Blaue Engel (The Blue Angel) . . . the ship that saved my life."[135] Figure 8-8 shows the two men, with Goldenbaum's granddaughter, holding the painting of PC 619. Figure 8-9 shows a crew member standing near the starboard wing of the bridge of PC 619. On the wing someone had painted the submarine they sank and the air craft that they shot down.

Fireworks for PC 617

After PC 617 completed her role as a control ship for LCTs in the invasion of France[136] at Omaha Beach, a German Junker JU 188 strafed the ship. During the night of 10 June 1944 the plane roared by low astern of the ship. The PC's gunners opened fire with 20-mm and 40-mm guns. MoMM 3/C James Rudolph Childress sighted and squeezed the trigger on his 20-mm Oerlikon machine gun. Shells pounded into the plane, and flames burst from the bomber. It swerved, tipped over on a wing, and plunged to earth.

All night of Independence Day, the men on ships, including PC 617, gazed at the flashes of light from Allied artillery that was dislodging Germans troops from Caen. It reminded them of fireworks during Fourth of July celebrations back home.[137] In the early hours of

5 July 1945, as darkness drifted away, they had their own fireworks.

A contact blossomed on the radar screen, and before the operator had a chance to evaluate the blip, the sonar operator heard an explosion to port. Lookouts had stared at "an object with a tail of flame strike the water with a great splash and tremendous explosion." Men leaped from their bunks. A second explosion heeled the ship over. On the bridge, Quartermaster Joseph P. Reeves, shouted, "General Quarters." Two HS 293 glide bombs had straddled the ship, missing by only twenty-five feet.

Because of the concussions of the near misses, the radio on the PC died. Lube oil lines shattered. Electric circuits popped open. Clocks, barometers, and fixtures twisted and fell from bulkheads. A generator lost its load. Lt. Squire Fort screamed, "The bastard's got us. We're sinking." Gunner's Mate Roy Adsmond swung his 20-mm gun at the low flying plane, squinted through the ring sight, and squeezed the trigger. His shells flashed against the fuselage of the plane, but it zoomed off and escaped. Later, men found metal debris from the bomb on the deck of the PC and saw holes punctured in the superstructure and other gear topside.

PCs Helped Rescue Survivors of S. S. *Leopoldville*

It was supposed to be a silent night a holy night Christmas eve of 1944 in Cherbourg, France for the crew of PC 564. In port for fuel and water after many days at sea, the men and officers looked forward to liberty in bombed Cherbourg and a quiet Christmas dinner. The 2,235 U. S. Army troops of the 262nd and 264th regiments of the 66th Panther Division were aboard Troopship S. S. *Leopoldville* only seven or eight miles from France. They also looked forward to a peaceful Christmas before deploying to the front.[138] Oberleutnant Gerhardt Meyer, his eyes glued to the periscope of U-486, planned otherwise.

Meyer stalked his target and launched a torpedo. Seconds later, at 1754 hours, the stillness of the night erupted in a blast as the German torpedo ripped open the hull of *Leopoldville* midships. Icy water poured in and bulkheads buckled. Soldiers, below decks, loaded with packs and Tommy guns, struggled to fight their way topside. The vessel settled lower.

Aboard PC 564, the radio blared with a voice order to "Peach," their code name. It ordered them to get underway immediately, rush to the sinking *Leopoldville*, and take charge of rescue operations that would include other small craft. Because of minor repairs being done on the engines on PC 564, she was out of compressed air for starting the engines. Twenty minutes later, when the engineers had recharged the air tanks enough to turn over the Diesel engines, the PC steamed out of the harbor. Captain James Spencer ordered the ship to flank speed.

Leopoldville had settled at the stern, and the bow had lifted almost forty-five degrees by the time the rescue ships arrived. Thomas Kay, a Navy gunlayer on a 3-inch gun on *Leopoldville*, shouted to the swarming soldiers at the top of his voice, "Right lads. It's time to go." As the rescue ships bounced in the surging seas men scrambled, jumped, and slid onto their decks. Some fell between the ships and the troopship and plunged into the frigid English Channel.

The rescue operations eventually grew to some thirty vessels, and high waves bashed the smaller rescue ships against *Leopoldville*. To hold their ship against the sinking vessel sailors on PC 564 tossed lines over to the sinking ship. With them they secured their ship against the larger ship's hull. As *Leopoldville* continued to sink, with many troops still lined up on deck awaiting rescue, it began to drag the PC down with it. Soon the PC also would go under if it did not get loose from *Leopoldville*. By then the lines were so taut the sailors could not untie them. The two ships settled lower in the water. Men on the PC grabbed fire axes, raced to the lines, and swung their axes. The lines held. Waves lapped higher against the side of the PC. Only a foot or so of freeboard remained. The men swung their axes again, and again. Finally, with a jolt, the lines split. PC 564, well down in the water by then, bobbed back up like a cork. Down sank *Leopoldville* fifty fathoms to the bottom.[139]

Until the following morning, the night echoed with the screams of freezing, injured, drowning soldiers and sailors. All night the rescue fleet continued plucking survivors from the water. Enlisted men and commissioned officers from the rescue ships plunged into the sea to save some of the swimming men. Heroism was routine that night, and sailors from the small rescue craft, including PC 564, saved hundreds of lives.

The PC Squadron Rested in France

After Allied troops secured areas of the coast of France, American ships began using the French harbors for anchorages to effect repairs and to resupply. PCs also found refuge in them for the same reasons. A few months later they also sought shelter there from the blustery wind, choppy seas, and freezing weather in the English Channel.

Upon the fall of Cherbourg to the Allied armies, the Navy found immediate use for the base there. Starting on 12 July 1944, the ships of PC Squadron One steamed into Cherbourg. They found it a safe haven where they could "drop the hook," make repairs, and give the crews liberty. Many PCs also berthed in Le Havre where their crews enjoyed going ashore and meeting the French people. Figure 8-10 shows a drawing, made by a PC sailor, of a lonely sailor returning to PC 617 from liberty in Le Havre on Christmas day 1944.

PCs Helped Defend the Channel Islands

When Hitler's fortified Channel Islands ran low on coal, Vizeadmiral Friedrich Hüffmeier dispatched an E-boat to raid Granville, France for coal. Lt. James S. Spielman, USNR, commanded PC 552. It had completed operations as one of the control ships in the landing at Normandy and the rescue of seventeen survivors of sunken LCTs. Now she had patrol duty from Mont St. Michel to Le Havre, a sector that included Granville. When the E-boat approached Granville, the PC responded to the raid by the Germans. PC 552 intercepted the E-boat and opened fire on it. The E-boat turned away, and Spielman's

PC chased it more than twenty miles before it outran his ship and escaped. This prompt action by PC 552 saved the coal stock at Granville.[140]

The Germans still needed the coal, so the German admiral tried again on the night of 8 March 1945. This time he deployed a tug boat, minesweepers, barges, and motor launches. Also, he planned to land commandos at Granville. At 2315 hours, the radioman on PC 564, which was on patrol off Granville, picked up an alert for his ship. The radio station blurted out the positions of three radar contacts between the islands of Chausey and Jersey. After they tracked and identified them as German, they sent orders to the PC to intercept them.[141] Lt. Percy Sandell, USNR, the Skipper of PC 564, rang General Quarters.[142] The PC charged toward the contacts. After a series of radar and navigational plots to intercept the targets, the Captain commanded, "All ahead two-thirds."

At a range of 4500 yards, Sandell ordered the crew on the three-inch gun to illuminate the targets. The night sky flashed to brilliance as PC 564 fired three star shells over the enemy ships. Fear raced through the men on the bridge as they stared at the sight of three German Gunboats knowing that even one Gunboat had them outgunned. Seconds later, a star shell from the German ships burst over the PC.

The PC opened fire, and after one round from the main gun it jammed. The German ships opened up with their larger guns, and their shells pounded the PC. A few minutes later a German 8.8 cm shell bored through the bridge of the PC and exploded. The blast, heat, and flying metal struck down all hands on the bridge, killing all but one person. As sailors raced to fight the fire another shell tore through the chart house. A third round splintered the ship's boat. Then, German shells riddled the 40-mm gun tub and crew. Motor Machinist's Mate 2/C Elmer "Scrappie" Hoover tumbled from his post as pointer. Shrapnel had riddled his body and splintered many of his bones. His buddies lashed him to a bomb rack as the ship rolled in the heavy sea. Bodies sprawled about the deck and the bridge. Because of the severe damage to the engine room, the steady roar of the PC's Diesel engines faded to silence. The Skipper ordered the men to, "Standby to abandon ship."

Sailors scurried about the deck twisting tourniquets, wrapping bandages, and shooting morphine into shivering men with legs and arms bloodied and dangling or blown away. Below decks, the engineers lit off the engines again. Under the direction of Lt. Sandell and Lt. Russell Klinger, the ship plowed ahead for the shore. It ground onto the rocks of La Baie du Verger near Cancale. Larry Jordan, Seaman 1st Class, wrote, "I never knew that land could look so good in all my life, but boy! that was the most beautiful land that I ever looked at!"

The shells of the German Gunboats killed fourteen men, wounded eleven, and left fourteen missing. Dazed survivors who heard only the last words of the Captain, ". . . abandon ship," jumped into the frigid water. From there they watched as Sandell, steering by hand, beached the heavily damaged ship. German sailors on the E-boat scooped up some of the men, who had gone overboard, before the ship ran aground. Those PC sailors ended the war in a German prison camp. A small group of men swam or went hand over hand along a line from the beached PC to shore. Though unable to speak French, they raised help from a French doctor and fishermen who went to rescue and care for the men still on the grounded ship.[143]

Figure 8-11 and Figure 8-12 show some damage on the PC. Later the Navy salvaged and towed PC 564 to England and repaired it. After the war her crew, including some survivors of the battle with the E-boat, sailed her back to the states.

For the action by and the loss of men from PC 564, the Commander, U. S. Naval Forces, France wrote to Commander-in-Chief, United States Fleet the following commendation. "The PC 564 closed the enemy rapidly, engaged vigorously, and did her best to break up the attack. The resultant loss of life and injuries to personnel is to be regretted, but the courage of the Captain and his crew was of a high order."[144]

Despite the battle at sea between the E-boat and PC 564, the Nazis landed their commandos at Granville, destroyed many shore facilities, and killed, wounded, and captured some Allied soldiers. PC 564 had delayed the German force long enough though so that by the time they loaded the coal the tide had gone out. With low water they could not get all their vessels out, so all the Germans stole was one collier with 112 tons of coal.

French PC Sank a U-boat

After she finished escort duties on the Atlantic Seaboard, PC 474 continued convoy and other duties in the Mediterranean. Finally, she hauled down her commissioning pennant on 1 June 1944 at Casablanca and became a unit of the French Navy as F. N. S. *L'Indiscret*.[145] Nine months later in March 1945, under her French crew, she and *Fowler* (DE 222) raced to the attack on an under water sound contact. The PC attacked the submarine, and her depth charge barrage killed U-869 and all hands.

Crews of PCs Marched in Victory Parades

After V-E Day the officers and enlisted men of various ships joined the French people and other Allied peoples in celebrating the defeat of Germany and its European Axis partners. Some PCs took part in the ceremonies, and sailors from the ships marched in parades in French cities. The ship's company of PC 619, for example, displayed their marching skills through the streets of Le Havre, France. They joined the victory celebration in that city as shown in Figure 8-13 and Figure 8-14.

PCs Were the First American Ships in a German Port

After the Nazis surrendered, PC 1176, with three other PCs, became part of the Allied occupation force in Bremerhaven. Those PCs were the first American ships to enter a German port since the start of the war.

Summary

PCs escorted ships to England, and, when there, they patrolled around the British Isles. In Mediterranean invasions and that at Normandy, PCs went in before landing craft as control ships, ran picket and rescue duty, destroyed mines, and screened large ships and convoys. Aircraft, U-boats, midget submarines, torpedo boats, and mosquito boats became victims of the depth charges and guns of PCs.

During those invasions and on D-day in France, many PCs acted as control vessels for each beach. This they did, though the invasion planners had not given their crews much training for that role. Despite this oversight, PCs steamed to their stations on time and led landing craft to their assigned beaches. In addition, they guided tank carriers to the beaches. While doing this, they provided gunfire support and dragged bleeding waterlogged soldiers from the water. Many times their crews hauled up corpses, collected dog tags, and body-bagged and buried at sea soldiers, marines, and sailors. Often gunners on PCs, exploded floating mines with 20-mm machine guns and rifles. When an army commander wanted to go ashore, a PC often delivered him. Away from the beaches PCs screened the larger ships. When relieved from the screen, they picked up and delivered mail and dispatches to the other ships.

Because PCs were seaworthy and could operate in any sea and weather conditions, yet had shallow draft and high maneuverability, the Navy used them for many chores. Along with the larger ships, PCs also did their part in the many naval actions in the European, African, Middle Eastern Theater of War.

Figure 8-1. PC 543 laying down a depth charge pattern on a submarine contact in the Mediterranean. Note the two depth charges in the air, to port and starboard of the ship, which were launched from K-guns. Painting courtesy of Bob Baldwin.

Figure 8-2. Photograph of a Painting by Carter Barber which shows his view from in the water how PC 496 looked as she went under. Photograph courtesy of Carter Barber.

H.M.S. "Safari" at left (beacon Submarine for landings at Gela, Sicily -10 July'43)
U.S. Destroyer Maddox goes up when a lone German Bomber drops a single Bomb in her
Depth Charge Magazine (astern of 543)

Figure 8-3. PC 543 with H. M. S. *Safari* at left (beacon submarine for
landings at Gela, Sicily - 10 July 1943). U. S. destroyer *Maddox*
(astern of PC 543) goes up when a German bomber drops a bomb
in her depth charge magazine. Drawing by and courtesy of Bob Baldwin.

Figure 8-4. PC 543 acting as a control ship for the landings at Anzio, Italy on
22 January 1944. In the background a British LCT(R) propels rockets onto the beach
before the first wave of troops goes in. Drawing by and courtesy of Bob Baldwin.

Figure 8-5. View aboard a PC heading into the assault area of Omaha Beach on D-day. Photograph courtesy of Douglas L. Roberts.

Figure 8-6. PC 1261 launched in Sturgeon Bay, Wisconsin on 28 February 1943. She was the first U.S. Navy ship sunk at Normandy on D-day. Photograph courtesy of the Institute for Great Lakes Research.

Figure 8-7. Photograph of PC 553 taken by the shipbuilder in 1942 before they turned it over to the Navy. The Captain was Jim Heatherington. Photograph courtesy of Harry Ayres.

Figure 8-8. Roy Goin and Hermann Goldenbaum, a German flier shot down and rescued by PC 619, hold one of Jim Kennedy's paintings. The young lady is Goldenbaum's granddaughter. Photograph courtesy of Ray Goin.

Figure 8-9. George Raab on PC 619 standing near the symbols for the submarine they sank and the air craft they shot down. Photograph courtesy of Ray Goin

200

Figure 8-10. Drawing of a lonesome sailor returning to PC 617 in Le Havre, France on Christmas day 1944. Drawing by and courtesy of Bill Buffington.

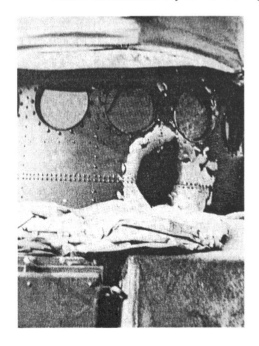

Figure 8-11. Damage to PC 564. Photograph courtesy of Stan Kusek.

Figure 8-12. Damage to PC 564. Photograph courtesy of Stan Kusek.

Figure 8-13. Officers and crew of PC 619 and other PCs join the victory parade in Le Havre, France after V–E Day. Photograph courtesy of Ray Goin.

Figure 8-14. Officers and crew of PC 619 and other PCs join the victory parade in Le Havre, France after V– E Day. Photograph courtesy of Ray Goin.

CHAPTER 9

PC Exploits — Asiatic, Pacific Theater of War

PCs in the Pacific Ocean

Many PCs finished their shakedown cruises and ASW training along the west coast of the United States at facilities from Seattle to San Diego. When the training was complete and the bugs worked out of their equipment, the U. S. Navy assigned some PCs to patrol the west coast and its major harbors. Others sailed west into the Pacific on their first assignments. From the Aleutian Islands to Guadalcanal PCs were among the first United States ships in the offensive actions against Japan.

After the European conflict progressed, the Navy no longer needed as many PCs in the Atlantic. It brought some of them back to the east coast and assigned them to various duties. Others received repairs and refits, and their crews got leaves. When the ships and their crews were ready, they transited the Panama Canal. Then they joined their sister ships that had already engaged the Japanese in the Pacific. Those PCs had proved their value in many different roles against German and Italian forces. Now they would do the same against Japan.

PCs spanned the Pacific Ocean and did many tasks. They escorted convoys that brought war supplies and troops to forward bases to launch the offensive against Japan. To protect merchant and naval vessels at overseas bases they patrolled for, hunted, harassed, and sank Japanese submarines. Like those PCs in the Atlantic, they also did picket duty and air-sea rescue. Then too, as in the European campaigns, they became invasion control ships. Some PCs that acted in this latter category the Navy had designed and constructed specifically for the task of invasion beach control. The Navy designated them PCCs as discussed in Chapter 3. Because they retained their PC hull numbers, I refer to them as PCs in this chapter.

Those PC hulls that the Navy converted to PGMs, as discussed in Chapter 3, also saw service in the Pacific. However, they entered the war too late to have a significant impact. Meant to be important as barge busters, they frequently found employment instead as mine destroyers.

One book cannot describe the recorded activities of all PCs in the Pacific, and authors have not written about many of their actions. The details of the operations of those particular ships, and the actions and emotions of the young men who served on them, are buried in the cryptic language of ships' logs. They remain unknown except in the memories of the men who were involved in them. To illustrate the types of actions in which PCs were involved in the Pacific, I followed, in this chapter, the guidelines I adopted in Chapters 6, 7, and 8.

Tokyo Rose Threatened PC Sailors

Sailors in the Pacific rarely made liberties in cities such as those in Africa, Italy, England, and France. Often they relaxed ashore on clammy fog shrouded islands in the north or on steamy islands in the south. North or south, though, many islands were unpopulated except by military personnel. The sailors did not have much contact with civilization as they used to know it. They did have, however, one contact with the outside world. Most of the men on Navy ships in the Pacific enjoyed a diversion not often heard by men in the American or European theaters of war.

While in port or even underway, the men could listen to the sweet offerings or the harangues and threats of Tokyo Rose. She never fooled anyone with her transparent propaganda, and her attempts at it usually stimulated as much laughter as the Abbott and Costello "Who's on First Base" routine. Also for many men she was the only source of the sounds of Glen Miller's "In the Mood" and other favorites she broadcast to make men melancholy and home sick.

In her attempts to frighten or disrupt American sailors, she most often singled out large Navy task forces or individual capital ships. She gave their locations, and predicted their destruction. Sailors heard her warn them with words like, "While you are dying, your wives and girl friends back home are dating rich draft-dodging civilians. Now your ship will be sunk and you will die." In general, the men paid little attention except to laugh at the woman. Not always though. Once she selected a PC for her threat and got the attention of that ship's crew.

For five days, PC 793 pounded its bow into the crests of forty-foot seas and rolled to her beam ends in the North Pacific. Eighty knot winds ripped icy blasts of spindrift from wave crests. The freezing water battered and doused the lookouts topside who grappled with stanchions and lifelines to keep waves from washing them overboard. For days the sailors did not sleep or have hot meals. Sea water and condensation drenched the compartments. PC 793 with PC 777 and PC 820 zigzagged around a convoy of troop ships. The convoy was en route to Attu in the Aleutian Islands. This island was the farthest American outpost in the North Pacific, less than five hundred miles from Japan. Huddled around the radio in the chartroom a group of men hung on the swing beat of Tommy Dorsey's trombone. The music was in a broadcast by Tokyo Rose. Then, the voice of the woman broke into the reverie and said words like, "To you men on PC 793 in the convoy to Attu, farewell." Heads snapped up. "Japanese submarines are waiting for you," she continued. "It is sad that you will not see your girls at home again. You will die for nothing." The sailors glanced from one to another each wondering how she got her information. They recalled the poster, like the one in Figure 9-1, tacked to walls in buildings and bulkheads in Navy stations that read, "Loose Lips Might Sink Ships."

Quickly the men who heard the warning passed the word to the entire crew. Every man reacted the same way. None of them showed fear only indignation, but they did forget their discomforts. The threat of a submarine was remote in such bad weather, but even so, lookouts stared more intently for periscopes. The radar operator scanned his screen with more care. The sonar operator leaned closer to his sound gear. All hands became more cautious and resolute on watch the rest of that trip.

The First PCs Through the Panama Canal

Sixteen days before the Japanese sneak attack on Pearl Harbor, workers in Bay City, Michigan at the Defoe Shipbuilding Company started construction of PC 477. On 30 March 1942 they completed her and she began her cruise. After shakedown in the Caribbean, she was the first PC, along with PC 476 and PC 479, to transit the Panama Canal[146] and to operate in the Hawaiian Islands. She was also the first PC to participate in action in the Solomon Islands. Her record included the campaigns for Guadalcanal, New Guinea, and the Philippines.

PC 477 in Action at Guadalcanal

Off Henderson Field, Guadalcanal, one year to the day after the attack on Pearl Harbor, PC 477 got her first kill. Gunnery Officer Art Bell, the OOD who was conning the ship on patrol at 0800, gazed at a torpedo that leapt from the water. It plunged back in, and raced for *Alchiba*, a Navy supply ship. Bell wrote, "Bam! It slammed into her port beam, . . . leaving a hole the size of a truck in *Alchiba's* hull." He rang General Quarters. The sonar operator rotated the wheel and sent out a pulse. Moments later a sound echo bounced back from the depths. Captain David C. Miller, who reached his station on the bridge, ordered the PC ahead at standard speed. The ship bore toward the contact at fifteen knots.

When the ship reached the target, Miller launched a pattern of ten depth charges set at one hundred feet. Concussions racked the PC, and her stern lifted as the ocean swelled and boiled behind her. Because of the disturbance caused by the explosions, the Soundman lost contact with the submarine.

Inside the two man Japanese submarine, which PC 477 had just attacked, the men struggled for their lives to keep their damaged craft from sinking. They used all their training and ingenuity for hours. Theirs was a "Divine Mission," and they labored and struggled not to waste their young lives without killing Americans. Six hours later the submarine floated to the surface unable to maneuver but still with a few torpedoes aboard. They could still make the Emperor proud and send themselves to their ancestors as heroes.

Observers in a plane spotted the "Pygmy" sub and signaled the PC. She raced at flank speed toward the submarine's position. Captain Miller sensed a chance, not just to destroy the submarine but to capture the vessel. He delayed firing his guns at her as he bore down.

"All guns manned and ready," Bell told the bridge.

"Bridge, aye, aye."

"Depth charges armed and ready," the speaker aft announced over the phones.

Bob Weeks, Ship's Cook, belted himself into a 20-mm machine gun forward, away from his galley where his meal was simmering. He stared at the submarine, frowned, and worried. The ship plunged ahead toward the submarine. All hands tensed. A torpedo from the wounded craft could blast the PC to splinters. Would the submarine fight? Who would die? Breathlessly, the men stared and waited as the PC churned toward the submarine.

Suddenly over the phone a voice asked, "Depth charges?"

"Depth charges, aye," the expectant voice answered.

"Listen depth charges, Weeks says to tell Lyons the mess cook to put some water on the beans."

As the PC neared the damaged submarine, a plane from Henderson Field roared over and swooped ". . . down like a hawk set to kill." Two bombs hurtled down and blasted up a huge geyser of water. When it settled, the submarine was gone. The pilot of the plane had prevented the possible capture of the submarine. Later, Admiral Spruance awarded PC 477 and the aircraft a joint kill.

PC 581 Captured Japanese Soldiers

PC 581 had a varied career. While on patrol along the northern California coast on 23 January 1943, the PC 581 sped to the rescue of twenty-five survivors of the abandoned USAT *San Diego*. Later, after a brief tour in the Aleutian Islands, PC 581 controlled landing craft to the beaches during the invasions of Saipan and Tinian. There she dodged enemy bombs and shells. While in that campaign, on 25 June her crew nabbed two Japanese soldiers who tried to escape from Tinian to Aguijan.[147]

A Submarine Kill in the Aleutians

PC 487, Lt. Wallace Gordon Cornell, USNR, Commanding, cruised forty miles northeast of Shemya Island in the fog-covered Aleutians on 10 June 1943. The sonar operator picked up propeller noise. Moments later a blip showed on radar. Cornell, certain that the target was a partially submerged Japanese submarine, rang General Quarters. Lookouts on the PC spotted two periscopes about 250 yards off the port bow. Coming hard to port, the PC raced ahead to the contact at full speed. As they approached, the submarine slid below the surface. Retaining the sound contact, the PC maneuvered into position. After the PC slowed to attack speed she steamed over the now submerged contact. The Skipper ordered his crew to splash a pattern of depth charges. The explosions from the spread of five depth charges shook the PC. They had bracketed the submarine and had gone off below it. The shock and force of the explosions blew the Japanese I-24 to the surface.[148]

Wheeling around, the PC stormed back toward the submarine. Men on the PC grabbed handholds and prepared for a ram. PC 487 lunged ahead as gunners on the PC pumped 3-inch and 20-mm shells into her hull. The PC scraped its keel over the submarine's awash deck. It churned across the submarine, slid past the boat, and whirled around. PC 487 raced back and drove its bow into I-24 just forward of its conning tower. The two vessels shuddered and heeled over, momentarily locked together. Then the submarine settled lower in the water. The PC moved away and hove to while her gunners poured more shells into the foundering submarine. Five 3"-50 shells ripped into its hull and conning tower. The submarine settled lower, and its bow tilted up. On the PC the crew stared as the cold water boiled over the 2,000 ton[149] Japanese submarine. The sea sucked it stern first below the frigid choppy surface of the North Pacific with all hands.

Members of the crew of PC 487 painted a Japanese flag above a painted symbol of a submarine on the stack of the PC as shown in Figure 9-2.

PC 1588 From the Aleutians to Iwo Jima

Another PC that started its duty in the Aleutians was *Annoy* (AM 84) a mine layer and sweeper built on a PC hull. Between 31 October 1942 and 5 October 1943 she ran convoys and did odd assignments in the North Pacific. The U. S. Navy sent the ship stateside, and on 17 November 1944 it completed the conversion of the AM 48 to PC 1588. She then sailed for the South Pacific and more convoy and air-sea rescue duty. At Iwo Jima the PC's gunners got action when they blasted at three Japanese suicide planes. As time went on, they fended off thirteen other attacks by Japanese aircraft.

PC 1134 Rescued the Crew of YP-281

During the morning watch on 5 January 1944 aboard PC 1134, the ship got underway to escort six small ships from Pago Pago to Suva Fiji.[150] For four days they zigzagged at four to five knots on one engine to screen the ships. Then the weather began to make up. Soon, howling winds whipped the sea, and 50-75 foot waves buried the forecastle under green water. The men could ". . . feel the deck plates snap and pop under our feet. The ship rolled violently."

Taking an even worse beating in the storm, YP-281 signaled the PC that they were taking on water and feared they would sink. The Captain of the PC knew nothing could be done at night, so all hands waited while the storm raged. When daylight arrived, the PC hove to near the YP and got a line over to the smaller vessel. Men on the YP lashed it to a life raft and tethered another line to it and their ship. With three to five men from the YP on the raft at a time the PC crew hauled them to the PC. As they closed on the rescue ship, waves bashed the raft against the ship that leaped up and plunged down as shown in Figure 9-3. Men gasped for breath as mist, foam, and waves pounded them. Sailors on the PC battled in knee-deep water against waves coming aboard that battered the men against bulkheads and knocked them down. Lashed to lifelines, some of the men on PC 1134 hung over the side. Others plunged into the sea to yank the drenched and weary survivors aboard as shown in Figure 9-4.

Hours later twenty-one tired haggard men of YP-128 gulped brandy and huddled in the relative safety of the PC. The exhausted sailors of PC 1134 trudged back to their watches to resume ship's duties. Then, the senior officer of the group (SOPA) declared the YP a menace to navigation and ordered the PC to sink it. Gunners on PC 1134 stumbled back to their stations and blasted the derelict with all the ship's guns. They, and the YP crew, watched as ". . . she turned belly up and slid silently under the waves."

PC 1135 Helped Sink a Japanese Submarine

On 24 May 1944, the PC 1135 helped *Manlove* (DE 36) attack a sonar contact. The two ships closed on the contact and laid a series of depth charge barrages. The explosions battered the submarine. Together the two ships sent the Japanese submarine I32 and its crew to the bottom of the Central Pacific in the Marshall Islands.[151]

PCs at the Invasion Beaches

At Hollandia, Saipan, the Philippines, Iwo Jima, Okinawa, and other islands PCs delivered blows to Japanese naval and ground forces. For example, en route to Guam with a convoy of Task Group 53.16, the PC 555 and PC 1125 helped repulse an attack by Japanese torpedo planes on 21 July 1944. The ships' gunners blasted two of the planes from the sky.[152] Other PCs that participated in the invasion of Guam included PC 549, PC 581, PC 1079, PC 1080, PC 1126, PC 1127, and PC 1136.

PC 1134 shared the action in eight invasions as a control ship. She survived five air raids by kamikazes and two by dive bombers, and her gunners got revenge by knocking down two Japanese planes at Leyte. On top of that she weathered two typhoons. Her career continued after V-J Day when PC 1134 made two trips up the Yangtze river in China. She was one of the first ships to go there since before the war.[153]

PCs Rescued Survivors of the Battle off Samur

On 25 October 1944, PC 1119, PC 623, and five gunboats LCI(R) 34, 71, 337, 340, and 341 got orders as TG 78.12 to search for survivors of the battle off Samur. At 2229 hours the next day, lookouts on the ships spotted red, green, and white flares and headed in their direction. An hour and a quarter later, PC 623 closed on a group of rafts loaded with survivors of sunken ships. Her Skipper ordered the other ships to join the PC.

As they rolled in long swells, the two PCs eased up to rafts loaded with bloody, soaked, shivering survivors. They were from the three ships, Escort Carrier *Gambier Bay* (CVE 73), *Samuel B. Roberts* (DE 413), and *Hoel* (DD 533). Men on the PCs hauled 183 of the survivors aboard. During later searches lookouts found more men in the sea, and the ships rescued them. PC 1119 eventually crammed aboard about 200 exhausted, shivering, and wounded sailors. Though the Captains of the ships could not make an exact count, the Skipper of PC 623 estimated the eight little ships rescued approximately 1,150 survivors.

During the rescue operation, crew members of PC 1119 and PC

623 slid into the dark water to help wounded men climb or be lifted aboard the PCs. On the ships, crew members donated their clothing and blankets to and tended to the survivors for thirty hours without rest.[154] Years later Allison Levy, an officer on PC 623, wrote these words. ". . . crew members gave the survivors the shirts off their back, their pants, their bed linens, their towels, their supplies and a lot of TLC. They deserve all the credit that can be bestowed upon them."[155]

Heavily loaded with sick and wounded survivors, their trial continued when at 0950 the next morning a Japanese plane soared over the formation of ships. The gunners on the PCs and LCIs poured shells at the plane that, to the relief of all hands, flew away.

One survivor, on board PC 1119, with his life secured, worried about his money. He climbed down into the engine room and draped dollar bills over the rails to dry them out. It worked, and he did not lose any of them. Another rescued sailor blew off steam by shouting, "That *#%!" MacArthur . . . . This is the third time he done this to me."[156]

Besides this action, PC 623 took part in many invasions, and its gunners downed three Japanese planes.[157]

Suicide Boats Sank PC 1129

After service in the Gulf of Mexico and at Pearl Harbor, PC 1129, shown in Figure 9-5 in 1943, steamed for the South Pacific. She ran convoys among various islands then joined the invasion forces at Palau, Leyte Gulf, Linguyan Gulf, and Nasugbu in the Philippine Islands. Her luck ran out in the Philippines though.

Under a full moon at 2300 on the night of 31 January 1945, sailors on DE *Laugh* spotted a group of small boats off Luzon in the Philippines. Her Commanding Officer ordered PC 1129 to investigate them.[158] The PC had been a landing craft control vessel at Nasugbu and was now on ASW patrol. She headed toward the boats, and when the PC approached the contacts, her crew recognized them as Japanese midget suicide boats. By then she was too close for evasive action, and about twenty-three to twenty-six suicide boats[159] surrounded the PC.

Her gunners poured fire at the boats and knocked out two of them as they swarmed around the PC. Her skipper tried to dodge them, but they rammed her. The PC shuddered as charges blew her hull open and killed one man in the engine room. Bloodied wounded men struggled topside. As the PC rolled onto its starboard side, the Captain ordered the crew to abandon the ship. Shipmates helped the wounded men into rafts then went over the side themselves. They huddled together in the water. Floating in life belts or on rafts and debris, the men stared as their ship flipped over, broke in half, and sank.

PC 1123 Supported Troops and Guerillas

Between Christmas and New Years days, in 1944 the PC 1123 joined a squadron of PT boats and F4U Corsair aircraft. Together they helped Australian soldiers mop up Japanese forces on the southern end of Bougainville. The PC, with three other small vessels, steamed in a circle offshore. On each turn, as they approached the shore, they blasted the area with their guns. Tragedy struck, however, when Australian Intelligence failed to coordinate the actions of the ships with troops ashore, and ninety of them died from friendly fire.[160]

At Polillo Island, about twenty-six miles east of Luzon in the Philippines the whole village and a Military Band greeted the arrival of PC 1123 on 5 May 1945. The PC was the largest ship the natives had seen since the war had started. The next day Lt. Col. Anderson and a dozen Philippine guerrilla fighters boarded the ship for transit to eastern Luzon. To support the guerrillas before they went ashore, the PC gunners poured gunfire into the beach area. That day and the next day the sailors also helped stranded Filipinos come aboard their ship. They came directly from the beach and in canoes. Among them were pregnant women, children, blind people, and some wounded civilians. The Japanese had hunted all of the people to slaughter them. So many Filipino natives came aboard, they filled the decks of the PC as shown in Figure 9-6.

After they loaded the PC, the roar of high speed boats approaching alerted Col. Anderson. He yelled to the Skipper of the PC that the craft were Japanese suicide boats. General Quarters rang through the ship, and all hands jumped for their battle stations. The crowded passengers screamed as an explosion aboard rattled the ship. One suicide boat bolted toward PC 1123 to ram her. The Captain of the PC swung the ship toward it, and the boat glanced off without exploding. The boats needed a head-on contact to detonate their charges. The Japanese sailors shoved their boat off from the PC with their hands and their boat bolted away. Gunners on the PC sighted on it and poured out streams of shells from the guns. The boat exploded throwing debris and flames across the water. Machine gun shells from the PC also sank a second boat, and the Philippine guerrillas in their motor launches finished off the third one. With that danger removed, PC 1123 delivered the hapless Filipinos to a safe haven.

PC 1119 in Action Again

During the invasion of Arawe, New Britain, PC 1119 received orders to bombard the beach in preparation for landings. Navigated by Lt. James H. Latimer, USNR, the ship closed to 1,000 yards of the shore. From there she poured 275 rounds of three-inch and 4,500 rounds of machine gun shells into a Japanese stronghold.[161] For two hours her gunners blasted caves, dugouts, foxholes, machine gun emplacements, and bivouac areas with her 3-inch gun and 20-mm and .50 cal. machine guns.

At Corregidor in February 1945, on a close-fire support run, she took a hit on the forward deck that wounded four men. During other actions her crew blasted from the sky four and one-half Japanese planes with antiaircraft fire. The "half plane" was a close call. A kamikaze pilot picked out the PC and swept toward the ship in a long glide. The ship heeled over as the Skipper swung her around in a power turn with her guns blazing. The kamikaze bore in despite the gun fire. A few hundred feet from the ship, chunks flew from the plane, but it kept coming. Only fifty feet from PC 1119, the Japanese kamikaze finally swerved and plunged into the sea.

Again, at Corregidor on 16 February 1945, the PC 1119, in

support of the landing, steamed within 100 yards of the beach. She went through a barrage of machine gun, mortar, and artillery shells to blast the Japanese. Enemy fire tore pieces from the ship and bloodied four crew members. Later, with a load of wounded soldiers and her own wounded crew members, PC 1119 dodged mortar shells in a flank speed race to a hospital LST at Mariveles Harbor.

Another memorable occasion for the crew was the transport, from Arawe, New Britain to New Guinea, of a USO group. It included a Metropolitan Opera singer and "The Duke," movie actor John Wayne. Figure 9-7 shows John Wayne with some of the crew on board PC 1119.

Nineteen Invasions, a Navy Unit Citation, and Three Bronze Stars for PC 1133

PC 1133 started ingloriously towed to sea from Bay City, Michigan down the Mississippi River and across the Pacific as a drag for a floating dry dock. The crew's frustrations at this unglamourous duty were relieved, however. Starting on 2 July 1944 she became a control ship for landings on New Guinea and in eighteen more invasions until 28 July 1945.[162] Between the invasions PC 1133 ran convoys, shot down Japanese aircraft, and bombarded beaches. She also engaged kamikazes, captured Japanese sailors, and rescued survivors of sunken American landing craft, as shown in Figure 9-8. The ship also received a Navy Unit Citation.[163]

Planners for the invasion of Noemfoor Island, Netherlands New Guinea, on 2 July 1944 did not know of a path through the corral reef for the amphibious tanks and landing craft. Someone had to discover one for the success of the operation. The Captain of PC 1133 asked for volunteers to find a path.

"I'll go," said the Executive Officer Lt. Dave Knapp. QM1/C Everitt D. Lewis, Jr. and Coxswain D. A. Byington also volunteered. The PC took them in close and put them over in a small boat. Scurrying toward the beach, with Japanese machine gun and rifle bullets whistling about them, they found a passage through the reef and dropped marker buoys in place. For their action, the Navy awarded each of the three men a Bronze Star Medal.

Along with an SC and three landing craft, the crew of PC 1133 watched as United States and Japanese ships slugged each other in the Battle of Surigao Strait. Evading Japanese destroyers that approached within a few miles of them, the PC loitered in the dark. Men on the PC stared as the battleship *Yamishiro* burst into flames. They also watched other ships of the Emperor's fleet slip under the waves.

On 26 October 1944 a Japanese plane swept toward a convoy of LSTs that PC 1133 was escorting. When the plane bore in to point blank range, the captain ordered the guns to fire. The 20-mm guns chattered and the 40-mm Bofors pounded out shells. Streams of tracers tore into the plane. Flames burst from it, and it plunged down into the sea 400 yards from the ship.

Besides the actions described above, PC 1119 earned three battle stars for eighteen invasions, two stars on her Philippines Liberation ribbon, and a Navy Unit Citation. For their combat actions, the crew of PC 1119 received three commendations and three Bronze Star Medals.[164] "The ship's record isn't too bad," wrote the Executive Officer of PC 1119, Lt. j. g. Coolbaugh, USNR. He added, "But after all, she is a sub-chaser, — and we never did actually get to chase a sub!" The only submarine the ship encountered was after the war when the Captain accepted the surrender of Japanese submarines in Subic Bay.

Thirty-nine Men Killed or Wounded on PC 1124

After a fifty-day trip from Miami, Florida to Brisbane, Australia, PC 1124 spent a year on convoy duty and ASW patrol in the South Pacific. Then she arrived in San Pablo Bay, Philippines on 24 November 1944 and tied up against *Severn* (AO 61), a fleet oiler.[165] Before the crew could relax, an air raid siren blared, and the men raced to their battle stations.

An American P-38 zoomed overhead chasing a Zero that

headed for the ships. The Japanese plane screeched down in a long dive from above PC 1124. At this time the *Severn* was loaded with water and was supplying a clutch of PCs and LSTs. The LSTs were temporary hospital ships.[166] In his anxiety to evade the P-38 and complete his mission, the Japanese pilot probably mistook the tender for a tanker. A gray bomb floated from the plane's belly and dropped toward the ships. The bomb plowed into the starboard side of the PC. It blew a gaping hole in the hull of the PC amidship, and peeled back deck plating. Figure 9-9 and Figure 9-10 show damage to the ship. The concussion and shrapnel from the exploding bomb killed five and wounded thirty-two men on the PC. Also, two crew members were missing and presumed to be dead. Fred Morrissey's body was afire from hot shrapnel, and he plunged into the water to put out the fires. Later, in the hospital a nurse said to him, "Honey, you look like you were caught with the farmer's daughter. He must have chased you and filled your fanny full of buck shot."

PCs in the North Pacific

In the Aleutians, after the Attu and Kiska invasions, at least twenty[167] Navy and Coast Guard PCs still soared over and plunged down fifty foot seas. They breasted 100 knot williwaws on ocean convoys, fleet and Air Corps picket duty, and island patrols. During the latter part of the war the United States was building up bases in the Aleutian Islands for the planned invasion of the Northern Islands of Japan. PCs were to play an important role in what Admiral Fletcher wrote when Japan surrendered as, ". . . future blows — now happily not needed."[168]

Under typical Aleutian conditions, a PC would hang on the crest of a wave, the forward half of its keel glaring at the sky. She would shiver from stem to stern. Then her bow would plunge down, screws flailing air, and bury to her bridge in green water. Groaning and twisting, the ship would struggle to the surface, seas pouring from her decks, and shudder into the next wave. Sailors spent their watches with one hand clenched around a stanchion and their knees flexed to absorb

FOUND IN THE NAVY NOW

1951 - 20th Century Fox Film Corp
Gary Cooper / Ray Collins /
Na Brian / Eddie Albert. Firewells
Rk Manuel / Harrington Zach

CHARLES BRONSON
~~The Feeling Fighters~~

THE SUBMARINE CHATER MANUAL
Come Michael R92

The Black Tracker Manual

the shocks. Waves hurled across the decks, smashed steel fixtures, tore loose 3"-50 guns, and tossed men about like corks. Seamen rigged safety lines on deck to keep waves from washing men overboard. Often seas were so high that, despite the safety lines, men could not go on deck and had to remain below. At those times some men stood multiple watches for long periods, even days.

These PCs rode winter gales on picket duty for Army Air Corps strikes at Japan. They screened the cruisers, carriers, and destroyers of the North Pacific Force when it bombarded the northern Japanese Kurile Islands. In convoys and on patrol, they staggered from concussions of their depth charges as they attacked sound contacts of submarines that threatened merchant men and transports.

Frogmen From PC 800 at Iwo Jima

After commissioning in Portland, Oregon and her shakedown off Oregon and at San Diego, PC 800 headed for Pearl Harbor. Months later the Navy ordered her on a mission to Iwo Jima. A few days before the scheduled invasion, her Skipper sneaked the PC in close to the island. There, he sent in a squad of frogmen to demolish underwater obstructions at the planned landing site.[169] After securing from this mission, which helped make possible the landing, the ship came back for the invasion. Her gunners lobbed shells into the island and at Mt. Suribachi to soften Japanese defenses.

After the invasion of Iwo Jima, PC 800 moved to the battle at Okinawa. There she manned the "inner ping line" off Okinawa to protect ships from submarine attacks. While on this duty, she also dodged kamikaze air attacks.

Other PCs at Iwo Jima

Off Iwo Jima in February 1945, battleships, carriers, cruisers, and destroyers pounded the island for days with shells and bombs. Then the assault waves of Marines went in to dig out the Japanese defenders. PC 779, after herding a flock of LSTs, loaded with Marines and their tanks, to the beaches, shifted to ASW patrol off the island.[170] Then as the blood-red sun rose, the PC got orders to join other ships to add gunfire support for the Marines ashore. PC 779 steamed to within 1,000 feet from the base of Mt. Suribachi, "Hot Rocks." There, her gunners poured shells into the Japanese positions. Because she was so close to the island, the Japanese gunners targeted the PC, and she scurried back and forth dodging Japanese shells. Smoke and the smell of cordite and battle decay flooded the air and drifted seaward from the island. The concussions of the shells from big guns on the island and from the ships off the beaches, and exploding ammunition dumps, rocked the little ship. Inexperienced boys, on 31 May 1943 when they had commissioned their ship in Portland, Oregon, the crew of PC 779, like many others, had become fighting men. They are shown placing their ship in commission in Figure 9-11.

After the initial landings at Iwo Jima, PC 779 and another PC swung in with a convoy. The convoy consisted of an AM and several badly damaged LCIs and LSMs the PCs were escorting to Saipan. On the third night out, at 1800 hours, an echo rang from the sound stack of PC 779. GQ blared and men raced to their battle stations. The ship tracked and finally attacked the submarine contact. Depth charges rattled off the racks and smoke billowed from the K-guns that tossed their depth charges out to the sides of the ship. The low rumble from the deep-set depth charges ruffled the surface. Men on PC 779 felt that the attack was not conclusive, but no one ever heard from the submarine again.

After the fifteen day convoy trip and a little rest, PC 779 returned to Iwo. There, she joined other ships in air-sea rescue and ASW patrols, often dodging Japanese bombs.

With her companion ships, PC 469, with its Coast Guard crew, snaked back and forth off Red Beach. They were under the menace of the guns on Mt. Suribachi. The men on the ship stared at the mountain top knowing that the Marines had to capture it.[171] Much later a man, peering through binoculars, yelled, "It's our flag." The other men on the PC turned toward Suribachi and cheered as the stars and stripes swung up and billowed in the breeze atop the mountain.

David E. Newby wrote about the invasion of Iwo Jima, "What followed is recorded in history. All the statistics are in the books: number of casualties, days before final victory, tactical reasons for taking a pile of worthless volcanic rock, risks versus value, and whatever. What is not recorded is emotion. The feelings of horror and anguish on hearing the reports of casualties coming through the radio shack."

PC 555 With the Big Boys

After she finished a tour of duty in the Solomon and Marshall Islands, PC 555 operated with large ships of Fast Transport Division 17 as a landing control ship. For this duty she received new signal flags from the fleet, and the Signalmen stowed them in the flag bags. Out the PC steamed accompanying the Division 17 ships. The first time the Signalman on the PC ran some of the flags up the halyards and two-blocked them, the bottoms of the flags dragged on the deck. By mistake, the flags the PC got were the size of those that flew on the tall masts of battleships.[172]

PCs at Okinawa

On 15 December 1944 at Mindoro, gunners on PC 1128 blasted a Japanese plane from the sky. Afterward, during the Okinawa campaign, on 26 March 1945, the fire support United States destroyer *Halligan* and mine sweeper *Skylark* were cruising in unswept waters. They were just short of the fifty fathom curve about three miles southeast of Maye Shima.[173] A mine detonated against *Halligan,* and the blast ignited a magazine on the ship. The resulting explosions blew off the forward section of the destroyer back to the first stack. *Skylark* also rammed a mine, and the explosion ripped her open. Both ships began to go down.

PC 1128, nearby, heeled into a quick turn and darted to the rescue of the crews of the sinking ships. She circled the ships and searched the water in the darkness for survivors.[174] After the crew of PC 1128 rescued six of them, she continued the search with PC 584 and LSM 194. Together they took off the remaining survivors still aboard the sinking ships. The Task Force Commander commended the crew of the LSM and the PCs for a "courageous job."

In January 1944 a seventy-knot wind ripped PC 1128 from her moorings and slammed her into a destroyer. The impact cut the PC's steering cables and power lines and tore a gash in the hull near the engine room. Water poured in, but using bedding, a collision mat, and pumps the crew saved the ship.

During the invasion of Okinawa, PC 463 and PC 469 distinguished themselves as control vessels keeping the landing craft arriving at Purple and Orange beaches, respectively.

At 1415 hours on 24 July 1945 DE *Underhill*, in company with PC 803 and PC 804, heard a sound contact and asked PC 804 to investigate.[175] Half an hour later the PC's sound operator heard an echo he confirmed as a submarine. The Commanding Officer on *Underhill* accepted the confirmation, raced in, and attacked the submarine with a depth charge barrage. Evidence that floated to the surface prompted the DE's Skipper to declare, "We sank a kaiten." (a human torpedo).

A few minutes later a lookout on the PC sang out that he had sighted a periscope and submarine near the surface. At 1507 *Underhill* steamed toward the contact to attack again. Suddenly her bow exploded throwing flame, debris, and torn bodies a thousand feet into the sky. A Japanese kaiten, the Japanese had launched from submarine I-53, had slammed into the bow of the DE. Another kaiten passed under PC 804 in an unsuccessful attempt to ram her also, but PC 803 attacked the submarine and drove it away.

PC 803 and PC 804 rushed to the aid of the sinking *Underhill*, and Sailors on the PC pulled one hundred and sixteen of the sinking ship's survivors from the sea. Of the DE's ship's company, ten officers and 102 men died. More would have died if it had not been for the two PCs stopping to haul the men from the water.

PC 586 Rates a Salute From a British Aircraft Carrier

While patrolling near an atoll in the Western Pacific in the spring of 1945, the PC 586 steamed on a collision course with a British carrier task force.[176] The Captain of the PC had given Ensign Sutherland, the OOD, strict orders. He was to steer a course so the choppy seas would not disturb the crew's noon chow or the Skipper's nap. The OOD followed orders.

Soon the PC approached close aboard of and bounced in the bow waves of a huge British aircraft carrier. The PC was in the middle of the task force. Men on the flying bridge of the PC knew that a United States ship does not initiate a salute to a friendly man-of-war. They also understood that the British, the long-term Queen of the Seas, had no need to render a salute. The men on the PC did want to greet the British, however, so those men on deck cheered and waved their caps at the carrier.

With slow majesty, the white ensign on the British carrier fluttered down in a salute. Heads held high, the cocky Yanks, whose average age was twenty years and whose ship the British could hoist aboard and stuff into a corner of the carrier's deck, dipped the PC's colors in reply.

Ernie Pyle's Last Ride on a Ship Was on a PC

PC 1603, shown in Figure 3-7, acted as a control ship in the Philippine invasions and in the Okinawa campaign where she also ferried personnel to the beaches. On one trip the ship transferred a news correspondent to an LCVP for his trip to Ie Shima.

As the correspondent departed the ship, one sailor asked, "Do you know who that was?"

Albert Young answered, "Negative."

The sailor replied, "That was Ernie Pyle."

Two days later, on the island of Ie Shima, a Japanese machine gunner found a target, squeezed out some rounds, and snuffed out the life of Ernie Pyle.

PC 1603 Took Two Suiciders

While moored at Taka Shima on 26 May 1945, part of the crew of PC 1603 sacked out forward, others wrote letters, a few shot at sharks, and most of them rested. It was a quiet and lazy day away from the noise, smoke, shells, and fear of the invasion beaches. The day was peaceful and still.[177]

Suddenly, a deafening roar and explosion blasted the calm. The ship shuddered and lurched violently tossing men against bulkheads. "We've taken a suicider," someone shouted. The tail of a Japanese Tommy jutted out from the port bow of the PC where it had dived down and hammered itself into the ship. The plane's engine had churned through the forward compartment where some men slept. Twisted steel plates, shredded clothing, blood, and human flesh splattered the area.

Searchers never found three of the men of PC 1603 who had been in that compartment. Two of those young men were the saxophone player and one of the crew members in the background in Figure 5-11.[178]

A second kamikaze roared in toward the PC as the crew rushed to battle stations and fired a few ineffective rounds of 20-mm shells at the plane. With a screech and blast the aircraft smashed into the starboard side forward at deck level. Flaming gasoline sprayed over the men scorching their bodies. The blast blew some men from the three-inch gun crew overboard. The plane's engine ripped through the pilot house and shredded its interior and the men inside.

Besides the direct impacts of the two "Divine Wind" planes on the PC, three or four bombs the kamikazes carried tore into the ship and ripped open bulkheads and hatches. The bombs slashed on through the hull and out the bottom without exploding. The "Old Salt" was almost correct when he had said that the thin hull of a PC offered protection against torpedoes because the tin fish could go through without exploding. He should have added, "aerial bombs." Still afloat, but damaged beyond repair, PC 1603 died later in the ship's graveyard at Kerama Retto.

PC 793 Got a "Probable"

One monotonous job assigned to PCs was ASW patrol outside a harbor. Often the ships stayed at sea four to seven days lumbering along at five to ten knots with the "Ping" of the sound gear echoing throughout the ship. When relieved, they had a day or two dockside to replenish and a day ashore for each of the two liberty sections.

PC 793, on Purple Patrol outside the harbor at Adak in the Aleutians on 27 April 1945, steamed back and forth at one third speed on one engine. She pinged for submarines on one leg of a triangle, the sides of which covered all access to the inner harbor. Another PC and the Coast Guard Cutter *Cyane* crept back and forth along the other legs of the triangle. In the harbor the fighting ships of the North Pacific Force, tankers, freighters, and troop ships lay at anchor.

It was an atypical day in the Aleutians, where fog, rain, sleet, and gusty winds usually prevailed. On this day a calm sea mirrored the blue sky and bright sun at midday. Ping . . . Ping . . . rang the sound pulses. Men settled into their routine. Then suddenly a clear metallic echo rang from the sound stack. Paul Jones, the Soundman blurted out, "Contact."

The OOD rang General Quarters. Men ran for their stations. The Captain, Gordon Secor, raced for the bridge.[179] He maneuvered the PC toward the contact that gave a "sharp clear echo" then opened the range to 1800 yards and started a firing run. At 1,430 yards Jones called out, "Doppler down. Moving right." Secor eased the ship to starboard to lead the target. Four minutes later, at 325 yards, the gunner fired the mousetraps. The bombs arced up, dropped, and plunged below the surface. Down they dropped to the full sixty fathoms at that position with no explosions.

Cyane and PC 793 ranged on the contact and alternated attacks without results, but kept getting sharp clear echoes. Then the PC moved in on its fourth attack. At 305 yards, Secor ordered the mousetraps fired. The bombs sailed away and dove into the cold sea. The Captain counted, one second, two seconds, three seconds . . . . Eleven fathoms down explosions pounded the contact. Moments later the water boiled and debris floated to the surface. *Cyane* and PC 793 never got another echo.

Two destroyers dashed to the scene and lashed the water with sound pulses for hours. Army air planes searched the area. They found nothing. Members of the ship's company on the PC convinced themselves that they had sunk a submarine. Ray Page, a signalman on PC 793 drew a picture of a Japanese submarine with a question mark above it. The sketch hung in the chart room of PC 793 and remained there until the Navy decommissioned the ship. The drawing is shown in Figure 9-12.

Atlantic Veteran PCs in the Pacific

After convoy runs from New York City to Guantanamo, Cuba, PC 1177 shifted to the Pacific where she saw action at Palau; Subic Bay, Philippines; Ulithi; and Okinawa. After the war she helped in the occupation force of Japan.

Another veteran of convoy duty with the Caribbean sea Frontier, PC 594 transited the Panama Canal on 28 January 1945. With the Fifth Fleet, she steamed into Tokyo Bay on 19 September 1945 to help in the occupation of Japan. Later, after a few months in China, PC 594 got orders for Operation Cross-Roads, the A-bomb test at Bikini. Before she left, though, the Navy canceled the assignment because of engine trouble on the PC.[180]

PC 1546 also shifted from East Coast convoy duty to the Pacific theater on 8 July 1945. She sailed on to Tientsin, Republic of China for liaison duty and to help in evacuating Japanese prisoners of war. On 15 March 1946, the Commander, Service Forces, U. S. Pacific Fleet assigned PC 1546 to the Marianas Trust Territory Government. Nine years later, on 26 February 1955 she finally sailed into San Francisco where the Navy decommissioned her.[181]

PC 466 at the Japanese Surrender Ceremony

"A feeling of exhilaration swept through the crew of USS PC

466 when it was announced on August 25th, that our ship had been chosen to join TF 33 and steam to Tokyo Bay to witness the Japanese surrender aboard USS *Missouri*." That was how Ken Kennedy described the news the Navy had delivered to the crew of PC 466.[182]

Because of that decision, on 2 September 1945, the PC 466 steamed into Tokyo Bay as shown in Figure 9-13. She was the last and the smallest ship in a fifteen-mile long convoy of vessels that included battleships, carriers, cruisers, and destroyers. Ensign Tom Conway conned the ship as she joined the rest of the representatives of the U. S. Navy and its Allies in the Japanese capital port.

Tokyo Bay was a long way from the George Lawley & Sons shipyard in Neponset, Massachusetts that had launched the PC on 29 April 1942. On 3 June 1942 she first flew her commissioning pennant and was one of the first PCs the United States Navy had sent to sea to hunt Nazi U-boats in the Atlantic. At that time probably no one envisioned PC 466 in the role of an emblem of the overwhelming victory of the United States Navy over the Empire of Japan.

Kennedy wrote in a letter home about his impression of Tokyo Bay and its surroundings, "Chills went up and down my spine. . . . total defeat was everywhere." Idle ships and half-sunken hulls of the once mighty Japanese Navy lay around the harbor. As he stared at them, Kennedy reflected that the men on PC 466 and the other ships were there as observers of ". . . the Navy's answer to Pearl Harbor."

The Last Prisoner of War

World War II ended more than four months after the atom bomb attacks on Japan and the Japanese signed the Instrument of Surrender on 2 September 1945. It was not until 31 December 1946, however, that the war ended officially.

During the last few days of November 1946, the Navy dispatched sailors from the U. S. Naval Barracks in Tsingtao, China to help secure a supply depot against Chinese Communist forces. Donald Blair of PC 803 was among them.[183] In the dark of night of 3 December 1946, screaming Red soldiers poured into the defenders.

Slashing and stabbing with bayonets, they overran the small group of defenders. Men bled, fell, and died.

Blair, struck unconscious during the battle, awoke wounded and bound in a bouncing truck with wounded Red soldiers. He was a prisoner of war. Though they had badly wounded Blair, the Communists beat him repeatedly to force information from him about American supply locations. When not beating him they threw him into a filthy, freezing, solitary confinement cell and nearly starved him to death.

Finally on 15 January 1947, after fifteen days of brutal treatment, the Communists released him to the U. S. Marines. It was Donald Blair, a member of the crew of PC 803, who was the last American to become a World War II prisoner of war.

Summary

In the Pacific PCs did chores similar to those they did in the Atlantic. In addition, many PCs guided landing craft to the beaches in invasions. Japanese records showed that they considered beach control ships, including PCs, as vital to the American offensive. The Imperial Navy worried so much about these ships that they assigned squadrons of suicide boats to eliminate them. For example, when United States forces secured the Kerama Retto Islands they captured more than 300 Japanese suicide boats. This action eliminated that Japanese menace to the beach control forces and undoubtedly saved many PCs from disaster and saved the lives of many servicemen. Despite Tokyo Rose and everything the Japanese or nature threw at them, the men who manned PCs in the Pacific helped to destroy Japanese forces and win the war.

Figure 9-1. World War II propaganda poster, "Loose Lips Might Sink Ships." Year and source unknown. Courtesy of J. D. Ross, WWII Propaganda Posters, located at http://home.fish.net.an/jd/posters.

Figure 9-2. Crew members of PC 487 record their first Japanese submarine kill.
U. S. Navy photograph.

Figure 9-3. Rescue raft from YP-281 pounding against the hull of PC 1134. Photograph courtesy of David L. Brown.

Figure 9-4. Crew members of PC 1134 hang over the side to rescue survivors of YP-281. Photograph courtesy of David L. Brown.

Figure 9-5. PC 1129 in 1943. Photograph courtesy of the Institute for Great Lakes Research.

Figure 9-6. The bow of PC 1123 crowded with Philippine natives in 1945. Photograph courtesy of Bill Truemper.

Figure 9-7. On board PC 1119 off Arawe, New Britain. Left to right: Buckley (sitting), Blasdell, Deaton, John Wayne, Merchant, and "Guns." Photograph courtesy of Leonard Kurtz.

Figure 9-8. Men from a burning LSM struggle in the water as a man on PC 1133 prepares to throw them a line.

Figure 9-9. Bomb damage on PC 1124 on November 24, 1944. The auxiliary engine room was destroyed. A man could walk through the hole in the hull. Photograph courtesy of David Brown.

Figure 9-10. Starboard side of PC 1124 showing damage and list to port. The engine room was blown open about two feet. Photograph courtesy of David Brown.

Figure 9-11. Officers and crew of USS PC 779 placing the ship in commission on 31 May 1943 at the Commercial Iron Works, Portland, Oregon. Photograph courtesy of Arthur Fisher.

Figure 9-12. A sketch posted in the chartroom of PC 793 where it remained more than a year. Drawing by and courtesy of Raymond Page.

APRIL 26, 1945

Figure 9-13. PC 466 in Tokyo Bay for the Japanese surrender ceremony.
Photograph courtesy of Kenneth Kennedy.

CHAPTER 10

PC Casualties

PCs Also Paid the Price of War

During World War II the United States Navy called on PCs to operate in all theaters of war, often under extreme conditions, and to "go in harm's way." In responding to orders, PCs encountered the expected and many unexpected hardships and hazards of the sea and of war. Nature's forces battered them. Accidents, collisions, and groundings damaged and sank some. Enemy weapons crippled and destroyed PCs. Often, though, even serious damage to PCs by wind, waves, and near-shore operations was such a routine occurrence, that may Captains of the ships only listed the damage in ships' logs and had the crews do the repairs. They did not describe the damage in official reports. Therefore, much of the damage done to PCs is not well known.

Similarly, many PC sailors became seriously ill or received injuries from the pounding they took in rough seas. Most of these cases went unrecorded or became casual entries in ships' logs. Also, waves swept some men from their decks and drowned them.

Many crew members sustained serious injuries and received wounds during actions against enemy forces. Some members of crews of PCs died in battle aboard the ships. Other PC sailors languished in hospitals or enemy prisons, and some men were missing in action. PCs and their crews, like the bigger ships and their sailors, also paid the price of war.

Heavy Seas, and Storms Damaged PCs

Because of their diminutive size relative to the rough seas in which they often operated, most PCs sustained considerable damage. Waves bent and tore their external structure, topside appurtenances, and armament. In bad weather, tons of green water cascaded over the small ships and rushed from stems to sterns. It collapsed uprights, buckled plating and bulkheads, and whipped men off the ships' decks into the sea. The bending and twisting of the ships, as they lunged over the crests of waves and plunged into their troughs, cracked and bent internal structures and equipment. Damage to hulls, piping systems, steering mechanisms, propellers, propeller shafts, and engine mounts also happened often. Heavy seas ripped lines, stanchions, ammunition ready lockers, and wherries from their decks. Some ships had their mousetraps ripped apart and even their forward 3"-50 guns wrenched askew or torn loose from their mountings.

Where waves tore deck gear or guns loose, water poured through the gaps in the decks and endangered the stability of the ships. Seamen, engineers, shipfitters, and any man who had the ability, turned to for repairs underway to keep the ships afloat and operating. While battling the storms that caused the damage, however, crews could not make complete repairs to the holes torn in the decks and bulkheads. At best, ships' companies dogged hatches closed to maintain watertight integrity, jury-rigged covers over the openings, operated bilge pumps, and weathered the storms.

After buffeting through heavy seas and storms that caused damage to the ships and exhausted the crews, PCs limped into the safety of a harbor. There, despite their need for rest, the crews often had to do much of the repair work themselves. Area commanders could not always provide availability and shore-based or repair-ship personnel to help with repairs. Larger ships often had priority over smaller ships including PCs. Of the 361 PCs (including PCCs, AMs, and PGMs) the Navy commissioned, seven ran aground, and storms sank or destroyed five more of them.

PCs Collided With Friendly Vessels

Despite generally excellent seamanship, PCs, like other ships, not always avoided other vessels, and they received damage from collisions. Because the Navy used them on missions in which they interacted at close quarters with larger ships for deliveries, transfers, and miscellaneous uses, they were subject to minor accidents. Often they delivered men to beaches and cruised in shallow water crowded with other craft, contact with which they could not always avoid. During invasions they operated in only a few fathoms of water with landing craft and other control ships buzzing around them. They also scurried about among large and small craft picking up survivors. These activities caused many accidents.

Besides those occurrences, collisions with other ships seriously damaged five PCs. Also, three other PCs went to the bottom after colliding with a submarine, a merchant ship, and a destroyer.

Enemy Actions Damaged or Destroyed PCs

Enemy actions also took their toll of PCs. In the Atlantic Ocean, English Channel, Mediterranean Sea, and Pacific Ocean they suffered battle casualties. Cannon and mortar shells, aircraft bombs, mines, and torpedoes blasted holes in the hulls and superstructures of PCs. Bullets ripped up deck gear and rigging. Some PCs had their hulls torn open, and they went to the bottom. Crew members drowned, bled and died aboard, or were lost or captured when their vessels sank.

When any event shattered a PC's 5/16 inch thin hull below the water line, the ship quickly capsized or sank. Men had little time in which to save their ship or even to abandon her. Scrambling up from the lower decks, as water frothed around his legs, against a ship going over on her beam, took all of a man's strength and speed. The sinking of a PC happened fast. It usually left no time for men to save the ship's gear or their personal possessions. The men had only enough time to try to save their lives. Not all of them succeeded. Enemy actions seriously damaged seven and sank eight PCs during WWII.

Typhoon Louise Ravaged Okinawa

After hostilities ceased, many U. S. Navy ships gathered at Okinawa. In that sanctuary they hoped for respite from years of battle with the Japanese. Their rest was short lived, however. On 9 October 1945 typhoon Louise struck. It was the worst storm in the history of Okinawa and ravaged the area. This storm damaged and destroyed some 200 United States naval vessels, and more than 100 bodies of drowned sailors washed ashore after the storm subsided.

PC 590 Broke Up

World War II had ended, but many ships still carried out some wartime activities. For example, the Coast Guard crew aboard PC 590 ran mail to a United States garrison on Mijako Island between Formosa and Okinawa. En route, during one trip, its gunners sank a few mines then headed back for Okinawa. Though the sea was smooth and hardly a breeze stirred, the ship's radio crackled with storm warnings. Typhoon Louise was building her fury and setting a course for the Okinawa area and the armada of United States ships stationed at and near the island. A short time after PC 590 entered Buckner Bay at Okinawa on 9 October 1945 and dropped the hook, the storm engulfed the area. "The sea began to rise and the wind grew in intensity . . . ."[184] Waves broke twenty-five feet above her bridge. Winds raged at force 11. The barometer dropped to 28.80. Solid water washed the men in the anchor detail on the forecastle thirty feet aft from their stations, and the anchor chain parted. "Our anchor chain broke under the strain of a monstrous sea, and things began to happen fast and furious."

"Looking to windward was almost literally impossible because of the driving spray." Using a combination of the wind, various speeds with the engines, and rudder action, the Captain conned PC 590 through a whirling maze of gale-blown vessels. The glass plunged to 28.20. Winds increased to more than 100 knots, and despite the Captain's and the crew's frantic attempts to save the ship, the wind forced the ship toward land.

Just when the power of the main Diesel engines was critical for maneuvering the ship, a huge wave washed over the engine exhaust-opening in the hull. Flames and smoke backfired into the engine room. A loud knock sounded in the starboard engine. Engine temperatures soared and threatened the loss of propulsion. The Motor Machs struggled to keep the main engines running. An oil line broke on an auxiliary engine, that drove an electric generator, and it wheezed to a stop. Lights on the ship failed. Battle lamps flared on the ship. In the engine room the snipes struggled to keep the main engines alive.

Moments later, the wind and waves pounded the ship onto a reef. It twisted, groaned, and shivered. With a shudder it ripped free. Then the wind and sea jarred it back onto the reef. The steering cable snapped. Jagged rocks ripped open the port side of the engine room, and water poured in. The engineers raced up the ladder to escape as water surged around their legs. Then the pumps failed, and the crew lost control of the rising water. At 1630, electric power drained from the circuits, and the radio and signal lamps died.

"Help. Help," a voice wailed, and a struggling sailor in a life jacket, whom waves had thrown overboard from another ship, swept past the PC. The crew on PC 590 tried to tend him a line, but the waves swept him away before they could help him. Ships drifting around, on possible collision courses with the foundering PC, blew whistles and sounded alarms. Small craft, propelled by the gale winds and pounding waves, tumbled past the PC.

A depth charge tore loose on the fantail of PC 590. Men battled their way aft and labored and strained against the thirty foot seas, the 100 knot wind, and the jerking roll of the ship to secure the charge. If it exploded, it could have blown away the stern of the ship.

Mona Island (ARG-91) hove to nearby, and her seamen sailed a messenger line to the PC. The crews on the two ships rigged a breeches buoy and boatswain's chair between the two vessels and started hauling the men from the PC to the rescue ship. During one transit, seas parted the line, and men dropped into the ocean. Sailors heaved on the lines and barely dragged the men up from the sea. The wind and waves almost swept some sailors on the foundering PC overboard or crushed them against the ship's structure. Eventually, though, the crew of *Mona Island* plucked the last group of sailors from PC 590 to safety. Moments later a crunching sound rose from the PC. Its keel snapped, and the ship broke in half. Figure 10-1 shows the broken ship on the rocks.

PC 800 Survived

At Okinawa, the crew of PC 800 also fought for their lives in that typhoon. Alton Fuller wrote,[185] ". . . 30 to 40-foot waves bashing the ship as it quivered, rolled, slammed into the troughs, then lifted skyward on the crests . . . . We all wondered if the next wave would cause the ship to flounder. But PCs are rugged, a credit to their builders . . . ."

PC 1558 and PC 1126 Pounded Onto a Reef

Six months after she left Mill Basin, Brooklyn, NY, the PGM 27 (PC 1558) huddled in Buckner Bay, Okinawa to ride out the typhoon.[186] Like the men on other ships, her crew topped off her tanks, moved heavy gear as close to the keel as possible, rigged lifelines, and battened down. Her Captain scoped out eighty-five fathoms of chain on both anchors in ten fathoms of water.

Despite running ahead on the engines, the anchor chains broke under the strain of the wind and seas. Unable to keep her bow into the sea, the ship rolled to 55 degrees. At 1845 hours the PGM ground onto a reef. An hour and a half later, PC 1126 slammed into the starboard quarter of the PGM. The two vessels remained locked together, and the crew of the PC jumped and hauled themselves aboard the PGM. Most of the men later transferred from the two grounded ships to *Sherburne* (APA 205). Eventually PGM 27 broke up but after the crew stripped her of whatever they could move by hand. The Navy later salvaged the damaged PC 1126.

The Typhoon Drove PC 1238 Aground and Sank PC 584 and PC 814

The winds also sank PC 584 and PC 814 and ground PC 1238 onto a reef in Buckner Bay, Okinawa.[187] She lay on her starboard side stranded like a beached whale with her engine room filled with oil and water and her other compartments flooded with water. She is shown in Figure 10-2. After the storm subsided, crew members climbed through a hole in the hull on the port side of PC 1238. They retrieved gear from the forward part of the ship, but they could not enter the flooded engine room.

The Storm Left PC 1239 High and Dry

The sister ship to PC 1238, the PC 1239, though anchored when the typhoon struck, was not in operating condition. The fury of the wind and high seas of the typhoon tore her from her moorings and swept the ship a quarter of a mile inland. After the typhoon she lay there high and dry.

Table 10-1 lists those vessels that sank or whose damage was serious enough for their Captains to have reported it.[188, 189]

Table 10-1. Casualties Reported to PCs

PC Number	Date	Location	Incident
PC 460	1/24/42	Gulf of Panama	Sunk by collision with a submarine
Ex PC 473, French, *L'Ardent*, W 39	1/31/45	Casablanca Harbor	Sunk by collision with SS *Empire Abbey*
Ex PC 482, French, *L'Enjoue*, W 44	1/9/945	Cape Spartel, Straits of Gibralter	Sunk by a torpedo from U-870
PC 487	6/10/43	Attu, Aleutian Islands	Damaged in ramming and sinking Japanese submarine I24

PC 496	6/4/43	Tunisia, Africa	Sunk by a torpedo from an Italian submarine
PC 546	8/11/43	Sicily	Damaged by bombs
PC 556	5/9/44	Naples, Italy	Damaged by bombs
PC 558	5/9/44	Mediterranean Sea	Sunk by a torpedo from U-230
PC 562	7/18/43	Sicily	Damaged by a mine
PC 564	3/9/45	France	Damaged by E-Boats
PC 578	2/24/45	Iwo Jima	Damaged by collision
PC 582	7/12/45	Philippine Islands	Damaged by grounding
PC 584	10/45	Okinawa	Sunk by typhoon Louise
PC 590	10/9/45	Buckner Bay, Okinawa	Grounded and broken up in typhoon Louise
PC 621	7/10/43	Off Sicily	Damaged by collision with an LST
PC 624*	44	Palermo	Damaged by rocks in a storm
PC 627	7/31/43	Palermo	Damaged by bombs
PC 814	12/12/45	Okinawa	Destroyed by typhoon "Louise"
PC 815	11/45	San Diego	Sunk by collision with DD, USS *Laffey*
PC 877	2/23/45	Iwo Jima	Damaged by collision
PC 1119	2/16/45	Luzon, Philippines	Damaged by shells from coastal defense guns
PC 1124*	11/24/44	Leyte, Philippines	Damaged by a dive bomber. The hulk was scrapped on 10 October 1945
PC 1126	10/9/45	Buckner Bay, Okinawa	Damage by grounding and collision during a typhoon

PC 1128	1/44	Dumbea Bay, New Caledonia	Damaged by collision with a destroyer in a hurricane
PC 1129*	1/31/45	Philippine Islands	Sunk by a Japanese suicide boat
PC 1133	3/26/45	Philippine Islands	Damaged by grounding
PC 1189 (PGM 17)	5/4/45	Okinawa	Destroyed by grounding
PC 1217	9/13/44	Florida, USA	Damaged by a hurricane
PC 1238	9/8/45	Okinawa	Damaged by grounding
PC 1239	9/8/45	Okinawa	Damaged by grounding
PC 1255 (PGM 18)	4/7/45	Okinawa	Sunk by a mine
PC 1261	6/6/44	Normandy, France	Sunk by shellfire from coastal defense guns
PC 1558 (PGM 27)	10/9/45	Buckner Bay, Okinawa	Destroyed by grounding during typhoon Louise
PC 1599	6/1/45	Okinawa	Damaged by grounding
PC 1603	5/26/45[190]	Off Okinawa	Damaged by a suicide plane. The hulk was sunk later
Total Number Damaged	**20**		
Total Number Sunk or Destroyed	**15**		
Total Number of Casualties	**35**		

* A drawing of PC 624 is shown in Figure 10-3. A photograph of PC 1124 being scrapped at Hollandia in March 1945 is shown in Figure 10-4. A photograph of PC 1129 is shown in Figure 9-5.

Table 10-2 contains a summary of the numbers of ships involved in each type of incident.

Table 10-2. Numbers of PCs Involved in Each Type of Casualty in Table 10-1.

Type of Casualty	Number of PCs Involved
Damaged by grounding	7
Damaged by collisions	4
Damaged by bombs	3
Damaged by shellfire	1
Damaged by a mine	1
Damaged by E-boats	1
Damaged by a hurricane	1
Damaged by ramming a Japanese submarine	1
Sunk by shellfire	1
Sunk by a mine	1
Sunk by a Japanese suicide boat	1
Sunk by collisions	3
Sunk or destroyed by grounding	5
Sunk by torpedoes from U-boats	2
Sunk by a torpedo from an Italian submarine	1
Sunk because of bomb damage	2
Total	**35**

PC Crew Battle Casualties

Besides the damage to and losses of ships, crew members of PCs received injuries that no one recorded or merely entered them as routine statements in ships' logs. Then too, seas swept men to their death. In combat, PC sailors received wounds and were killed, lost, or captured. The numbers of casualties, from enemy action, to members of the crews of those PCs whose stories are recounted in previous chapters total forty-nine wounded, thirty-six killed, and twenty captured or missing in action. This count is not a total list of casualties on all PCs. See Appendix I to get more information on casualties. Nevertheless, the number of casualties given here does highlight the fact that these small ships engaged the enemy during the war.

Summary

PCs suffered battle casualties from torpedoes, mines, bombs, planes, suicide boats, shore batteries, and in the ramming of a Japanese submarine. Storms, groundings, and collisions destroyed or did major damage to other PCs.[191,192] They and their crews suffered casualties while hounding and attacking German U-boats, for which the Navy had conceived them. Beyond that service, though, they suffered casualties as they herded convoys, patrolled for submarines, and led attacks on beachheads.

Typhoons, hurricanes, williwaws, collisions, and enemy action sank or destroyed sixteen PCs of the 361 PC-type ships the Navy commissioned. Most of those that sustained severe damage underwent repairs and went back to service. This record of survival and recovery is a tribute to the cleverness of their design, the excellent construction of them by shipyard workers, the ruggedness of the vessels, and the ability and courage of the commissioned officers and enlisted men who manned them.

Figure 10-1. PC 590 after she foundered and broke in half off Okinawa during the typhoon on 9 October 1945. Photograph courtesy of Ed Emanuel.

Figure 10-2. PC 1238 aground at Okinawa after typhoon Louise. Photograph courtesy of Robert B. Dunlap.

Figure 10-3. Drawing of PC 624 which ran aground off Palermo, Sicily in 1944. Drawing by and courtesy of Bob Baldwin.

Figure 10-4. PC 1124 being scrapped at Hollandia, New Guinea in March 1945 after being damaged by a Japanese dive bomber. Photograph courtesy of Mrs. Connie Whitman from Joseph Whitman's collection.

CHAPTER 11

The Naming, Decommissioning, and Disposition of PCs

The Greatest Navy Was Dismantled

Soon after the guns went silent on V-J Day, 15 August 1945, the greatest navy ever to have spanned the world's seas began to dismantle itself. Millions of men and women shed their United States Navy blues for civilian clothes. "Ruptured Ducks," symbols of past military service, sprouted on jacket lapels and sweaters after the United States Armed forces gave millions of men and women their discharges.

Then, after this release of many of the Navy's personnel, the Navy quickly returned many larger more costly to operate ships and unneeded craft to the United States. Hundreds of Navy vessels, from battleships to landing craft, became immobilized for lack of military objectives, trained crews, and an adequate operating budget. Quick decommissioning of ships became the order of the day.

The United States Navy decommissioned most of its capital ships and hero ships with great ceremonies. Removal from active service of the other thousands of work horse ships of the Navy, however, was done with much less formality. For example, after World War II ended, the Navy decommissioned most of the 300 of the PCs, that were still afloat in the United States Navy,[193] with none of the fanfare the larger ships received. The decommissioning of PCs was not as exciting as was their commissioning when the Navy started throwing them to sea in 1942 to fight Nazi U-boats.

After the war ended, the Navy released many PCs from their duties. Their crews quickly unfurled their long homeward-bound pennants and plotted courses for "stateside" like PC 478 shown in Figure 11-1 and PC 466 shown in Figure 11-2. After years overseas for many men on the ships, coming back to the States for liberty, leave, and discharge was a long awaited and happy moment. Figure 11-3 shows some ship's company and watch-standing passengers, who brought PC 820 back to Seattle, enjoying their first liberty in the United States in two years.

Disposition of PCs

The Navy did not send home or decommission all PCs immediately. A few of them continued naval service for as many as ten years in the Pacific Islands. Others served even longer in various places and with other countries. Of those that returned to the United States, cocoons enshrouded some in the reserve fleet. Others went to Reserve Training facilities. One felt the heat and blast of an atomic bomb at Bikini. Navy guns blasted some as target ships. Salvagers' torches tore others to scrap. Foreign navies received a few as gifts or purchased them. Commercial fishermen and other commercial ventures bought some and converted them for different uses. Those not destroyed continued varied and long lives, even until this decade, fifty years after the shipyards had launched them.

When the Navy disposed of PCs they sent many of them to The Maritime Commission for disposition. This agency maintained records of the ships only up to the first sale by them or by some other means of disposal. After that first event the United States government relinquished control, and, in most respects even knowledge of them. Tracing the histories of PCs from then on is difficult for various reasons. Their new owners modified or altered them, some beyond recognition as a PC. For example, Figure 11-4 and Figure 11-5 show ex-PC 1172, named *Gleaner*. Its owner converted it into a landing barge by hacking off the bow forward of the 3"-50 mount and the stern aft of the engine room.

New owners did not always keep records of how they disposed of the ships. Some business owners' names changed, and some stopped operating, so learning where the ships went after a first sale is difficult. Despite these and other problems, however, people have traced the histories of many PCs after the United States government disposed of them.

Illustrations of the Disposition of Some PCs

Illustrations of the varieties of events that some PCs underwent after World War II ended are given below in increasing order of the ships' numbers. These accounts are not inclusive, but they represent the diversity of ways in which the Navy disposed of the PCs. For the dates of the starts of their construction, launching, christening, commissioning, decommissioning, and disposal of them and all other World War II PCs see Appendix D. It lists them alphabetically by the shipyards that built them.

PC 477 Became Scrap Metal for Japan

With more than four years of service battling the Japanese in the Pacific, the Navy declared the battered and weary PC 477, ". . . excess and not essential to the defense of the United States." On 15 August 1946 a sailor lowered her commissioning pennant at Terminal Island, California, and the Navy struck her from the Naval Register. On 4 December 1946, J. C. Berkwit and Company purchased her for salvage. West Coast scrappers sold her remains as scrap metal to Japan. This fate is an ominous reminder of how the United States supplied steel to Japan before World War II and, thereby, helped her build a war machine.

PC 542 Had an Interesting Experience

PC 542 joined the French Navy in September 1944 but only after three weeks of an "interesting experience" with a half American and half French crew aboard.[194] The French named the PC, *Tirailleur*. Thirteen years later, after her exploits in the Mediterranean, including her gunners blasting two German planes from the sky, the French Navy condemned the ship.

PC 548 Ended At the Atom Bomb Test

After convoy duty on the east coast of the United States, PC 548 served in the South Pacific in invasions in the Philippines, the Marshall Islands, and at Iwo Jima. After her return to the United States, the government put her in moth balls at San Francisco. Then the Navy recalled her and sent her west again. PC 548 ended her life at the atom bomb test at Eniwetok.[195]

PC 550 Transferred to France

On 15 June 1944, after her European service, sailors struck the commissioning pennant of PC 550 (PGM 32) in Oran, Algiers, North Africa. Her American crew fell in at quarters on the ship and a French crew assembled on the dock, as shown in Figure 11-6. The American sailors heard Lt. B. J. Belmore, Commanding Officer, read orders transferring the ship to the French Navy as shown in Figure 11-7. Ship's company then walked down the gangway the last time, and a crew of French sailors strode onto the decks of the then named *Le Vigilant*. Figure 11-8 shows the new Captain, Lt. Robert Serrett, French Navy, leading his men aboard. Finally, PC 550 was stricken from the records as a Navy ship on 1 August 1959.[196]

PC 564 Joined the Submarine Force

In June 1945 PC 564 received an overhaul in the United States and started duty with the Commander, Submarine Force in New London Connecticut. Later, the Navy named her *Chadron*. In 1964 the U. S. Navy sent her to the Korean Navy, where they named her *Sol Ak* (PC 709). She served on coastal patrol and training for the Korean Navy.[197]

PC 567 Earned its Wings

On 15 March 1963, the PC 567 suffered what many sailors considered the worst fate for a ship to experience. She joined the United States Air Force.[198] The men who served on PCs in heavy seas probably thought, however, the time was long overdue for people to recognize a PC as having airborne capabilities.

PC 568 Was the Last to Go

The Navy struck the last PC from the Naval Vessel Register on 1 November 1965. The last PC left the Navy in March 1968[199] when PC 568 joined eight other PCs in the Philippine Navy. They renamed PC 568 the *Nueva Viscaya*.

PC 576 Was Sold for $8,000

Completed on 10 September 1942 at a cost of $628,500 in Wilmington, Delaware, PC 576 plied the Eastern Sea Frontier and the Caribbean from Tompkinsville, NY to Trinidad and Guantanamo.[200] On 23 January 1947, the Secretary of the Navy authorized her decommissioning, and the Navy struck PC 576 from the Naval Register on 5 March 1947. They sold her to John A. Papado of New York, New York on 2 July 1948 for $8,133.55. That loss of $620,366.45 was typical of the losses the government incurred for the disposal of each PC.

PC 618 Was One of the Last PCs in the Navy

Sailors on board PC 618 (USS *Weatherford*) lowered her commissioning pennant in 1965 after the ship had put in twenty-three years of service. Her longevity testifies to the excellent design and construction of the ship and its versatility. The Navy struck her from the Register on 1 November 1965, and she became a salvage training hulk until 11 January 1968. Then she ended her career of twenty-six years as a target ship.

PC 807 Also Served in the Korean Conflict

PC 807 raised its commissioning pennant on 20 February 1945 at the Commercial Iron Works in Portland, Oregon. Her tour of duty included Pearl Harbor, Eniwetok, Guam, Saipan, and Okinawa. After the war, PC 807 served as flagship for the Liberation landings at Jinsen, Korea, and Taku Bar. Then she sailed up the Pei Ho River to Tangku, China. In April 1946 she made her last trip which was to San Pedro, California for decommissioning. Then the Maritime Commission sold PC 807 for scrap in July 1948.[201]

PC 823 Honored a Merchant Marine Sailor

In November 1946, the Merchant Marine Academy at Kings Point, Long Island, New York acquired PC 823 for its Naval Science Training program. It named it *Ensign Whitehead* in memory of a graduate of the academy who was killed during World War II.

On 17 October 1949 the Academy sold PC 823 to the Korean Navy for $18,000, and they commissioned her as PC 701 and named her *Bak Du San*. The name is Korean for Whitehead Mountain, in essence continuing her former name. On the first day of the Korean conflict, 25 June 1950, ex-PC 823 fought the most important naval engagement of the Korean War. Shells from her guns sank a North Korean ship loaded with 600 unconventional warfare troops. They were on their way to capture Pusan in the south and deny the port to the United States through which the United States could send in supplies. On other sorties ROK sailors on the PC poured gunfire into enemy soldiers . They also took part in the landings at Inchon that severed the North Korean army's supply lines and forced their retreat. Finally on 1 July 1959 the ROK Navy sold *Bak Du San* for scrap.[202]

PC 1089 (PGM 13) Ran Out of Luck

Known by her ship's company as the "Lucky 13," the PGM 13 (PC 1089) survived many close calls during and after the war. She served in "Mac Arthur's Navy" in the occupation of Japan from

September 1945 and operated off Korea sinking mines. On 6 May 1946, after she returned to the Philippines, the Navy decommissioned the ship. She went to the Taiwan Navy as *Tung Ting* and then as *Ling Chiang*. On 20 January 1995 a Communist Chinese Navy Motor Torpedo Boat sank her.[203]

PC 1141 Served Twelve Years in the Pacific

PC 1141 escorted twelve convoys from New York to Guantanamo Bay, Cuba. Then she transited the Panama Canal and steamed independently to Pearl Harbor. She continued convoy work and ran air-sea rescue and other missions in the Pacific until April 1954. The navy named her *USS Pierre* in 1956, decommissioned her on 25 October 1958, and transferred the ship to the Indonesian Navy. They renamed her *R. I. Tjakalang*. No record of the ship exists after 1970.[204]

PC 1172 Went From Tokyo Bay to Alaska as a Barge

Following Atlantic seaboard convoy duty, PC 1172 sailed to the Pacific and into Tokyo Bay on 29 September 1945. After that she operated in the Caroline and Marshall Islands on Trust Territory Patrol Duty for ten years.[205] On 26 February 1955 she returned to the United States and joined the Naval Reserve Fleet at Astoria, Oregon. The Navy struck her from the register on 1 July 1960.

She went to Hatch and Kirk of Astoria, Oregon on 20 May 1961 who stripped her and sold the parts. They sold the engines, reduction gears, shafts, and screws to The Luzon Stevedores in Manila, The Philippines. Then, in 1969, they cut off her stern and bow and made her into a landing barge with a bow ramp. With new engines installed, she worked on seismic studies in the Arctic for three years and then as a clam digger for Peninsula Packing of Alaska. In 1994 the remains of *Gleaner*, ex-PC 1172, sat waiting its next adventure[206] as shown in Figure 11-4 and Figure 11-5.

PC 1243 Went to China and Came Back

After six months with the Commander Gulf Sea Frontier, PC 1243 transited the Panama Canal and headed into the Pacific. She saw service at Saipan, Tinian, Eniwetok, and Guam, and she helped in the Japanese surrender at Yap.[207] In September 1946 the Navy assigned her to the Chinese Navy Program. PC 490 replaced PC 1243 in the Chinese Navy, and PC 1243 returned to the Foreign Liquidation Commission. On 17 February 1947 the Navy declared her, not essential to defense, decommissioned her on 1 April 1947, and struck her from the records on 23 April 1947. The Negros Navigation Co. Of San Francisco, California purchased PC 1243 on 27 August 1947.[208]

PC 1263 Went to China

Upon completion of duties at Normandy in the invasion of France, PC 1263 departed Europe 6 June 1945 for Miami, Florida. The Navy named her *USS Milledgeville* on 15 February 1959. She served as a training ship until 16 February 1959 when the navy decommissioned her. The Republic of China accepted PC 1263 for the Chinese Nationalist Navy under the Military Assistance Program on 1 July 1959 and named her *To Kiang* (PC125).[209]

PC 1565 (PGM 29) Went to Bikini and Greece

After a brief tour in the Pacific, PGM 29 (PC 1565) returned to San Francisco for a new crew. Then she headed for the Atom Bomb test at Bikini. On return from the tests, the ship went to the Naval Reserve. Then the United States Navy transferred her to Greece. The Greek Navy scrapped the ship in 1979.

PC 1590 Acted as a Target Ship

The Navy commissioned PC 1590 on 21 September 1942 as *USS Constant* (AM 86) and classified her as PC 1590 on 1 June 1944. The Navy decommissioned her on 19 June 1946 but then commissioned her again on 5 May 1950 for the reserves. After decommissioning a second time on 22 October 1954, the Navy sank her as a target ship.

PCs Transferred to Other Countries

During and after World War II the United States transferred some PCs to other countries. In most cases these countries altered the ships and numbered and named them. Figure 11-9 shows ex-PC 543, for example, months after the French Navy acquired her. The forty-five ships the Navy transferred during the war, with their new names, and in some cases new numbers, are given in Table 11-1. Table 11-2 lists these ships by country.

Table 11-1. PCs Transferred to Other Countries by the United States During WWII

NUMBER	COUNTRY	NAME AND NEW NUMBER
PC 467	Norway	
PC 468	The Netherlands, then Nigeria	*Queen Wilhelmina,* then *Ogaja*
PC 471	France	*Eveille*
PC 472	France	*Ruse*
PC 473	France	*Ardent*
PC 474	France	*Indiscret*
PC 475	France	*Resolu*
PC 480	France	*Emporte*
PC 481	France	*Effronte*
PC 482	France	*Enjoue*
PC 542	France	*Tirailleur*
PC 543	France	*Voluntaire*
PC 544	Brazil	*Guapore*

PC 545	France, then Morocco	*Goumier*, then *Agadir*
PC 546	France	*Franc Tireur*
PC 547	Brazil	*Gurupi*
PC 550	France	*Vigilant*
PC 551	France	*Mameluck*
PC 554	Brazil	*Goiana*
PC 556	France	*Carabinier*
PC 557	France	*Dragon*
PC 559	France	*Voltigeur*
PC 561	Brazil	*Grauna*
PC 562	France	*Atentif*
PC 591	France	*Spahi*
PC 604	Brazil	*Guaiba*
PC 605	Brazil	*Gurupi*
PC 607	Brazil	*Guajara*
PC 621	France	*Fantassin*
PC 622	Greece	*Vassilefs Georghios*
PC 624	France	YW 120, YWN 120
PC 625	France	*Grenadier*
PC 626	France	*Lansquenet*
PC 627	France	*Cavalier*
PC 1226	France	*Legionnaire*
PC 1227	France	*Lancier*
PC 1234	Uruguay	*Maldonado*

PC 1235	France	*Hussard*
PC 1236	Brazil	*Graju*
PC 1248	France	*Sabre*
PC 1249	France	*Pique*
PC 1250	France	*Cimeterre*
PC 1560	France	*Coutelas*
PC 1561	France	*Dague*
PC 1562	France	*Javelot*
TOTAL		**45**

**Table 11-2. Numbers of PCs Sent to Other Countries During WWII
(Taken from Table 11-1)**

COUNTRY	PC NUMBERS	NUMBERS of PCs
Brazil	PC 544, 547,554, 561, 604, 605, 607, 1236	8
France	PC 471-475, 480-482, 542, 543, 545, 546, 550, 551, 556, 557, 559, 562, 591, 621, 624-627, 1226, 1227, 1235, 1248-1250, 1560-1562	33
Greece	PC 622	1
Netherlands	PC 468	1
Norway	PC 467	1
Uruguay	PC 1234	1
TOTAL		**45**

The 110 PCs the United States transferred to other countries after World War II are given, with their new names and numbers, in Table 11-3.

Table 11-3. PCs Transferred to Other Countries After WWII

NUMBER	COUNTRY	NAME AND NEW NUMBER
PC 465	Venezuela	*Pulpo*, P7
PC 483	Venezuela	*Damaron,*
PC 484	Venezuela	*Togogo*
PC 485	Korea	*Han Ra San*
PC 487	Venezuela	*Mejilon*
PC 490	China	*Wu Sung*
PC 492	China	*Fukiang*
PC 495	Thailand	*Sarasin*
PC 564	Korea	*Sol Ak*, PC 709
PC 565	Venezuela	*Alcatraz*
PC 566	Venezuela	*Calamar*
PC 568	Philippines	*Nueva Viscaya*, PS 80
PC 570	Thailand	*Longlom*
PC 572	Venezuela	*Tooele*
PC 575	Thailand	*Thayanchon*
PC 580	Indonesia	*Hui*
PC 581	Indonesia	*Torani*
PC 582	Venezuela	*Albatros*
PC 593	China	*Fuchiang*
PC 595	China*	
PC 600	Korea	*Myo Hyang San*

PC 608	Mexico	GC 31
PC 609	Thailand	*Khamronsin*
PC 613	Dominican Republic	*27 de Febrero*
PC 614	Mexico	GC 32
PC 616	Thailand	*Tongpliu*, PC6
PC 619	Venezuela	*Pulpo* nee *Gaviota*
PC 786	China	*Hsiang Kiang*
PC 787	Indonesia	*Alu Alu*
PC 790	Cuba**	*Baire*
PC 794	Mexico	GC 34
PC 796	France	*Pnom-Penh*
PC 797	France	*Hue*
PC 798	France	*Luang-Prabang*
PC 799	Korea	*Kum Kang San*
PC 802	Korea	*Samkaksan*
PC 809	Portugal	*Sal*
PC 810	Mexico	G 37
PC 811	Portugal	*Madeira*
PC 812	Portugal	*Principe*
PC 813	Mexico	GC 33
PC 819	Mexico	GC 37
PC 820	Mexico	GC 30
PC 824	Mexico	GC 35
PC 1077	Venezuela	*Caracoi*

PC 1078	China	*Chih Kiang*
PC 1086	Indochina then Cambodia	*Flamberge* then E 311
PC 1087	China	*Tung Kiang*
PC 1088 (PGM 12)	China	Defected to Taiwan
PC 1089 (PGM 13)	China	*Ling Chiang* nee *Tung Ting*
PC 1090 (PGM 14)	China	Defected to Taiwan
PC 1091 (PGM 15)	China	Defected to Taiwan as *Kan Tang*
PC 1121	Philippines***	*Camarines Sur*
PC 1122	Philippines***	*Monicken*
PC 1130	Indochina then Viet Nam	*Intrepide* then *Van Kiep*
PC 1131	Philippines	*Bohol*, PS 22
PC 1133	Philippines	*Zamboanga del Sur*, PS 23
PC 1134	Philippines	*Batangas*, PS 24
PC 1139	Indochina then Cambodia	*Impetueux*
PC 1141	Indonesia	*Tjakalang*
PC 1142	China	*Pei Kiang*
PC 1143	Indochina then Viet Nam	*Glaive* then *Tuy Dong*
PC 1144	Indochina then Viet Nam	*Mousquet* then *Chi Lang*
PC 1145	Korea	*Oteasan*
PC 1146	Indochina then Viet Nam	*Trident* then *Tay Ket*
PC 1148 (PGM 16)	Greece	*Antiploiarkhos Laskos*

PC 1149	China	*Hai Kiang*
PC 1167	Indochina then Viet Nam	*Dong'Da*
PC 1168	China	*Ching Kiang*
PC 1169	China	*Liu Kiang*
PC 1171	Indochina then Cambodia	*Inconstant* then E 312
PC 1175	China	*Han Kiang*
PC 1176	Venezuela	*Petrel*
PC 1182	China	*Yuan Kiang*
PC 1183	Indonesia	*Tenggiri*
PC 1185	Thailand	*Phali*, PC4
PC 1202	Dominican Republic	*Patria* nee *Capitan Wenceslas Arvels*
PC 1208	China	*Li Kiang*
PC 1210	Mexico	G 38
PC 1211	Spain	*Javier Quiroga*
PC 1218	Thailand	*Sukrip*, PC5
PC 1224	Mexico	GC 36
PC 1232	Taiwan****	*Chang Kiang*
PC 1233	Taiwan****	*Kung Kiang*
PC 1241	Philippines	*Nueva Ecija*, PS 25
PC 1245	France	
PC 1247	China	*To Kiang* nee *Chialing*
PC 1252	Venezuela	Not put into service
PC 1253	Thailand	*Liulom*, PC7

PC 1254	Taiwan****	*Po Kiang*
PC 1256	Portugal	*Sao Tome*
PC 1257	Portugal	*Santiago*
PC 1259	Portugal	*Sao Vicente*
PC 1262	Taiwan****	*Chung Kiang*
PC 1263	Taiwan****	*To Kiang*
PC 1546	Korea	*Kum Chong San*
PC 1549	China	*Chien Tang*
PC 1551 (PGM 20)	China	*Ying Chiang* nee *Pao Ying*
PC 1552 (PGM 21)	Greece	*Antiploiarkhos Pezopoulos*
PC 1553 (PGM 22)	Greece	*Ploiarkhos Meletopoulos*
PC 1556 (PGM 25)	Greece	*Plotarkhis Arslandoglou*
PC 1557 (PGM 26)	China	*Ou Chang* nee *Hung Tse*
PC 1559 (PGM 28)	Greece	*Plotarkhis Blessas*
PC 1563	Phillippines	*Negros Oriental*, PC26
PC 1564	Philippines	*Capiz*, PS 27
PC 1565 (PGM 29)	Greece	*Plotarkhis Chantzikonstandis*
PC 1567 (PGM 31)PC	China	*Chu Kiang*
PC 1569	Viet Nam	*Van Don*
PC 1597	Dominican Republic	*Engage Cibus Constitucion*
PC 1646	Chile	*Papudo*, No. 37
TOTAL		**110**

* Friedman, Norman, *U. S. Small Combatants* (US Naval Institute, Annapolis, MD, 1987) lists this ship as going to France as CH 132 and then to China in August 1958.

    ** Other sources list it as sold to Honduras and named *Tribesman*, then obtained by Cuba in 1956.

    *** Private communication from the Headquarters Philippine Navy dated 12 November 1992 does not list PC 1121 and PC 1122. It lists PC 1171 as *Negros Oriental* (PS 26) commissioned on 6 November 1976. This ship may have replaced PC 1563 that was stricken by the Philippine Navy on 24 January 1963.

    **** Friedman lists these ships as going to China

    The list of those PCs transferred to other countries after World War II, given by country, is shown in Table 11-4.

Table 11-4. Numbers of PCs Sent to Other Countries After WWII (Taken from Table 11-3)

COUNTRY	PC NUMBERS	NUMBERS OF PCs
Indochina then Cambodia	1086, 1139, 1171	3
Chile	1646	1
China	490, 492, 593, 595, 786, 1078, 1087–1091, 1142, 1149, 1168, 1169, 1175, 1182, 1208, 1247, 1549, 1551, 1557, 1567	23
Cuba	790	1
Dominican Republic	613, 1202, 1597	3
France	796, 797, 798, 1245	4
Greece	1148, 1552, 1553, 1556, 1559, 1565	6
Indonesia	580, 581, 787, 1141, 1183	5
Korea	485, 564, 600, 799, 802, 1145, 1546	7
Mexico	608, 614, 794, 810, 813, 819, 820, 824, 1210, 1224	10

Philippines	568, 1121, 1122, 1131, 1133, 1134, 1241, 1563, 1564	9
Portugal	809, 811, 812, 1256, 1257, 1259	6
Spain	1211	1
Taiwan	1232, 1233, 1254, 1262, 1263	5
Thailand	495, 570, 575, 609, 616 1185, 1218, 1253	8
Venezuela	465, 483, 484, 487, 565, 566, 572, 582, 619, 1077, 1176, 1252	12
Indochina then Viet Nam	1130, 1143, 1144, 1146, 1167, 1569	6
TOTAL		**110**

Some United States Navy PCs Got Names

Fifteen years after the steel-hulled PCs began the search for and destruction of Nazi submarines, and then served in many other capacities in all theaters during World War II, the United States Navy finally allowed that these ships deserved names. Ten years after World War II ended, on 15 February 1956, the Navy assigned the names of small cities to those PCs that were still operating with the United States Navy.[210] Those 102 ships, and the names assigned to them, are shown in Table 11-5.

Table 11-5. Names Assigned to PCs After WW II

PC	USN NAME	PC	USN NAME	PC	USN NAME
461	*Bluffton*	620	*Bethany*	1175	*Vandalia*
465	*Paragold*	776	*Pikeville*	1176	*Minden*
466	*Carmi*	777	*Waynesurg*	1177	*Guymon*

470	*Antigo*	778	*Gallipolis*	1178	*Kewaunee*
483	*Rolla*	779	*Mechanicsburg*	1179	*Morris*
484	*Cooperstown*	780	*Maynard*	1180	*Woodstock*
486	*Jasper*	781	*Metuchen*	1181	*Wildwood*
487	*Larchmont*	782	*Glenolden*	1186	*Ipswich*
553	*Malone*	785	*Frostburg*	1191	*Bel Air*
560	*Oberlin*	808	*Ripley*	1193	*Ridgway*
564	*Chadron*	817	*Welch*	1196	*Mayfield*
565	*Gilmer*	822	*Asheboro*	1198	*Westerly*
566	*Honesdale*	845	*Worland*	1201	*Kittery*
567	*Riverhead*	1077	*Edenton*	1209	*Medina*
568	*Altus*	1079	*Ludington*	1212	*Laurinburg*
569	*Petoskey*	1081	*Cadiz*	1213	*Louden*
571	*Anoka*	1087	*Placerville*	1216	*Elkins*
572	*Tooele*	1119	*Greencastle*	1225	*Waverly*
579	*Wapakoneta*	1120	*Carlinville*	1228	*Munising*
580	*Malvern*	1125	*Cordele*	1229	*Wauseon*
581	*Manville*	1135	*Canastota*	1230	*Grinnell*
582	*Lenoir*	1136	*Galena*	1231	*Tipton*
586	*Patchogue*	1137	*Worthington*	1237	*Abingdon*
588	*Houghton*	1138	*Lapeer*	1240	*Culpeper*
589	*Metropolis*	1140	*Glenwood*	1242	*Port Clinton*
592	*Towanda*	1141	*Pierre*	1244	*Martinez*
597	*Kerrville*	1142	*Hanford*	1246	*Canandaigua*
601	*Arcata*	1145	*Winnemucca*	1251	*Ukiah*

602	*Alturas*	1149	*Susanville*	1252	*Tarrytown*
603	*Solvay*	1169	*Escondido*	1260	*Durango*
606	*Andrews*	1170	*Kelso*	1263	*Milledgeville*
617	*Beeville*	1172	*Olney*	1546	*Grosse-Pointe*
618	*Weatherford*	1173	*Andalusia*	1547	*Corinth*
619	*Dalhart*	1174	*Fredomia*	1569	*Anacortes*

Three PCs Remain

A few decades after World War II ended, the United States Navy eventually struck all PCs from its records. The U. S. Government disposed of them in various ways as described above in this chapter and in Appendix D. Scuttlebutt among former PC sailors infers that some PCs are still with foreign navies and in the United States as fishing boats or yachts. Despite these speculations, however, I know of only three PCs extant, all of which are in the United States. These three ships are rusted gutted hulks that have not seen the ocean in decades. They lay forgotten, ignored, and desolate in backwaters and are not salvageable. They are PC 1120, PC 1217, and PC 1264. Their final days are outlined below.

PC 1120 Went Fishing, Fought Whalers, and Hosted Hippies

An example of one PC with a long and checkered career[211] is PC 1120. The United States Navy commissioned her on 18 December 1942 in Bay City, Michigan, and she served in the Pacific during the war. They named her USS *Carlinville* on 15 February 1956. The United States Navy struck the ship from the register on 1 April 1959 after her more than sixteen years of service. The Pacific Diesel Company sold the PC, and it became a fishing boat in Kodiak, Alaska. Then it was reborn as the M. V. *Island Transport* in Hawaii. The Greenpeace Organization bought the ship for $70,000 at a bankruptcy auction, and, under Panamanian registry, renamed her *Ohana Kai*, which is Hawaiian for "children of the sea." Figure 11-10 shows the former PC 1120 in her Greenpeace form and colors in 1977. After one cruise, Greenpeace sailed the ship to San Francisco and discarded it. The ship became a derelict. Figure 11-11 shows PC 1120 during those idle days but still sporting a Greenpeace whale insignia painted on her starboard bow.

Then Claus von Wendel, a German merchant mariner, purchased the ship. He towed it to the Berkeley North Marina Basin in San Francisco where he gutted her and used it as a home and hippie hangout with himself as the guru.

In 1988, the PC 1120 was up to her gunnels in water in Berkeley's North Marina Basin at the end of University Avenue.[212] The hull was torn, gutted, and rusted. She sat with her keel on the bottom seven feet below the surface. Murky water filled the engine room. Diesel fuel and lube oil oozed from her rusted and broken pipes and machinery, polluting the waters of the basin. Only the chart house and mast remained topside. The owner scrapped her because ". . . [the PC is] illegal fill in public waters," said Charles Sager, asset manager for Catellus, the company that owns the land under the marina. All who saw PC 1120 considered her unsalvageable. Her owner scrapped the ship in 1991 at Alameda, California.

PC 1217 Sits on Staten Island, NY

Out of Luders Marine Construction Co. in May 1944, the PC 1217 ran convoys and submarine patrols. During a voyage from Cuba to Africa, waves smashed the ship's hull plates, shorted her electrical circuits, and surged eight feet of water into the PC's bilges. "The force of the waves [during the hurricane] snapped in half and sank *USS Warrington*, a destroyer the PC was accompanying. More than 300 of *Warrington's* sailors drowned. "We were better off aboard our ship [the PC]," Joseph Hartmann wrote.[213] The PC and her crew survived. Again, the clever PC design and rugged construction held her together and afloat while a larger ship, a destroyer, foundered.

Fifty years later, rotted and half buried in mud and slime, the carcass of PC 1217 slumps in murky water amid other decaying hulks. Jagged rusted holes pockmark the hull. Scavengers stripped out her guts. Seven members of her former crew, in 1995, trekked to the ship through weeds and a rutted road in Witte Marina, Rossville, Staten Island, New York. They went to pay their last respects to the ship on which they had served.[214] "It was pretty dramatic," Walter Mackey said. The PC seemed to surge from her grave as though soaring once again over the five-story waves and breasting the 150 knot winds she battled during the Atlantic Hurricane in 1944. Figure 11-12, Figure 11-13, Figure 11-14, and Figure 11-15 show the remains of the ship.

With a shake of his head Cliff Jones said, as he gazed at the rotting hull of PC 1217, "That was a brand new ship when we started. Boy were we proud of it."

PC 1264 Decays in a Scrap Yard

Resting in the same scrap yard in Staten Island, New York, near the hulk of PC 1217, is PC 1264. She gained renown as the first American ship that operated with an all black crew. Their exploits are outlined in Chapter 7. Figure 11-16 and Figure 11-17 show starboard and port views of what remains of the decaying ship.

Summary

When World War II ended, the United States Navy transferred some of its ships to Allied navies and placed many others on the inactive role. Shrouds entombed thousands of those deactivated Navy ships, which nested in silent fleets throughout the country, mothballed for possible future use. This was a wise policy because the Navy recommissioned many of them for the Korean and Viet Nam Wars and later conflicts. The reuse of the United States Navy World War II battleships, even fifty years after the end of World War II, is a prime example of the wisdom of retaining those ships. Of the other immobilized ships, the Navy reincarnated some years after the war by selling or giving them to friendly nations. With those foreign Navies they continued their lives for many years. Other deactivated Navy vessels felt the sting of welders' torches as they dismembered them into scrap metal.

PCs received the same considerations given to the larger ships. Some PCs also went to Naval Reserve and training programs. The Navy mothballed a handful of them. Private companies purchased some PCs for commercial use and modified them into fishing boats, ferries, yachts, and barges. Also, the Navy transferred many of them to other countries.

The Navy donated and assisted in preparing ships of various types as monuments and historical museums to be preserved for future generations of people to visit. Various public and private organizations reclaimed more than sixty United States Navy ships including carriers, battleships, cruisers, destroyers, submarines, patrol torpedo boats (PT), landing craft, and liberty ships. With public and private assistance and devoted work by former crew members, interested sailors, and other persons they made these ships into memorials to provide future generations of people with knowledge of the ships of World War II.[215]

This memorialization and preservation of ships, however, did not happen for PCs. The government did not honor one PC by offering it as a historical monument to their gallant performance and to the young men who sailed them, during World War II. After the United States Navy struck PCs from its records, the PC Patrol Craft of World War II surrendered to history — unsung.

Figure 11-1. A homeward-bound pennant streams behind PC 478 as she leaves Haha Jima for stateside. Photograph courtesy of Walter Haag.

Figure 11-2. PC 466, her homeward-bound pennant trailing aloft, enters San Francisco Bay after being the first PC to enter Tokyo Bay for the Japanese surrender ceremony to end World War II. Photograph courtesy of Ken Kennedy.

Figure 11-3. Some of ship's company and passengers on PC 820 enjoying their first liberty in Seattle after returning to the United States in March 1946. From the left are Bill Korff, Albert Cloud, Bill Veigele, unknown lady, Jack Brown, unknown, unknown, Tony Fazzolari. Names are courtesy of William A. Mueller. Photograph is from the author's collection.

Figure 11-4. Starboard bow view of *Gleaner*, ex-PC 1172, circa 1961, converted into a landing barge. Photograph courtesy of Robert W. Daly.

Figure 11-5. Port bow view of *Gleaner, ex*-PC 1172, circa 1961, converted into a landing barge. Photograph courtesy of Robert W. Daly.

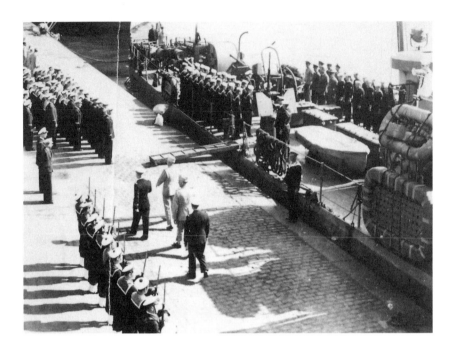

Figure 11-6. American crew of PC 550 on board and French crew on the dock waiting to take over the ship. Official U. S. Navy photograph courtesy of B. J. Belmore.

Figure 11-7. LT B. J. Belmore, C. O., PC 550, reading decommissioning orders. Official U. S. Navy photograph courtesy of B. J. Belmore.

Figure 11-8. French Navy LT Robert Serrett leading his crew aboard former PC 550, now named *Vigilant*. Official U. S. Navy photograph courtesy of B. J. Belmore.

Figure 11-9. Ex-PC 543 as the French ship *Voluntaire*. Notice the removal of her guns and the portholes inserted in the hull. Photograph courtesy of Robert W. Daly, Sr.

Figure 11-10. Photograph of *Ohana Kai* (ex PC 1120) under Greenpeace ownership, about 1977. Note the raised bow, white paint, and whale and dolphin insignias on the starboard bow. Photograph courtesy of Nora McCarthy of Greenpeace.

Figure 11-11. *Ohana Kai* (ex PC 1120) after use by Greenpeace, circa 1979. Photograph courtesy of John Tombaugh.

Figure 11-12. The remains of PC 1217 at Witte Marina on Staten Island, New York on 9 June 1995. Photograph courtesy of Walter Mackey.

Figure 11-13. Starboard bow view of the remains of PC 1217 in Staten Island, NY in 1995. Photograph courtesy of Walter Mackey.

Figure 11-14. Bow view, looking aft, on PC 1217 showing the hole in the deck where the 3"-50 gun had been removed. Photograph courtesy of Walter Mackey.

Figure 11-15. Inside the bridge of PC 1217 showing the binnacle and magnetic compass compensating balls. Photograph courtesy of Walter Mackey.

Figure 11-16. Starboard view of the remains of PC 1264 in Witte Marina on Staten Island, New York, 1995. Photograph courtesy of Walter Mackey.

Figure 11-17. Port view of the remains of PC 1264 in Witte Marina on Staten Island, New York, 1995. Photograph courtesy of Walter Mackey.

CHAPTER 12

The Patrol Craft Sailors Association

Complement of the PC Fleet

Though it varied slightly among ships, the typical complement on a PC during World War II was sixty enlisted men and five commissioned officers. The initial total complement of the 361 PCs[216] commissioned by the United States Navy during World War II therefore was almost 24,000 men and officers. With transfers of crew members off the ships and new men brought aboard them, by the end of the war, an estimated 50,000 United States Navy men served on PCs. This number of men is equivalent to the numbers of men who served on any other type of United States Navy ship during the war. PC sailors, therefore, represented a significant fraction of the Navy's personnel and contributed a large share to the prosecution of the war.

History Has Ignored PCs and PC Sailors

Because the capital ships captured the attention and imagination of observers, those ships got most of the acclaim during and after hostilities. In their anxiety to analyze the great sea battles and naval campaigns of World War II, reporters, naval reviewers, and historians focused their studies and written accounts on the big ships. They wrote mostly about the carriers, battleships, cruisers, destroyers, and submarines. The public followed the lead of these persons and acclaimed, honored, and eulogized the large ships. Though PCs fought in all the major campaigns, and in many lesser actions, with the larger ships, people gave PCs little thought. PCs went almost unnoticed and no one glorified them during or after the war. Like their ships, the men who served on them, also received little recognition.

PC Sailors Remembered Their Ships and Shipmates

Though writers ignored and forgot PCs, the men who served on them did not forget. Many PC sailors remembered, with affection, the months and years they had walked the decks of their ships. They did not forget their adventures, their ships, or their shipmates. Like most service men and women, though, after the war they delighted in their release from the Navy and their return home. When they did get home, the war and their time in the Navy sank back into their memories while they resumed their civilian lives.

Decades rumbled past. Wars in Korea and Vietnam flared and burned for years. The Cold War between the Free World and Communism demanded the resources and attention of the United States and its citizens. During these decades the former PC sailors had finished school, gotten married, established careers, raised families, and began to enter the latter part of their lives. World War II receded into their past, and other world conflicts and personal issues became more urgent. With the passage of time for these men, World War II became history rather than recent experience.

Despite all the time that had passed, however, the mens' memories of those years aboard PCs during the war endured. With time, though, many of them became uncertain about the accuracy of their memories. After all, one hears that, "We remember best those things that did not happen."

Those men began to wonder if that adage were true. They wondered if they had really lived the adventures they still had stored in their memories. Were their memories wrong? Were they only embellished truths? Did waves tower over our mast in heavy seas? What was the taste of powdered eggs? What did we feel during an attack? Did we almost capsize in that storm? Did we sink that submarine? Could friendships still be as firm as they were then? Could we recapture the excitement of those days and renew the friendships we once had aboard the ships?

Many ex-PC sailors began to search out their shipmates. They hoped that they could meet with them, exchange thoughts of the past, reminisce, and pay respect to their lost ships and dead shipmates. It seemed impossible to many of them, though, that they could find former shipmates thirty or forty years after they had last been together. However, some men persisted. Through hard work they located and contacted a few shipmates and organized groups from their particular ships and held reunions.

When one of these groups met, each man was stunned as he gazed at the other men across the chasm of time. They saw not the young men of their memory, like those from PC 793 in Figure 12-1 taken in 1944. Instead they saw men with wrinkles and gray hair, like some of those same men, shown in Figure 12-2 taken at their first reunion in June 1980. Soon, though, receding hairlines and sagging waistlines no longer mattered. The former young men were together again. Their friendships would continue from when they had left off, thirty-five years ago, as though it were yesterday. Photographs albums snapped open. Sea stories poured out. Men recalled storms at sea, torpedo juice, depth-charge attacks, poker games, convoys, movies, air raids, mid-watches, pin-up girls, the "ping" of the sound gear, and their postwar plans.

Those persons who attended the first reunions learned that the young men's faces in their memories no longer existed. Their only substance is that which peers out from old, faded, black and white photographs. But other features did not diminish. The men had retained attitudes that they had developed during years together at sea in a war. They still felt camaraderie, respect for each other despite individual differences, and pride for having served their country.

They gained even more, though, from being together again. They realized that their memories of life aboard ship were accurate.

Their lives had been exciting enough so that their memories did not need embellishment. Also they reminded each other that, though life aboard a PC was frustrating, uncomfortable, and hazardous, it was spiced with adventures and thrills. Each man who had been aboard a PC had been privileged to share those adventures and thrills with other young men. When they met as older men, they understood that a young man can have no greater experience from which to generate rewarding memories and lasting friendships than that of wartime life aboard a small ship.

Establishment of the Patrol Craft Sailors Association

Though some individual ship's companies arranged reunions, they realized that after forty or fifty years they found it difficult to get more than a handful of men and their wives together. Also, they wanted to meet other PC sailors from ships with which they had operated and who had shared similar or different experiences. They wanted to meet other PC sailors and swap sea stories. For these reasons various groups tried to organize larger meetings, but they had little success.

Wesley G. Johnson, a Lieutenant on PC 564, and Patrick Ward, a Yeoman 2/C on PC 565, had been organizing reunions of their respective ships. They longed to broaden their contacts with other "Donald Duck Navy" sailors. In May 1986, they took a large step and joined their desires and energies. In November 1986 they mailed a letter to former patrol craft sailors stating that, "We have assigned to ourselves, a membership of two, in a new veteran's association . . . . The Patrol Craft Sailors' Society, ... Our motto: 'We were Too Good To Be Forgotten.'"[217] These farsighted and dedicated men formed the Patrol Craft Sailors Society.[218]

Beginning with their declared membership of two, they sent letters to thirty-one former PC sailors. They wrote about the organization, announced a news organ they would publish titled "The Patrol Craft Sailors Times," and invited those other former PC sailors to join the Society. Pat Ward and Wes Johnson also declared as an objective that the organization should ". . . locate, acquire, and restore a representative PC to serve as our flagship, museum, and historic ship." With this society they hoped to expand on the individual ship reunion efforts, bring former patrol craft sailors together, and reach their objective of getting and restoring a PC as a historical monument.

Despite that modest beginning the flame caught. In one year the organization had grown to 600 members. The founders altered its name, and RADM Alban Weber, a former officer on PC 564, began incorporation procedures. It would be the not-for-profit Patrol Craft Sailors Association (PCSA). The motto they chose, "Too Good To Be Forgotten," is shown in the organization's logo in Figure 12-3. The organizers of the PCSA formed the first board of directors in 1987 consisting of Wes Johnson, Pat Ward, and Alban Weber. Other men, such as Ollie Durham, Bill Buffington, and Joe Kelliher joined them in the PCSA to help in distributing the first publication and staging the first reunion. In January 1987 they distributed the first issue of what they named the Patrol Craft Sailors Times. In November 1987, the third issue of the Newsletter outlined the results of the last board meeting that by then had fourteen members.[219] The PCSA held its first reunion in Jacksonville, Florida from 17 through 21 March 1988, and the PCSA has held reunions every year since then. Activities at the reunions have included visits to Navy bases and ships, including tours on the Navy's latest ships designated PC (Patrol Coastal).

By 1998, the PCSA swelled to almost 3,000 members.[220] Some of those members are active duty sailors and officers who are now serving on the new PCs currently on duty in the US Navy. The PCSA continues to publish a quarterly Newsletter that contains news of naval affairs and contributions from members of the PCSA that recount experiences aboard patrol craft.

Patrol Craft Sailors Search for a PC

Since the beginning of the PCSA, its members have been trying to obtain a PC as a memorial to represent not only PCs but all World War II patrol craft. A few of the men have worked independently, and some have banded together to find a PC in the United States. Their efforts, though intensive and varied, have not succeeded. To date they have found only those three battered hulks, PC 1120, PC 1217, and PC 1264 mentioned in Chapter 11. Figure 12-4 shows a group of ex-PC sailors who visited those skeletons of their former ships in Staten Island, New York. During their visit they learned that neither of those ships is in condition to salvage and restore.

In an attempt to find a PC outside the United States, PCSA members have communicated with navies of other countries to which the United States government transferred or sold PCs. A few PCs may still be operational in foreign countries. Their owners have not been contacted and convinced of the urgency to contribute one of those ships to the PCSA to preserve it as a memorial to the patrol craft of World War II.

The PCSA Contributed to the Navy Memorial

Instead of restoring and displaying a PC, the PCSA elected to represent itself at the Navy Memorial in Washington, D.C. The organization solicited money from its members, and donated it for two items at the Memorial. One item is a panel on the grand staircase that depicts a PC sand-etched in glass. The other item is a seat in the Arleigh and Roberta Burke Theater at the Navy Memorial.

The PCSA Established a Museum/Library/Archive

Without having a PC as a memorial and museum and concerned that with their advancing years their histories would be lost, members of the PCSA established a museum, library, and archive. It is a repository for stories, anecdotes, artifacts, ship models, photographs, paintings, drawings, and other memorabilia of patrol craft and patrol craft sailors of World War II. Eventually it will expand its collection to include items from United States patrol craft since World War II. The museum will retain and catalog all items so they will be available for future viewing and for research. On 10 June 1994, the PCSA dedicated the museum in the Historical Museum of Bay County in Bay City, Michigan.[221] The location is appropriate because Bay City is the birthplace of World War II PCs. Figure 12-5 shows the Bay County Museum that houses the PCSA exhibit.

More than 500 members, wives, and guests of the PCSA attended the dedication ceremony. They heard Mr. William Defoe, Chairman of the Board (retired) of the Defoe Shipbuilding company, present the keynote address. In his speech he recounted the history of the PC building program at the Defoe Shipbuilding Company.[222]

For the dedication of the PCSA museum, and in recognition of the contribution of patrol craft to World War II, the United States Postal Service issued four different commemorative stamps and a First Day Cover. The First Day Cover shows PC 1125 underway. Figure 12-6 shows the picture of PC 1125 the Postal Service used on the First Day Cover. One of the four stamps depicts a patrol craft chasing a U-boat in the Atlantic Ocean in 1943. After the dedication ceremony the museum opened the PCSA exhibit and sold the covers and stamps to the public.

The museum staff reported that the exhibit that ran during the remainder of the summer, after the dedication of the PCSA library and museum, was one of the most heavily attended of all their displays. Despite its popularity, because of lack of funds, limited space at, and renovation of the Bay County museum, the PCSA exhibit ended after the summer of 1994. All items from the exhibit are now in the archives awaiting completion of the renovation of the museum to provide space for a permanent PCSA display. Many members of the PCSA have contributed items to the museum. The museum staff has been cataloging the artifacts, photographs, and written material in a library and archive. As an example of items contributed by members of the PCSA, Figure 12-7 shows a model of PC 479, built by Tom Polock, that is in the exhibit at the museum. For more information about the museum, how to use its services, or to make contributions and donations, see Appendix J.

PCSA Members Endowed the Museum

When the PCSA established its museum, it donated money to operate the exhibit for a short time. In 1996 the Board of Directors of the PCSA decided it should endow the PCSA museum/library/archive to pay for its continued operation. They determined that $25,000 invested conservatively would provide minimal support, and the PCSA started a fund drive. By January 1998 the fund exceeded $40,000, and the PCSA deposited the money in an endowment fund. The Bay County Museum will use the funds to establish a permanent PCSA exhibit and provide research services for persons interested in the history of PCs and all patrol craft of World War II.

The PCSA Published Two History Books

For the reunion in 1989 the Board of Directors of the PCSA elected to record the biographies and photographs of members, photographs of their ships, and stories and anecdotes of the wartime activities of the men who served on patrol craft during World War II. Members submitted these items, and in 1990 the Turner Publishing Company published the first *Patrol Craft Sailors Association History Book*. Five years later the PCSA and Turner repeated the process for a second history book.[223]

DoD Invited the PCSA Into the Commemorative Community Program

To commemorate the fiftieth anniversary of the surrender of the Axis powers to the Allied Nations, the Department of Defense (DoD) established the World War II Commemorative Community Program. The purpose of this program is to honor America's veterans and their families and those who served on the home front in the war effort. In 1993, the DoD honored PC and other patrol craft sailors. They officially recognized the Patrol Craft Sailors Association as a member of the 50th Anniversary of the World War II Commemorative Community. A letter from Les Aspin, Secretary of Defense, designated the PCSA as an official WWII Commemorative Community. Now, the Patrol Craft Sailors Association flies the World War II Commemorative flag and displays the 50th anniversary logo for the PCSA shown in Figure 12-8. In memory of the service of men and women in the armed forces during the war, the flag sports a replica of the WWII Victory lapel pin, the "Ruptured Duck," that the United States government issued to honorably discharged service men and women.

Conclusions

Many men who served on other types of ships during and after World War II said that their time aboard a PC was their favorite duty. They liked life on PCs better than on the other ships. Art Bell,[224] for example, wrote, "... I don't think cruisers, battleships or carriers knew we [PCs] even existed. We were the forgotten Navy. But I served on three destroyers, had command of one, had command of a destroyer transport, took two trans-Pacific cruises on two different aircraft carriers, had command of the PC 477 for a while and cruised in the battleship New York. I thought they were all great ships, but without any doubt in my mind, the best of all was the PC 477 .... It wasn't because of size, armament or equipment — it was due to the people who manned her."

Those "people" who manned PCs retained their friendships and camaraderie. They do it by holding individual ship reunions and through membership in and contributions to the Patrol Craft Sailors Association and its activities. By participating in these activities these former PC sailors are doing their part to preserve the story of the "Forgotten Fleet" of PCs of World War II.

Figure 12-1. The Engineering Division from PC 793 at Adak, Alaska in 1944. The author is in the front row fourth from the left. Photograph from the author's collection.

Figure 12-2. First reunion of the PC 793 Association in June 1980 at Kansas City. From left to right in the back row are Paul Alexander, Paul Jones, Ralph Jones, John Ebel, Kenneth King, and John Blake. In the front row from left to right they are Bob Johnson, Bill Veigele, Joe Wilkinson, Bill O'Connor, and Ray Page. Photograph from the author's collection.

Too Good To Be Forgotten

Figure 12-3. Logo of the Patrol Craft Sailors Association.
Courtesy of the Patrol Craft Sailors Association.

Figure 12-4. Seven Navy buddies take a melancholy look at PC 1217 in 1995, fifty years after they piloted her through the stormy waters of the Atlantic and Pacific Oceans during World War II. The remains of their ship, in the background of the picture, are in a scrap yard in Staten Island, New York. Photograph courtesy of Walter Mackey.

Figure 12-5. The Bay County Historical Museum in Bay City, Michigan. It is the home of the Patrol Craft Sailors Association Museum. Photograph courtesy of the Bay County Historical Museum.

Figure 12-6. United States Postal Service Commemorative First Day Cover showed this photograph of PC 1125 and a stamp showing a patrol craft, escorting a convoy, attacking a U-boat in the Atlantic Ocean in 1943. Photograph courtesy of Wilfred R. Tlusty.

Figure 12-7. Model of PC 479 at the Patrol Craft Sailors Association Museum. Thomas A. Pollock built the model. Photograph from the author's collection.

Figure 12-8. PCSA World War II Commemorative Community Program logo. Courtesy of the Patrol Craft Sailors Association.

EPILOGUE

Thursday, 16 May 1946, the morning sun cast a red glow on the low skyline of Seattle, Washington. PC 793 lay in the murky water of Elliot Bay, Puget Sound. Nearby loomed the carrier *Essex*. Gathered about her were *Alabama*, *Ticonderoga*, *Indiana*, *West Virginia*, *Hancock*, *Eisley*, *Baltimore*, and *Bon Homme Richard*. Each ship in turn would end its fighting life in a burst of public recognition and pomp and be remembered forever. On that Thursday it was also the turn of the crew on PC 793 to haul down its flags. In her case, though, unlike the larger ships but like other PCs, she would end her Navy career and pass into obscurity — unsung.

At the bow and stern of the PC, sailors in dress blues and white hats waited. They would hoist her flags as they had every morning for two years, when the ship was in port. A boatswain's pipe whistled, and sailors two-blocked the ensign and jack at the flagstaff aft and the jackstaff forward. At 0915 the crew mustered on deck. Unlike at her commissioning ceremony, no band played. No crowd swarmed onto the deck. No one proclaimed the bravery of her crew or murmured prayers for its safety.

The Captain of the ship, a short-timer who had been aboard only a few months, read an Authority Letter of Decommissioning from the Thirteenth Naval District. The Quartermaster strode to the staff, untied the knot in the line, and struck the colors. Only fifteen minutes after the ceremony had started, the blue and white stripes and stars of the ship's long, tapered, commissioning pennant fluttered down. Six days less than three years after her keel first struck water, and two years and six days after the Captain had posted the first watch, the crew left the ship.

On the ship, stillness hung about the decks and in the mess hall. Silence crept into the bridge and the crew's quarters. No machinery turned. No coffee was poured. From across the bay a tugboat horn blared, and, nearby, a boatswain's pipe shrilled. The sounds did not disturb the silent echoes in the ship, of the young men who had forged friendships by sharing the monotony, thrills, and fears of life at sea.

In a similar manner, the Navy ended the careers of the 300 PCs that were still afloat in the United States Navy at the end of World War II. For some of those PCs, the end came soon after the war. For others, their lives as naval vessels continued for decades. In time though, all PC crews hauled down their ships' commissioning pennants and strode ashore — for the last time. When those young men went ashore, they ended the story of the "Forgotten Fleet" of the PC Patrol Craft of World War II.

APPENDIX A

Classes and Characteristics of World War II PCs

The classes of PCs that were built during World War II are shown in Table A-1.

Table A-1. Classes of PCs

PC CLASS	HULL NUMBERS
451	451
452	452
461	461-496, 542-627, 776-825, 1077-1091, 1119-1149, 1167-1265, 1546-1569
1586(AMs)	1586-1603

Characteristics of the PC 451 Class:
Length Overall: 169' 7"
Extreme Beam: 20' 9"
Standard Displacement: 270 tons
Maximum Draft: 8'
Accommodations: Officers, 4; Enlisted men 61
Armament: (2) 3"-50 caliber guns
Designed Speed: 22.5 knots
Engines: (2) General Motors Diesels
Propulsion: (2) Shafts

Characteristics of the PC 452 Class:

Length Overall: 173' 8"
Extreme Beam: 22' 7"
Standard Displacement: 280 tons
Maximum Draft: 6' 5"
Accommodations: 65 Officers and Enlisted Men
Armament: (2) 3"-50 caliber guns
Designed Speed: 22.5 knots
Engines: (2) De Laval type, GT
Boilers: C. E. Type, forced Circulation
Propulsion: (2) Shafts

Characteristics of the PC 461 Class:

Length Overall: 173' 8"
Extreme Beam: 23 feet
Displacement: 284 tons
Displacement on Load Draft: 360 tons
Full Load Displacement: 450 tons
Maximum Draft: 10' 10"
Average Draft: 7 feet
Endurance: 3,000 Nautical Miles at 12 knots.
Armament: (1) 3"-50 caliber gun, (1) single 40-mm Bofors machine gun, (5) 20-mm Oerlikon machine guns, (2) forward throwing mousetraps, (2) K-guns, and (2) Stern mounted depth charge racks
Designed Speed: 20.2 knots
Flank Speed: 21 knots
Sperry Gyrocompass, Mark XIV, Model 1.
Fuel Capacity: 20,378 gallons
Lubricating Oil Capacity: 2,942 gallons
Fresh Water Capacity: 4,386 gallons
Propellers: (2) Bronze, 72" diameter, three blades.
Engines: Diesel (2), Directly reversible. Types used were:

Fairbanks Morse & Co. Model 38D-a, two stroke cycle, 10 cylinder, opposed piston. (PC 461-470, 483-487, 563-572, 578-582, 600-603, 616-619, 1077-1082, 1176-1180, 1231-1233, 1251-1254, 1260-1263.

General Motors Corp. Model 16-2588-A, four stroke cycle, 16 cylinder, "V" type. (PC 471-479, 548-560, 583-590, 596-599, 606, 620-623, 1086-1149, 1167-1175, 1225-1230, 1241-1247, 1546-1569.

Hooven, Owens, Rentshler Co. (H.O.R.) Model 9DA-A, two stroke

cycle, double acting, 9 cylinder. The remainder of the PCs.
Propulsion: Shafts (2), One hydraulic coupling and reduction gear on each shaft.
Shaft Horsepower: 2,280 Horsepower
Auxiliary Engines for Ships' Service. Diesel (2). Types:
> Ships with F. M. or G. M. main engines used G. M. Model 6-71.
> Ships with H. O. R. main engines used Buda·Model 6DHG-691.
> All ships used two 60-kilowatt, 120 volt direct current generator
sets.

Characteristics of the PC 1586 Class:

Length Overall: 173' 8"
Extreme Beam: 23'
Standard Displacement: 450 tons
Maximum Draft: 11' 7"
Accommodations: Officers, 4; Enlisted men 61
Armament: (1) 3"-50 caliber gun, (1) Single 40-mm machine gun
Designed Speed: 16.8 knots
Engines: (2) Diesel: Cooper Bessemer (PC 1586-1599); Alco (PC 1600-1603)
Propulsion: (2) Shafts: SHP 1,770 (PC 1586-1599); 1,440 (PC 1600-1603)

EDWIN P HOYT

U BOATS OFFSHORE —
WHEN HITLER STRUCK AMERICA
STEIN + DAY, 1978

APPENDIX B

Thirty Engineering Drawings Showing PC Design Details

Robert Baldwin, a nineteen year old sailor on PC 543 during World War II, walked the entire ship with a tape measure, pencil, and sketch pad. He searched every area and compartment and sketched and recorded details of the ship with their measurements. After discharge from the Navy, years later, he converted his sketches to the thirty engineering drawings shown in this appendix. The Plates are numbered 1 through 30, not including number 20. One other supplemental drawing shows the starboard exterior of the superstructure of a PC.

A set of blueprints for plan and elevation views and external and internal details of a PC is available from John Tombaugh, 5009 W. Beaman Lane, Rochester, IN 46975.

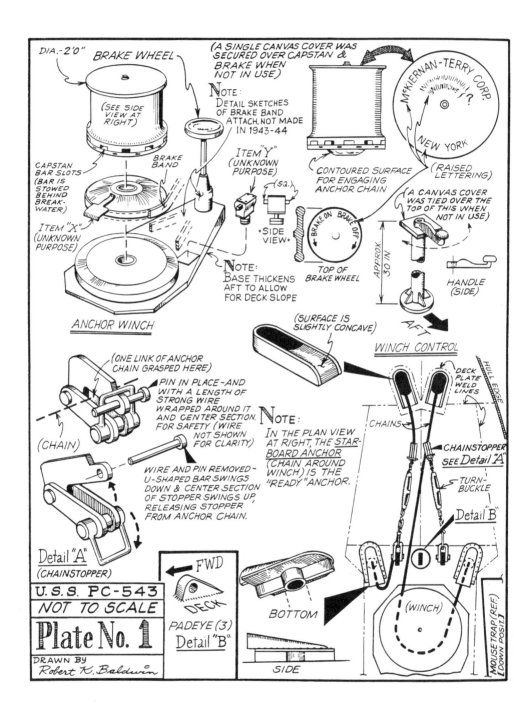

DIA.- 2'0"

BRAKE WHEEL

(A SINGLE CANVAS COVER WAS SECURED OVER CAPSTAN & BRAKE WHEN NOT IN USE)

(SEE SIDE VIEW AT RIGHT)

NOTE: DETAIL SKETCHES OF BRAKE BAND ATTACH. NOT MADE IN 1943-44

McKIERNAN-TERRY CORP.

?

NEW YORK

(RAISED LETTERING)

CAPSTAN BAR SLOTS (BAR IS STOWED BEHIND BREAK-WATER)

BRAKE BAND

ITEM "Y" (UNKNOWN PURPOSE)

(SQ.)

CONTOURED SURFACE FOR ENGAGING ANCHOR CHAIN

(A CANVAS COVER WAS TIED OVER THE TOP OF THIS WHEN NOT IN USE)

ITEM "X" (UNKNOWN PURPOSE)

• SIDE VIEW •

NOTE: BASE THICKENS AFT TO ALLOW FOR DECK SLOPE

BRAKE ON   BRAKE OFF

TOP OF BRAKE WHEEL

APPROX. 30 IN.

HANDLE (SIDE)

ANCHOR WINCH

AFT

(SURFACE IS SLIGHTLY CONCAVE)

WINCH CONTROL

(ONE LINK OF ANCHOR CHAIN GRASPED HERE)

PIN IN PLACE - AND WITH A LENGTH OF STRONG WIRE WRAPPED AROUND IT AND CENTER SECTION FOR SAFETY (WIRE NOT SHOWN FOR CLARITY)

DECK PLATE WELD LINES

HULL EDGE

(CHAIN)

CHAINS

WIRE AND PIN REMOVED - U-SHAPED BAR SWINGS DOWN & CENTER SECTION OF STOPPER SWINGS UP, RELEASING STOPPER FROM ANCHOR CHAIN.

NOTE: IN THE PLAN VIEW AT RIGHT, THE STAR-BOARD ANCHOR (CHAIN AROUND WINCH) IS THE "READY" ANCHOR.

CHAINSTOPPER SEE Detail "A"

TURN-BUCKLE

Detail "B"

Detail "A" (CHAINSTOPPER)

U.S.S. PC-543

NOT TO SCALE

Plate No. 1

DRAWN BY Robert K. Baldwin

FWD

DECK

PADEYE (3) Detail "B"

BOTTOM

SIDE

(WINCH)

MOUSETRAP (REF.) (DOWN POSIT.)

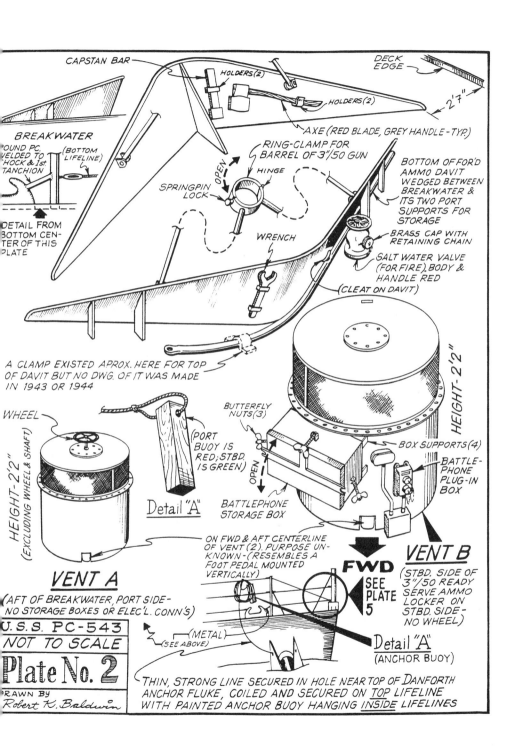

CAPSTAN BAR

HOLDERS(2)

HOLDERS(2)

DECK EDGE

2'7"

BREAKWATER

ROUND PC. WELDED TO CHOCK & 1st. STANCHION

(BOTTOM LIFELINE)

DETAIL FROM BOTTOM CENTER OF THIS PLATE

AXE (RED BLADE, GREY HANDLE - TYP.)

RING-CLAMP FOR BARREL OF 3"/50 GUN

OPEN

HINGE

SPRINGPIN LOCK

WRENCH

BOTTOM OF FOR'D AMMO DAVIT WEDGED BETWEEN BREAKWATER & ITS TWO PORT SUPPORTS FOR STORAGE

BRASS CAP WITH RETAINING CHAIN

SALT WATER VALVE (FOR FIRE), BODY & HANDLE RED

(CLEAT ON DAVIT)

A CLAMP EXISTED APROX. HERE FOR TOP OF DAVIT BUT NO DWG. OF IT WAS MADE IN 1943 OR 1944

HEIGHT - 2'2"

WHEEL

HEIGHT - 2'2" (EXCLUDING WHEEL & SHAFT)

(PORT BUOY IS RED; STBD. IS GREEN)

BUTTERFLY NUTS(3)

OPEN

BOX SUPPORTS(4)

BATTLE-PHONE PLUG-IN BOX

BATTLEPHONE STORAGE BOX

Detail "A"

ON FWD & AFT CENTERLINE OF VENT (2). PURPOSE UN-KNOWN - (RESEMBLES A FOOT PEDAL MOUNTED VERTICALLY)

VENT A

(AFT OF BREAKWATER, PORT SIDE - NO STORAGE BOXES OR ELEC'L. CONN'S)

FWD

SEE PLATE 5

VENT B

(STBD. SIDE OF 3"/50 READY SERVE AMMO LOCKER ON STBD. SIDE - NO WHEEL)

Detail "A"

(ANCHOR BUOY)

(METAL) (SEE ABOVE)

THIN, STRONG LINE SECURED IN HOLE NEAR TOP OF DANFORTH ANCHOR FLUKE, COILED AND SECURED ON TOP LIFELINE WITH PAINTED ANCHOR BUOY HANGING INSIDE LIFELINES

U.S.S. PC-543

NOT TO SCALE

Plate No. 2

DRAWN BY

Robert K. Baldwin

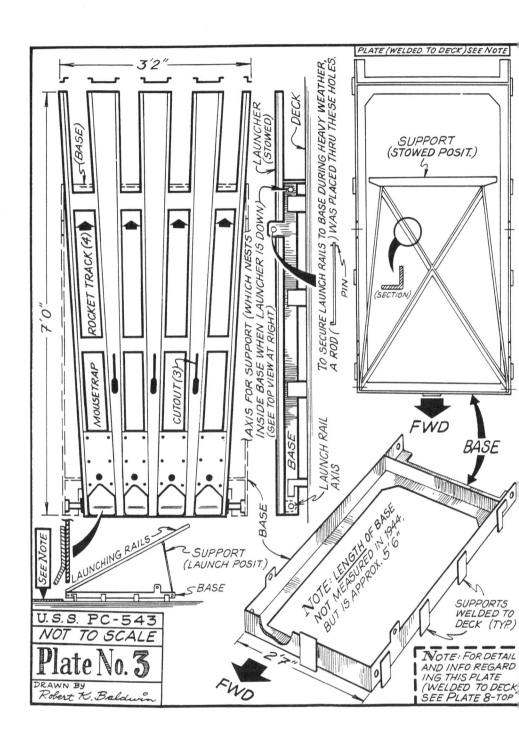

3'2"

(BASE)

ROCKET TRACK (4)

MOUSETRAP

CUTOUT (3)

7'0"

LAUNCHER (STOWED)

DECK

AXIS FOR SUPPORT (WHICH NESTS INSIDE BASE WHEN LAUNCHER IS DOWN) (SEE TOP VIEW AT RIGHT)

TO SECURE LAUNCH RAILS TO BASE DURING HEAVY WEATHER, A ROD ( ) WAS PLACED THRU THESE HOLES.

PIN

BASE

LAUNCH RAIL AXIS

BASE

SEE NOTE

LAUNCHING RAILS

SUPPORT (LAUNCH POSIT.)

BASE

U.S.S. PC-543

NOT TO SCALE

Plate No. 3

DRAWN BY
Robert K. Baldwin

PLATE (WELDED TO DECK) SEE NOTE

SUPPORT (STOWED POSIT.)

(SECTION)

FWD

BASE

NOTE: LENGTH OF BASE NOT MEASURED IN 1944, BUT IS APPROX. 5'6".

SUPPORTS WELDED TO DECK (TYP.)

2'7"

FWD

NOTE: FOR DETAIL AND INFO REGARDING THIS PLATE (WELDED TO DECK) SEE PLATE 8-TOP

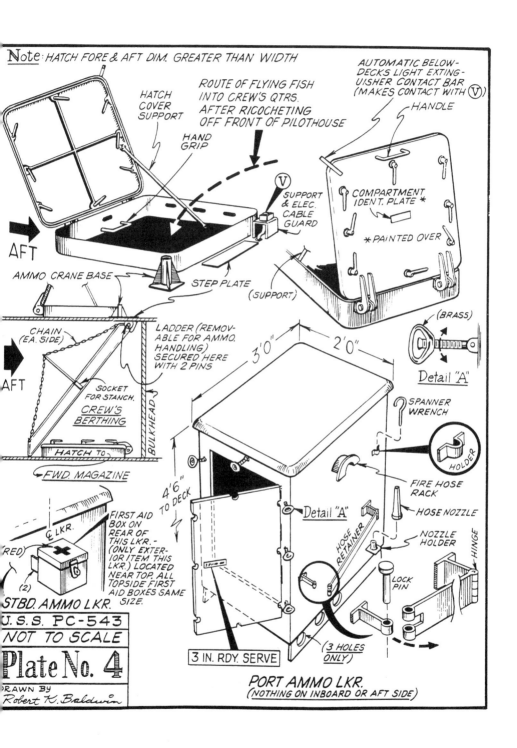

Note: HATCH FORE & AFT DIM. GREATER THAN WIDTH

HATCH COVER SUPPORT

ROUTE OF FLYING FISH INTO CREW'S QTRS. AFTER RICOCHETING OFF FRONT OF PILOTHOUSE

HAND GRIP

AUTOMATIC BELOW-DECKS LIGHT EXTING-UISHER CONTACT BAR (MAKES CONTACT WITH Ⓥ)

HANDLE

Ⓥ SUPPORT & ELEC. CABLE GUARD

COMPARTMENT IDENT. PLATE *

* PAINTED OVER

AFT

AMMO CRANE BASE

STEP PLATE

(SUPPORT)

(BRASS)

Detail "A"

CHAIN (EA. SIDE)

LADDER (REMOV-ABLE FOR AMMO. HANDLING) SECURED HERE WITH 2 PINS

AFT

SOCKET FOR STANCH.

CREW'S BERTHING

BULKHEAD

3'0"

2'0"

SPANNER WRENCH

HOLDER

FIRE HOSE RACK

HATCH TO

HOSE NOZZLE

FWD. MAGAZINE

Detail "A"

NOZZLE HOLDER

HINGE

FIRST AID BOX ON REAR OF THIS LKR. - (ONLY EXTER-IOR ITEM THIS LKR.) LOCATED NEAR TOP. ALL TOPSIDE FIRST AID BOXES SAME SIZE.

4'6" TO DECK

LKR.

(RED)

HOSE RETAINER

LOCK PIN

(2)

STBD. AMMO LKR.

U.S.S. PC-543

NOT TO SCALE

Plate No. 4

DRAWN BY
Robert K. Baldwin

3 IN. RDY. SERVE

(3 HOLES ONLY)

PORT AMMO LKR.
(NOTHING ON INBOARD OR AFT SIDE)

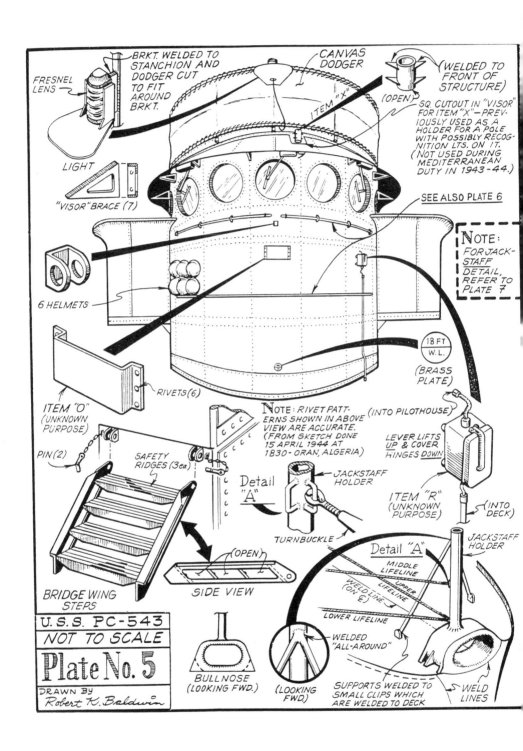

FRESNEL LENS

BRKT. WELDED TO STANCHION AND DODGER CUT TO FIT AROUND BRKT.

CANVAS DODGER

ITEM "X"

(OPEN)

(WELDED TO FRONT OF STRUCTURE)

SQ. CUTOUT IN "VISOR" FOR ITEM "X" — PREVIOUSLY USED AS A HOLDER FOR A POLE WITH POSSIBLY RECOGNITION LTS. ON IT. (NOT USED DURING MEDITERRANEAN DUTY IN 1943–44.)

LIGHT

"VISOR" BRACE (7)

SEE ALSO PLATE 6

NOTE: FOR JACK-STAFF DETAIL, REFER TO PLATE 7

6 HELMETS

18 FT W.L.

(BRASS PLATE)

ITEM "O" (UNKNOWN PURPOSE)

RIVETS (6)

PIN (2)

SAFETY RIDGES (3 ea)

NOTE: RIVET PATTERNS SHOWN IN ABOVE VIEW ARE ACCURATE. (FROM SKETCH DONE 15 APRIL 1944 AT 1830 - ORAN, ALGERIA)

(INTO PILOTHOUSE)

LEVER LIFTS UP & COVER HINGES DOWN

Detail "A"

JACKSTAFF HOLDER

ITEM "R" (UNKNOWN PURPOSE)

(INTO DECK)

TURNBUCKLE

(OPEN)

BRIDGE WING STEPS

SIDE VIEW

Detail "A"

JACKSTAFF HOLDER

MIDDLE LIFELINE

UPPER LIFELINE

WELD LINE (ON ℄)

LOWER LIFELINE

U.S.S. PC-543

NOT TO SCALE

Plate No. 5

DRAWN BY
Robert K. Baldwin

BULL NOSE (LOOKING FWD.)

WELDED "ALL-AROUND"

(LOOKING FWD.)

SUPPORTS WELDED TO SMALL CLIPS WHICH ARE WELDED TO DECK

WELD LINES

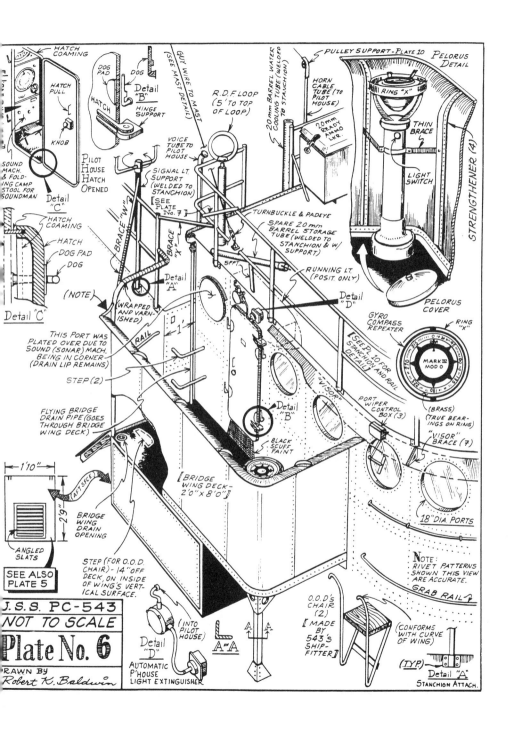

HATCH COAMING

DOG PAD
DOG

Detail "B"

HATCH

HINGE SUPPORT

HATCH PULL

KNOB

SOUND MACH. & FOLD-ING CAMP STOOL FOR SOUNDMAN

Detail "C"

PILOT HOUSE HATCH OPENED

GUY WIRE TO MAST (SEE MAST DETAIL)

R.D.F LOOP (5' TO TOP OF LOOP)

20mm BARREL WATER COOLING TUBE (WELDED TO STANCHION)

PULLEY SUPPORT – Plate 10

PELORUS Detail

HORN CABLE TUBE (TO PILOT HOUSE)

RING "X"

20mm READY AMMO LKR.

THIN BRACE

LIGHT SWITCH

STRENGTHENER (4)

VOICE TUBE TO PILOT HOUSE

SIGNAL LT. SUPPORT (WELDED TO STANCHION) [SEE PLATE No. 7]

HATCH COAMING

HATCH DOG PAD
DOG

Detail "C"

(NOTE)

BRACE "W"

BRACE "X"

TURNBUCKLE & PADEYE

SPARE 20mm BARREL STORAGE TUBE (WELDED TO STANCHION & W/ SUPPORT)

RUNNING LT. (POSIT. ONLY)

Detail "D"

PELORUS COVER

GYRO COMPASS REPEATER

RING "X"

[SEE PL. 10 FOR STANCHION AND RAIL DETAIL]

Detail "A"

(WRAPPED AND VARN-ISHED)

SFT.

1'

RAIL

THIS PORT WAS PLATED OVER DUE TO SOUND (SONAR) MACH. BEING IN CORNER (DRAIN LIP REMAINS)

STEP (2)

Detail "B"

"VISOR"

PORT WIPER CONTROL BOX (3)

MARK III MOD O

(BRASS) (TRUE BEAR-INGS ON RING)

"VISOR" BRACE (7)

FLYING BRIDGE DRAIN PIPE (GOES THROUGH BRIDGE WING DECK)

BLACK SCUFF PAINT

18" DIA PORTS

1'10"

2'9"

(AFT SIDE)

ANGLED SLATS

SEE ALSO PLATE 5

BRIDGE WING DRAIN OPENING

[BRIDGE WING DECK – 2'0" x 8'0"]

NOTE: RIVET PATTERNS SHOWN THIS VIEW ARE ACCURATE.

GRAB RAIL

STEP (FOR O.O.D. CHAIR) – 14" OFF DECK, ON INSIDE OF WING'S VERT-ICAL SURFACE.

O.O.D's CHAIR (2) [MADE BY 543's SHIP-FITTER]

(CONFORMS WITH CURVE OF WING)

(TYP.)

Detail "A"

STANCHION ATTACH.

J.S.S. PC-543

NOT TO SCALE

Plate No. 6

DRAWN BY
Robert K. Baldwin

(INTO PILOT HOUSE)

Detail "D"

AUTOMATIC P'HOUSE LIGHT EXTINGUISHER

A-A

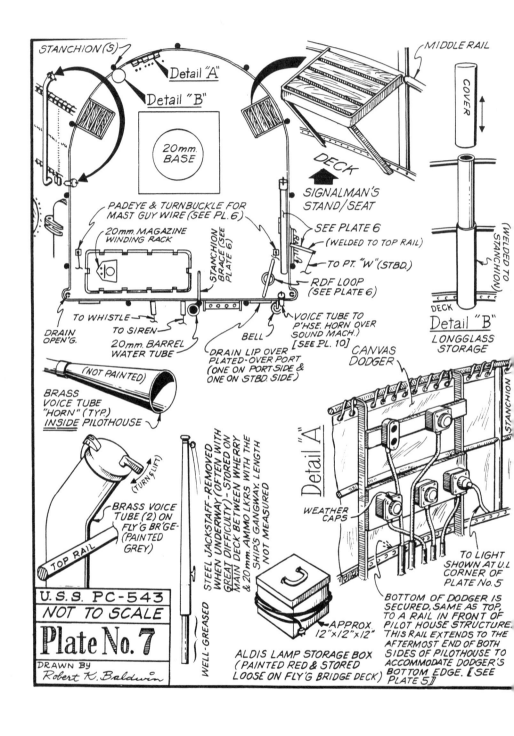

STANCHION(S)

Detail "A"

Detail "B"

20mm. BASE

MIDDLE RAIL

COVER

DECK

SIGNALMAN'S STAND/SEAT

PADEYE & TURNBUCKLE FOR MAST GUY WIRE (SEE PL. 6)

20mm. MAGAZINE WINDING RACK

STANCHION BRACE (SEE PLATE 6)

SEE PLATE 6
(WELDED TO TOP RAIL)

TO PT. "W" (STBD.)

RDF LOOP (SEE PLATE 6)

(WELDED TO STANCHION)

DECK

Detail "B"
LONGGLASS STORAGE

TO WHISTLE

TO SIREN

DRAIN OPEN'G.

20mm. BARREL WATER TUBE

BELL

DRAIN LIP OVER PLATED-OVER PORT (ONE ON PORTSIDE & ONE ON STBD. SIDE)

VOICE TUBE TO P'HSE. HORN OVER SOUND MACH.) [SEE PL. 10]

(NOT PAINTED)

BRASS VOICE TUBE "HORN" (TYP.) INSIDE PILOTHOUSE

CANVAS DODGER

Detail "A"

WEATHER CAPS

STANCHION

(TURN & LIFT)

BRASS VOICE TUBE (2) ON FLY'G BR'GE (PAINTED GREY)

TOP RAIL

STEEL JACKSTAFF-REMOVED WHEN UNDERWAY-(OFTEN WITH GREAT DIFFICULTY)-STORED ON MAIN DECK BETWEEN WHERRY & 20mm AMMO LKRS WITH THE SHIP'S GANGWAY. LENGTH NOT MEASURED

WELL-GREASED

TO LIGHT SHOWN AT U.L. CORNER OF PLATE No. 5

BOTTOM OF DODGER IS SECURED, SAME AS TOP, TO A RAIL IN FRONT OF PILOT HOUSE STRUCTURE. THIS RAIL EXTENDS TO THE AFTERMOST END OF BOTH SIDES OF PILOTHOUSE TO ACCOMMODATE DODGER'S BOTTOM EDGE. [SEE PLATE 5]

APPROX. 12"x12"x12"

ALDIS LAMP STORAGE BOX (PAINTED RED & STORED LOOSE ON FLY'G BRIDGE DECK)

U.S.S. PC-543
NOT TO SCALE
Plate No. 7
DRAWN BY
Robert K. Baldwin

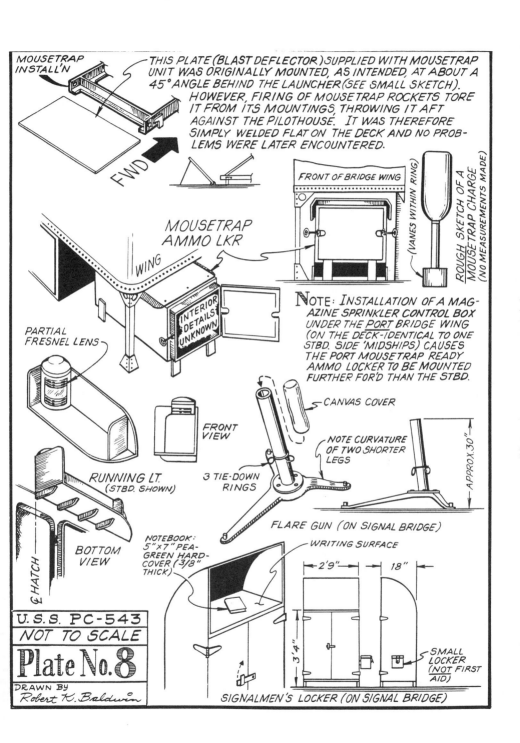

MOUSETRAP INSTALL'N

THIS PLATE (BLAST DEFLECTOR) SUPPLIED WITH MOUSETRAP UNIT WAS ORIGINALLY MOUNTED, AS INTENDED, AT ABOUT A 45° ANGLE BEHIND THE LAUNCHER (SEE SMALL SKETCH). HOWEVER, FIRING OF MOUSETRAP ROCKETS TORE IT FROM ITS MOUNTINGS, THROWING IT AFT AGAINST THE PILOTHOUSE. IT WAS THEREFORE SIMPLY WELDED FLAT ON THE DECK AND NO PROBLEMS WERE LATER ENCOUNTERED.

FWD

FRONT OF BRIDGE WING

MOUSETRAP AMMO LKR

WING

(VANES WITHIN RING)

ROUGH SKETCH OF A MOUSETRAP CHARGE (NO MEASUREMENTS MADE)

INTERIOR DETAILS UNKNOWN

NOTE: INSTALLATION OF A MAGAZINE SPRINKLER CONTROL BOX UNDER THE PORT BRIDGE WING (ON THE DECK-IDENTICAL TO ONE STBD. SIDE 'MIDSHIPS) CAUSES THE PORT MOUSETRAP READY AMMO LOCKER TO BE MOUNTED FURTHER FOR'D THAN THE STBD.

PARTIAL FRESNEL LENS

FRONT VIEW

CANVAS COVER

NOTE CURVATURE OF TWO SHORTER LEGS

APPROX. 30"

RUNNING LT. (STBD. SHOWN)

3 TIE-DOWN RINGS

FLARE GUN (ON SIGNAL BRIDGE)

℄ HATCH

BOTTOM VIEW

NOTEBOOK: 5"x7" PEA-GREEN HARDCOVER (3/8" THICK)

WRITING SURFACE

2'9"   18"

3'4"

SMALL LOCKER (NOT FIRST AID)

U.S.S. PC-543
NOT TO SCALE
Plate No. 8
DRAWN BY
Robert K. Baldwin

SIGNALMEN'S LOCKER (ON SIGNAL BRIDGE)

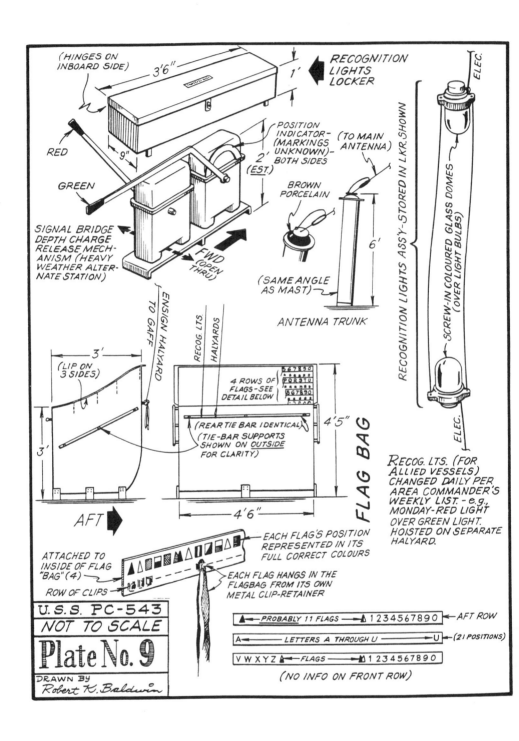

(HINGES ON INBOARD SIDE)

3'6"

1'

RECOGNITION LIGHTS LOCKER

9"

RED

GREEN

SIGNAL BRIDGE DEPTH CHARGE RELEASE MECHANISM (HEAVY WEATHER ALTERNATE STATION)

POSITION INDICATOR-(MARKINGS UNKNOWN)-BOTH SIDES

2' (EST.)

(TO MAIN ANTENNA)

BROWN PORCELAIN

FWD (OPEN THRU)

(SAME ANGLE AS MAST)

ANTENNA TRUNK

RECOGNITION LIGHTS ASS'Y-STORED IN LKR. SHOWN

ELEC.

SCREW-IN COLOURED GLASS DOMES (OVER LIGHT BULBS)

ELEC.

6'

ENSIGN HALYARD TO GAFF

RECOG LTS HALYARDS

3'

(LIP ON 3 SIDES)

3'

4 ROWS OF FLAGS-SEE DETAIL BELOW

567890
PQRSTU
567890

(REAR TIE BAR IDENTICAL)

(TIE-BAR SUPPORTS SHOWN ON OUTSIDE FOR CLARITY)

4'5"

FLAG BAG

4'6"

AFT

RECOG. LTS. (FOR ALLIED VESSELS) CHANGED DAILY PER AREA COMMANDER'S WEEKLY LIST. - e.g., MONDAY-RED LIGHT OVER GREEN LIGHT. HOISTED ON SEPARATE HALYARD.

ATTACHED TO INSIDE OF FLAG "BAG"(4)

ROW OF CLIPS

EACH FLAG'S POSITION REPRESENTED IN ITS FULL CORRECT COLOURS

EACH FLAG HANGS IN THE FLAGBAG FROM ITS OWN METAL CLIP-RETAINER

U.S.S. PC-543

NOT TO SCALE

Plate No. 9

DRAWN BY
Robert K. Baldwin

◄— PROBABLY 11 FLAGS —◄ 1 2 3 4 5 6 7 8 9 0	◄—AFT ROW
A◄— LETTERS A THROUGH U —►U	(21 POSITIONS)
V W X Y Z ◄—FLAGS —◄ 1 2 3 4 5 6 7 8 9 0	

(NO INFO ON FRONT ROW)

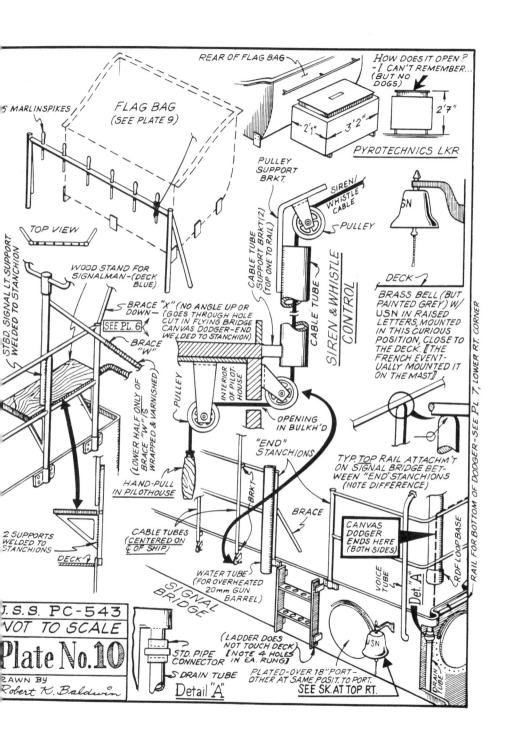

REAR OF FLAG BAG

FLAG BAG
(SEE PLATE 9)

5 MARLINSPIKES

HOW DOES IT OPEN?
- I CAN'T REMEMBER...
(BUT NO DOGS)

2'7"

2'1" 3'2"

PYROTECHNICS LKR

TOP VIEW

STBD. SIGNAL LT. SUPPORT
WELDED TO STANCHION

WOOD STAND FOR
SIGNALMAN-(DECK
BLUE)

BRACE "X" (NO ANGLE UP OR
DOWN — (GOES THROUGH HOLE
CUT IN FLYING BRIDGE
CANVAS DODGER-END
WELDED TO STANCHION)

SEE PL. 6

BRACE
"W"

(LOWER HALF ONLY OF
BRACE "W" IS
WRAPPED & VARNISHED)

HAND-PULL
IN PILOTHOUSE

2 SUPPORTS
WELDED TO
STANCHIONS

DECK

PULLEY
SUPPORT
BRKT.

CABLE TUBE
SUPPORT BRKT(2)
(TOP ONE TO RAIL)

SIREN/
WHISTLE
CABLE

PULLEY

CABLE TUBE

SIREN & WHISTLE CONTROL

PULLEY

INTERIOR
OF PILOT-
HOUSE

OPENING
IN BULKH'D

"END"
STANCHIONS

BRKT

CABLE TUBES
(CENTERED ON
Ç OF SHIP)

BRACE

TYP. TOP RAIL ATTACHM'T
ON SIGNAL BRIDGE BET-
WEEN "END" STANCHIONS
(NOTE DIFFERENCE)

CANVAS
DODGER
ENDS HERE
(BOTH SIDES)

VOICE
TUBE

RDF LOOP BASE

SN

DECK

BRASS BELL (BUT
PAINTED GREY) W/
USN IN RAISED
LETTERS, MOUNTED
IN THIS CURIOUS
POSITION, CLOSE TO
THE DECK. [THE
FRENCH EVENT-
UALLY MOUNTED IT
ON THE MAST]

RAIL FOR BOTTOM OF DODGER–SEE PL. 7, LOWER RT. CORNER

WATER TUBE
(FOR OVERHEATED
20mm GUN
BARREL)

SIGNAL
BRIDGE

U.S.S. PC-543
NOT TO SCALE

Plate No.10

DRAWN BY
Robert K. Baldwin

STD. PIPE
CONNECTOR

DRAIN TUBE

Detail "A"

(LADDER DOES
NOT TOUCH DECK)
[NOTE 4 HOLES
IN EA. RUNG]

USN

Det. "A"

PLATED-OVER 18" PORT –
OTHER AT SAME POSIT. TO PORT.
SEE SK. AT TOP RT.

DRAIN
TUBE

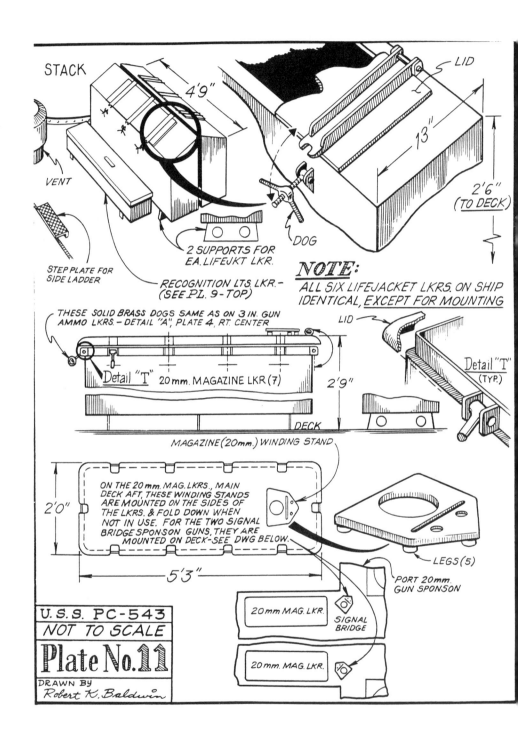

STACK

4'9"

LID

13"

2'6" (TO DECK)

VENT

DOG

STEP PLATE FOR SIDE LADDER

2 SUPPORTS FOR EA. LIFEJKT. LKR.

RECOGNITION LTS. LKR.— (SEE PL. 9-TOP)

NOTE:

ALL SIX LIFEJACKET LKRS. ON SHIP IDENTICAL, EXCEPT FOR MOUNTING

THESE SOLID BRASS DOGS SAME AS ON 3 IN. GUN AMMO LKRS.— DETAIL "A", PLATE 4, RT. CENTER

LID

Detail "T" 20 mm. MAGAZINE LKR (7)

Detail "T" (TYP.)

2'9"

DECK

MAGAZINE (20mm.) WINDING STAND

2'0"

ON THE 20 mm. MAG. LKRS., MAIN DECK AFT, THESE WINDING STANDS ARE MOUNTED ON THE SIDES OF THE LKRS. & FOLD DOWN WHEN NOT IN USE. FOR THE TWO SIGNAL BRIDGE SPONSON GUNS, THEY ARE MOUNTED ON DECK—SEE DWG BELOW.

5'3"

LEGS (5)

PORT 20mm. GUN SPONSON

20mm MAG. LKR.

SIGNAL BRIDGE

20mm MAG. LKR.

U.S.S. PC-543

NOT TO SCALE

Plate No. 11

DRAWN BY
Robert K. Baldwin

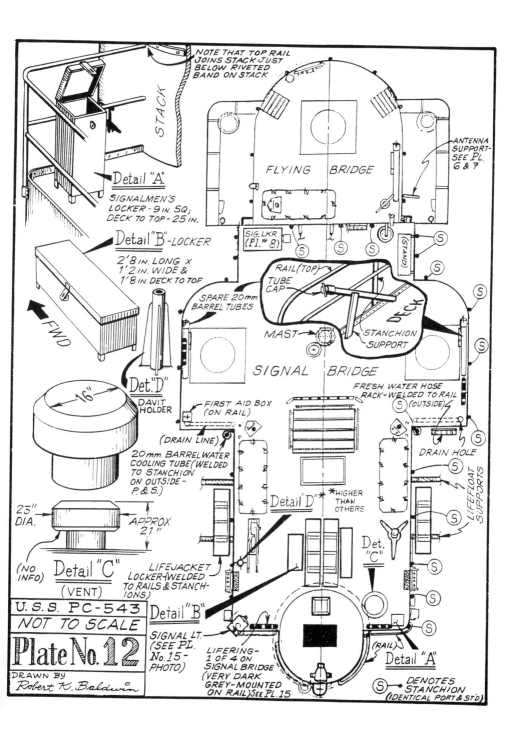

NOTE THAT TOP RAIL
JOINS STACK JUST
BELOW RIVETED
BAND ON STACK

STACK

FLYING   BRIDGE

ANTENNA
SUPPORT-
SEE PL.
6 & 7

Detail "A"

SIGNALMEN'S
LOCKER - 9 IN. SQ;
DECK TO TOP - 25 IN.

SIG. LKR.
(PL.# 8)

(STAND)

Detail "B"-LOCKER

2' 8 IN. LONG X
1' 2 IN. WIDE &
1' 8 IN. DECK TO TOP

RAIL (TOP)

TUBE
CAP

SPARE 20mm
BARREL TUBES

DECK

FWD

MAST

STANCHION
SUPPORT

SIGNAL   BRIDGE

16"

Det. "D"

DAVIT
HOLDER

FIRST AID BOX
(ON RAIL)

FRESH WATER HOSE
RACK-WELDED TO RAIL
(OUTSIDE)

DRAIN HOLE

(DRAIN LINE)

20mm. BARREL WATER
COOLING TUBE (WELDED
TO STANCHION
ON OUTSIDE-
P. & S.)

LIFEFLOAT
SUPPORTS

25"
DIA.

APPROX
21"

Detail "D"   *HIGHER
THAN
OTHERS

Det.
"C"

(NO
INFO)

Detail "C"
(VENT)

LIFEJACKET
LOCKER-(WELDED
TO RAILS & STANCH-
IONS)

U.S.S. PC-543
NOT TO SCALE

Detail "B"

SIGNAL LT.
(SEE PL.
No. 15 -
PHOTO)

LIFERING-
1 OF 4 ON
SIGNAL BRIDGE
(VERY DARK
GREY-MOUNTED
ON RAIL) SEE PL. 15

(RAIL)

Detail "A"

Plate No. 12

DRAWN BY
Robert K. Baldwin

S   DENOTES
STANCHION
(IDENTICAL PORT & ST'D)

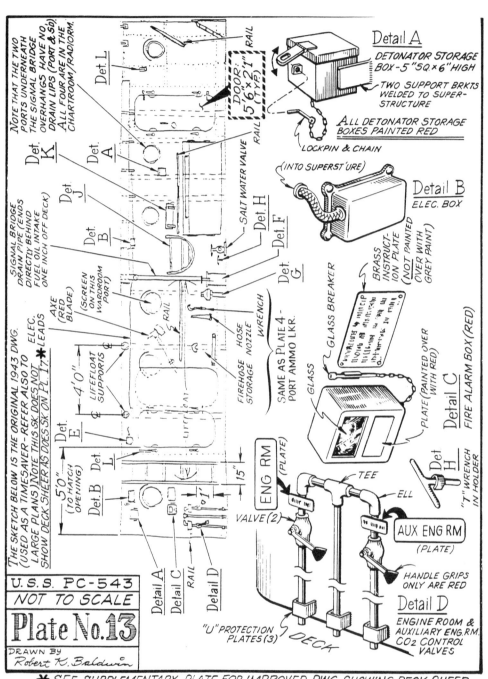

Detail A
DETONATOR STORAGE
BOX - 5" SQ. × 6" HIGH

TWO SUPPORT BRKTS
WELDED TO SUPER-
STRUCTURE

ALL DETONATOR STORAGE
BOXES PAINTED RED

LOCKPIN & CHAIN

DOOR: 5'6" × 21" RAIL (TYP.)

NOTE THAT THE TWO PORTS UNDERNEATH THE SIGNAL BRIDGE OVERHANGS HAVE NO DRAIN LIPS (PORT & S'D). ALL FOUR ARE IN THE CHARTROOM/RADIORM.

Det. L

Det. K

Det. A

Det. J

Det. B

SALT WATER VALVE

RAIL

Det. H

Det. F

(INTO SUPERST'URE)

Detail B
ELEC. BOX

Det. G

SIGNAL BRIDGE DRAIN PIPE (ENDS DIRECTLY BEHIND FUEL OIL INTAKE ONE INCH OFF DECK)

AXE (RED BLADE)

(SCREEN ON THIS WARDROOM PORT)

RAIL

LIFEFLOAT SUPPORTS

4'0"

FIREHOSE HOSE STORAGE NOZZLE WRENCH

SAME AS PLATE 4 - PORT AMMO LKR.

BRASS INSTRUCT-ION PLATE (NOT PAINTED OVER WITH GREY PAINT)

GLASS BREAKER

GLASS

FIRE ALARM BOX (RED)
Detail C

PLATE (PAINTED OVER WITH RED)

THE SKETCH BELOW IS THE ORIGINAL 1943 DWG. (USED AS A TIMESAVER - REFER ALSO TO LARGE PLANS) NOTE THIS SK DOES NOT SHOW DECK SHEER AS DOES SK ON PL. 17.

ELEC. LEADS ✱

Det. E

Det. L

Det. B

5'0" (TO HATCH OPENING)

15"

1"

Det. A

RAIL

ENG RM (PLATE)

TEE

ELL

AUX ENG RM (PLATE)

Det H

"T" WRENCH IN HOLDER

VALVE (2)

HANDLE GRIPS ONLY ARE RED

"U" PROTECTION PLATES (3)

DECK

Detail D
ENGINE ROOM & AUXILIARY ENG. RM. CO₂ CONTROL VALVES

U.S.S. PC-543
NOT TO SCALE
Plate No. 13
DRAWN BY
Robert K. Baldwin

Detail A
Detail C
RAIL
"Detail D"

✱ SEE SUPPLEMENTARY PLATE FOR IMPROVED DWG. SHOWING DECK SHEER

Although not pertinent to building a model, you will probably be interested in knowing that the hulls of many, if not all, of these submarine chasers were built upside down to speed their production.

Since there is far more welding on any overhead compared to the amount of welding on a deck (which must, of course, be kept as unobstructed as possible for walking) building hulls upside down allows welders to work at their feet rather than over their heads, a far easier and faster operation.

Many PC boats built along rivers were launched down ways sideways since some river construction sites did not have the room for conventional launching. Thus, the hull of a PC was started on one set of ways and then was "rolled over" to adjoining ways (see sketches at bottom, this page). The prefabricated superstructure was then lowered by cranes onto the hull.

The boxed sketch at lower left is based solely on recollections of a comprehensive magazine article (since lost) showing the construction of PCs at Defoe Boat and Motor Works - later Defoe Shipbuilding Company, but now out of business.

This article was illustrated with a number of fine photographs and appeared in either a January or February issue of YACHTING magazine in 1942. The sketches are, therefore, far from accurate as to details.

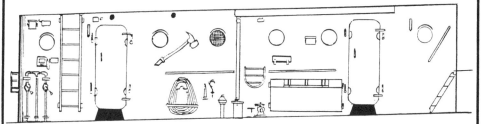

IMPROVED SK. OF SUPERSTRUCTURE (STBD. SIDE) FROM THAT ON PLATE 13 SHOWING A TRUE VIEW WITH MAIN DECK SHEER

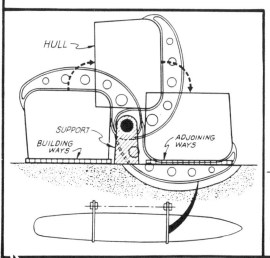
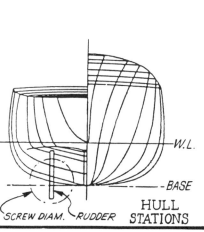

HULL

SUPPORT

BUILDING WAYS

ADJOINING WAYS

SCREW DIAM.   RUDDER

W.L.

BASE

HULL STATIONS

SUPPLEMENTARY PLATE

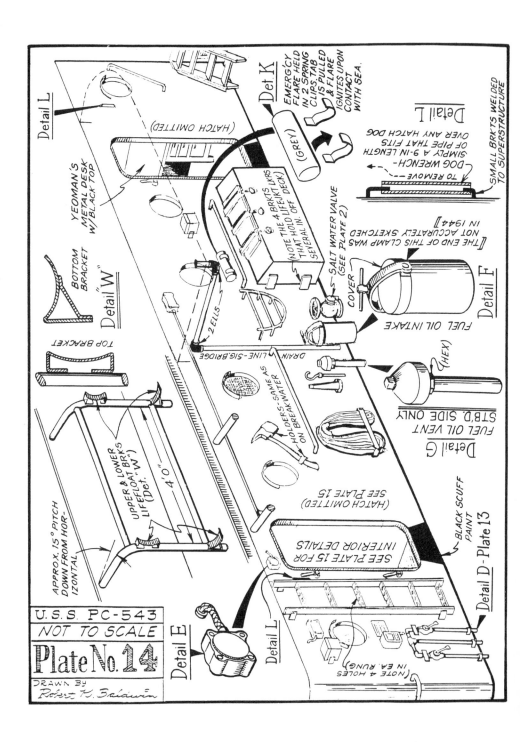

Detail L

(HATCH OMITTED)

Det K

EMERG'CY
FLARE HELD
IN 2 SPRING
CLIPS. TAB
IS PULLED
& FLARE
IGNITES UPON
CONTACT
WITH SEA.

(GREY)

Detail L

DOG WRENCH—
SIMPLY A 9-IN LENGTH
OF PIPE THAT FITS
OVER ANY HATCH DOG

TO REMOVE

SMALL BRKTS WELDED
TO SUPERSTRUCTURE

YEOMAN'S
METAL DESK
W/BLACK TOP

NOTE THE 4 BRKTS LKRS
THAT HOLD THE LIFEFLOAT
SEVERAL IN. OFF DECK

SALT WATER VALVE
(SEE PLATE 2)

COVER

[THE END OF THIS CLAMP WAS
NOT ACCURATELY SKETCHED
IN 1944]

FUEL OIL INTAKE

Detail F

BOTTOM
BRACKET

Detail "W"

2 ELLS

TOP BRACKET

DRAIN LINE-SIG.BRIDGE

(HEX)

FUEL OIL VENT
STB'D. SIDE ONLY

Detail G

HOLDERS-SAME AS
ON BREAKWATER

UPPER & LOWER BRKS
LIFEFLOAT "W"
(Det.)

4'0"

SEE PLATE 15
(HATCH OMITTED)

BLACK SCUFF
PAINT

APPROX. 15° PITCH
DOWN FROM HOR-
IZONTAL

SEE PLATE 15 FOR
INTERIOR DETAILS

Detail D- Plate 13

Detail E

Detail L

(NOTE 4 HOLES
IN EA. RUNG)

U.S.S. PC-543

NOT TO SCALE

Plate No. 14

DRAWN BY
Robert K. Baldwin

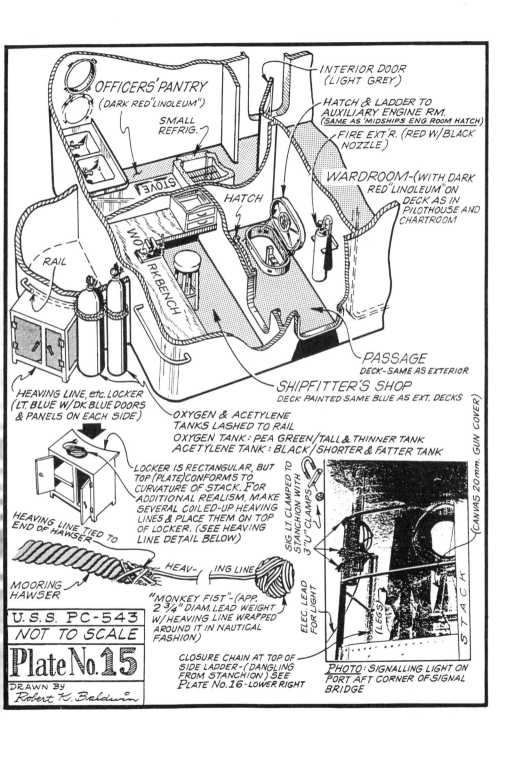

OFFICERS' PANTRY
(DARK RED "LINOLEUM")

SMALL REFRIG.

INTERIOR DOOR (LIGHT GREY)

HATCH & LADDER TO AUXILIARY ENGINE RM.
(SAME AS 'MIDSHIPS ENG. ROOM HATCH)

FIRE EXT'R. (RED W/BLACK NOZZLE)

STOVE

HATCH

WORK BENCH

RAIL

WARDROOM-(WITH DARK RED "LINOLEUM" ON DECK AS IN PILOTHOUSE AND CHARTROOM

PASSAGE
DECK-SAME AS EXTERIOR

HEAVING LINE, etc. LOCKER
(LT. BLUE W/DK. BLUE DOORS & PANELS ON EACH SIDE)

SHIPFITTER'S SHOP
DECK PAINTED SAME BLUE AS EXT. DECKS

OXYGEN & ACETYLENE TANKS LASHED TO RAIL
OXYGEN TANK: PEA GREEN/TALL & THINNER TANK
ACETYLENE TANK: BLACK/SHORTER & FATTER TANK

LOCKER IS RECTANGULAR, BUT TOP (PLATE) CONFORMS TO CURVATURE OF STACK. FOR ADDITIONAL REALISM, MAKE SEVERAL COILED-UP HEAVING LINES & PLACE THEM ON TOP OF LOCKER. (SEE HEAVING LINE DETAIL BELOW)

HEAVING LINE TIED TO END OF HAWSER

MOORING HAWSER

HEAV- ING LINE

SIG. LT. CLAMPED TO STANCHION WITH 3"U" CLAMPS

(CANVAS 20mm. GUN COVER)

ELEC. LEAD FOR LIGHT

(LEGS)

STACK

"MONKEY FIST"-(APP. 2 ¾" DIAM. LEAD WEIGHT W/HEAVING LINE WRAPPED AROUND IT IN NAUTICAL FASHION)

U.S.S. PC-543
NOT TO SCALE
Plate No. 15
DRAWN BY
Robert K. Baldwin

CLOSURE CHAIN AT TOP OF SIDE LADDER-(DANGLING FROM STANCHION) SEE PLATE No. 16-LOWER RIGHT

PHOTO: SIGNALLING LIGHT ON PORT AFT CORNER OF SIGNAL BRIDGE

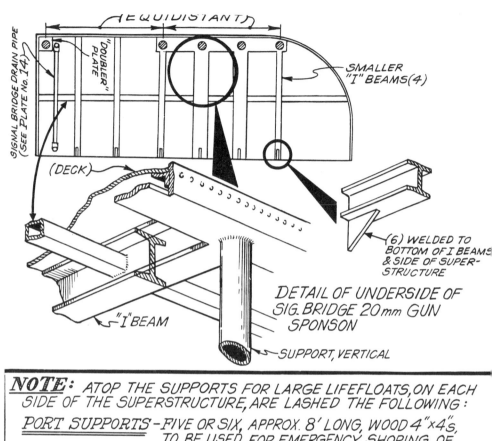

SIGNAL BRIDGE DRAIN PIPE (SEE PLATE No. 14.)

(EQUIDISTANT)

"DOUBLER" PLATE

SMALLER "I" BEAMS (4)

(DECK)

(6) WELDED TO BOTTOM OF I BEAMS & SIDE OF SUPER-STRUCTURE

"I" BEAM

DETAIL OF UNDERSIDE OF SIG. BRIDGE 20 mm GUN SPONSON

SUPPORT, VERTICAL

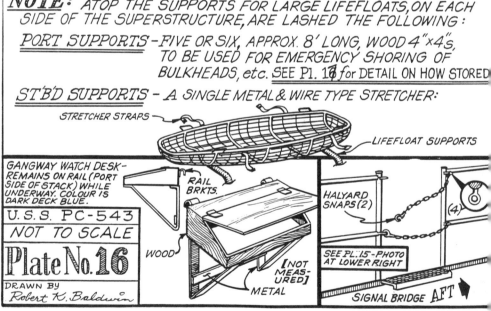

NOTE: ATOP THE SUPPORTS FOR LARGE LIFEFLOATS, ON EACH SIDE OF THE SUPERSTRUCTURE, ARE LASHED THE FOLLOWING:

<u>PORT SUPPORTS</u> – FIVE OR SIX, APPROX. 8' LONG, WOOD 4"x4"s, TO BE USED FOR EMERGENCY SHORING OF BULKHEADS, etc. SEE Pl. 18 for DETAIL ON HOW STORED

<u>ST'B'D SUPPORTS</u> – A SINGLE METAL & WIRE TYPE STRETCHER:

STRETCHER STRAPS

LIFEFLOAT SUPPORTS

GANGWAY WATCH DESK- REMAINS ON RAIL (PORT SIDE OF STACK) WHILE UNDERWAY. COLOUR IS DARK DECK BLUE.

RAIL BRKTS.

HALYARD SNAPS (2)

(4)

U.S.S. PC-543

NOT TO SCALE

Plate No. 16

DRAWN BY Robert K. Baldwin

WOOD

METAL

[NOT MEAS-URED]

SEE PL. 15 - PHOTO AT LOWER RIGHT

SIGNAL BRIDGE AFT

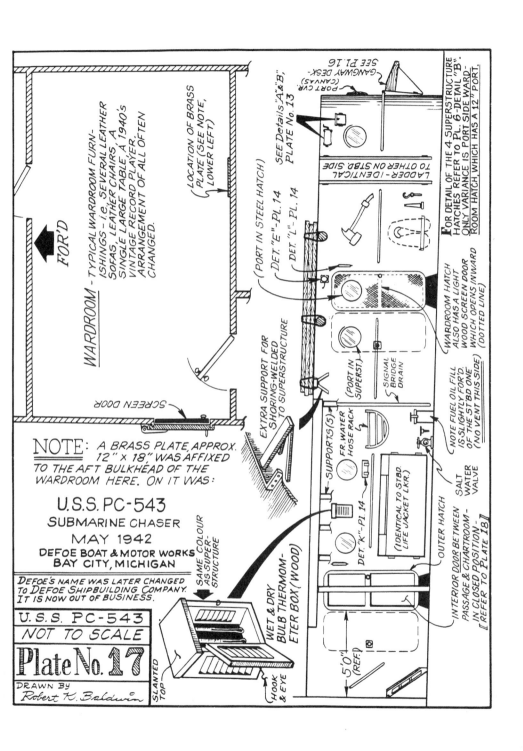

FOR'D

WARDROOM - TYPICAL WARDROOM FURN-
ISHINGS - i.e. SEVERAL LEATHER
SOFAS, LEATHER CHAIRS, A
SINGLE LARGE TABLE, A 1940's
VINTAGE RECORD PLAYER.
ARRANGEMENT OF ALL OFTEN
CHANGED.

(LOCATION OF BRASS
PLATE (SEE NOTE,
LOWER LEFT)

SCREEN DOOR

NOTE: A BRASS PLATE, APPROX.
12" X 18" WAS AFFIXED
TO THE AFT BULKHEAD OF THE
WARDROOM HERE. ON IT WAS:

U.S.S. PC-543
SUBMARINE CHASER
MAY 1942
DEFOE BOAT & MOTOR WORKS
BAY CITY, MICHIGAN

DEFOE'S NAME WAS LATER CHANGED
TO DEFOE SHIPBUILDING COMPANY.
IT IS NOW OUT OF BUSINESS.

U.S.S. PC-543
NOT TO SCALE
Plate No. 17
DRAWN BY
Robert K. Baldwin

SAME COLOUR
AS SUPER-
STRUCTURE

WET & DRY
BULB THERMOM-
ETER BOX (WOOD)

HOOK
& EYE

SLANTED
TOP

EXTRA SUPPORT FOR
SHORING-WELDED
TO SUPERSTRUCTURE

(PORT IN STEEL HATCH)
DET. "E" - PL. 14
DET. "L" - PL. 14

SEE Details "A" & "B",
PLATE No. 13

PORT CVR
(CANVAS)
GANGWAY DESK -
SEE PL.16

LADDER - IDENTICAL
TO OTHER ON STBD. SIDE

FOR DETAIL OF THE 4 SUPERSTRUCTURE
HATCHES REFER TO PL. 6-DETAIL "B" -
ONLY VARIANCE IS PORT SIDE WARD-
ROOM HATCH, WHICH HAS A 12" PORT.

WARDROOM HATCH
ALSO HAS A LIGHT
WOOD SCREEN DOOR
WHICH OPENS INWARD
(DOTTED LINE)

(PORT IN
SUPERST.)

SIGNAL
BRIDGE
DRAIN

NOTE FUEL OIL FILL
IS SLIGHTLY FOR'D
OF THE STBD ONE
(NO VENT THIS SIDE)

SALT
WATER
VALVE

SUPPORTS (5)

FR. WATER
HOSE RACK

DET "K"-PL 14

(IDENTICAL TO STBD.
LIFE JACKET LKR.)

OUTER HATCH

INTERIOR DOOR BETWEEN
PASSAGE & CHARTROOM -
IN CLOSED POSITION -
[REFER TO PLATE 18]

5'-0"
(REF.)

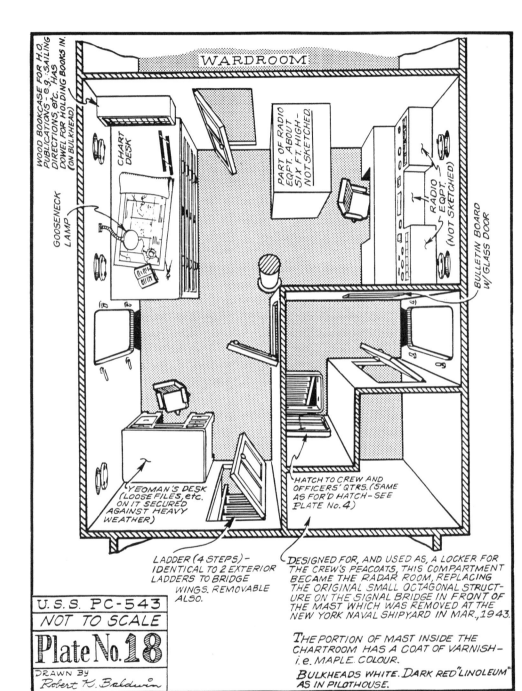

WARDROOM

WOOD BOOKCASE FOR H.O. PUBLICATIONS - e.g., SAILING DIRECTIONS, etc. HAS DOWEL FOR HOLDING BOOKS IN. (ON BULKHEAD)

GOOSENECK LAMP

CHART DESK

PART OF RADIO EQPT. ABOUT SIX FT. HIGH - NOT SKETCHED

RADIO EQPT. (NOT SKETCHED)

BULLETIN BOARD W/ GLASS DOOR

YEOMAN'S DESK (LOOSE FILES, etc. ON IT SECURED AGAINST HEAVY WEATHER)

HATCH TO CREW AND OFFICERS' QTRS. (SAME AS FOR'D HATCH - SEE PLATE No. 4.)

LADDER (4 STEPS) - IDENTICAL TO 2 EXTERIOR LADDERS TO BRIDGE WINGS. REMOVABLE ALSO.

DESIGNED FOR, AND USED AS, A LOCKER FOR THE CREW'S PEACOATS, THIS COMPARTMENT BECAME THE RADAR ROOM, REPLACING THE ORIGINAL SMALL OCTAGONAL STRUCTURE ON THE SIGNAL BRIDGE IN FRONT OF THE MAST WHICH WAS REMOVED AT THE NEW YORK NAVAL SHIPYARD IN MAR., 1943.

THE PORTION OF MAST INSIDE THE CHARTROOM HAS A COAT OF VARNISH - i.e. MAPLE COLOUR.

BULKHEADS WHITE. DARK RED "LINOLEUM" AS IN PILOTHOUSE.

U.S.S. PC-543
NOT TO SCALE
Plate No. 18
DRAWN BY
Robert K. Baldwin

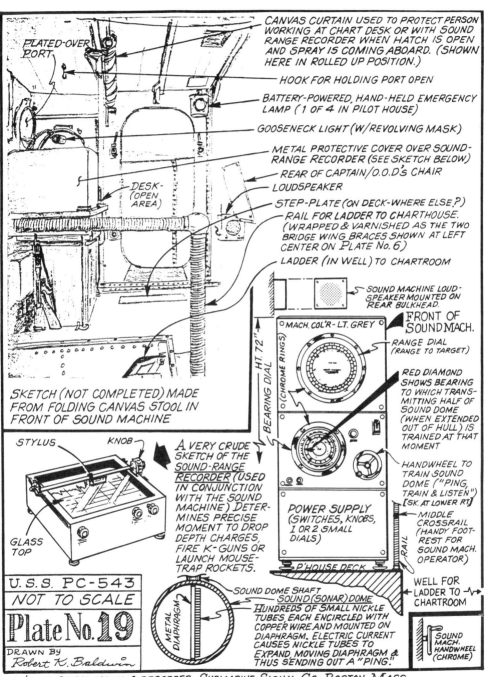

CANVAS CURTAIN USED TO PROTECT PERSON WORKING AT CHART DESK OR WITH SOUND RANGE RECORDER WHEN HATCH IS OPEN AND SPRAY IS COMING ABOARD. (SHOWN HERE IN ROLLED UP POSITION.)

HOOK FOR HOLDING PORT OPEN

BATTERY-POWERED, HAND-HELD EMERGENCY LAMP (1 OF 4 IN PILOT HOUSE)

GOOSENECK LIGHT (W/REVOLVING MASK)

METAL PROTECTIVE COVER OVER SOUND-RANGE RECORDER (SEE SKETCH BELOW)

REAR OF CAPTAIN/O.O.D's CHAIR

LOUDSPEAKER

STEP-PLATE (ON DECK-WHERE ELSE?)

RAIL FOR LADDER TO CHARTHOUSE. (WRAPPED & VARNISHED AS THE TWO BRIDGE WING BRACES SHOWN AT LEFT CENTER ON PLATE No. 6)

LADDER (IN WELL) TO CHARTROOM

PLATED-OVER PORT

DESK-(OPEN AREA)

SKETCH (NOT COMPLETED) MADE FROM FOLDING CANVAS STOOL IN FRONT OF SOUND MACHINE

SOUND MACHINE LOUD-SPEAKER MOUNTED ON REAR BULKHEAD.

FRONT OF SOUND MACH.

MACH. COL'R - LT. GREY

RANGE DIAL (RANGE TO TARGET)

RED DIAMOND SHOWS BEARING TO WHICH TRANS-MITTING HALF OF SOUND DOME (WHEN EXTENDED OUT OF HULL) IS TRAINED AT THAT MOMENT

HANDWHEEL TO TRAIN SOUND DOME ("PING, TRAIN & LISTEN") [SK. AT LOWER RT]

MIDDLE CROSSRAIL (HANDY FOOT-REST FOR SOUND MACH. OPERATOR)

HT. 72"

BEARING DIAL

(CHROME RINGS)

STYLUS

KNOB

A VERY CRUDE SKETCH OF THE SOUND-RANGE RECORDER (USED IN CONJUNCTION WITH THE SOUND MACHINE) DETER-MINES PRECISE MOMENT TO DROP DEPTH CHARGES, FIRE K-GUNS OR LAUNCH MOUSE-TRAP ROCKETS.

GLASS TOP

POWER SUPPLY (SWITCHES, KNOBS, 1 OR 2 SMALL DIALS)

RAIL

P'HOUSE DECK

WELL FOR LADDER TO CHARTROOM

U.S.S. PC-543

NOT TO SCALE

Plate No. 19

DRAWN BY
Robert K. Baldwin

SOUND DOME SHAFT

SOUND (SONAR) DOME

METAL DIAPHRAGM

HUNDREDS OF SMALL NICKLE TUBES, EACH ENCIRCLED WITH COPPER WIRE AND MOUNTED ON DIAPHRAGM. ELECTRIC CURRENT CAUSES NICKLE TUBES TO EXPAND, MOVING DIAPHRAGM & THUS SENDING OUT A "PING".

SOUND MACH. HANDWHEEL (CHROME)

MF'R. OF SOUND MACH. & RECORDER: SUBMARINE SIGNAL CO., BOSTON, MASS.

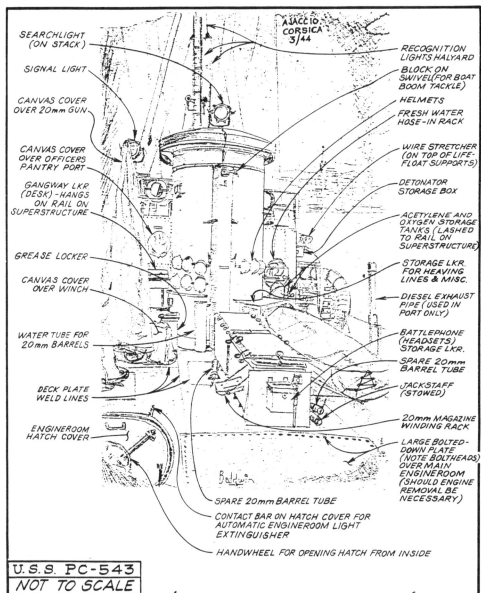

SEARCHLIGHT (ON STACK)

SIGNAL LIGHT

CANVAS COVER OVER 20mm GUN

CANVAS COVER OVER OFFICERS PANTRY PORT

GANGWAY LKR. (DESK) - HANGS ON RAIL ON SUPERSTRUCTURE

GREASE LOCKER

CANVAS COVER OVER WINCH

WATER TUBE FOR 20mm BARRELS

DECK PLATE WELD LINES

ENGINEROOM HATCH COVER

AJACCIO CORSICA 3/44

RECOGNITION LIGHTS HALYARD

BLOCK ON SWIVEL (FOR BOAT BOOM TACKLE)

HELMETS

FRESH WATER HOSE - IN RACK

WIRE STRETCHER (ON TOP OF LIFE-FLOAT SUPPORTS)

DETONATOR STORAGE BOX

ACETYLENE AND OXYGEN STORAGE TANKS (LASHED TO RAIL ON SUPERSTRUCTURE)

STORAGE LKR. FOR HEAVING LINES & MISC.

DIESEL EXHAUST PIPE (USED IN PORT ONLY)

BATTLEPHONE (HEADSETS) STORAGE LKR.

SPARE 20mm BARREL TUBE

JACKSTAFF (STOWED)

20mm MAGAZINE WINDING RACK

LARGE BOLTED-DOWN PLATE (NOTE BOLTHEADS) OVER MAIN ENGINEROOM (SHOULD ENGINE REMOVAL BE NECESSARY)

Baldwin

SPARE 20mm BARREL TUBE

CONTACT BAR ON HATCH COVER FOR AUTOMATIC ENGINEROOM LIGHT EXTINGUISHER

HANDWHEEL FOR OPENING HATCH FROM INSIDE

U.S.S. PC-543

NOT TO SCALE

Plate No. 21

DRAWN BY
Robert K. Baldwin

ALTHOUGH NOT A PLAN, THIS SKETCH (DONE WHILE SITTING ON 'MIDSHIPS 20mm READY SERVE LOCKERS — A POPULAR CHATTING PLACE) SHOULD PROVIDE THE MODEL BUILDER WITH ORIENTATION.

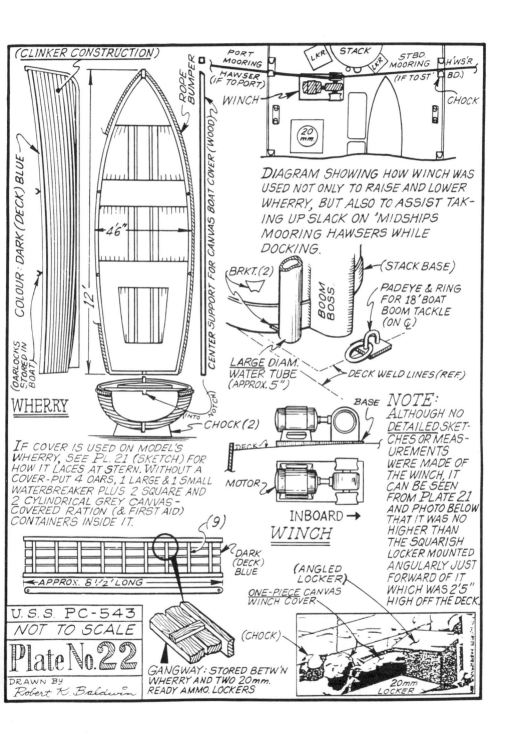

(CLINKER CONSTRUCTION)

ROPE BUMPER

COLOUR: DARK (DECK) BLUE

CENTER SUPPORT FOR CANVAS BOAT COVER (WOOD)

4'6"

12'

(OARLOCKS STORED IN BOAT)

WHERRY

INTO NOTCH

CHOCK (2)

IF COVER IS USED ON MODEL'S WHERRY, SEE PL. 21 (SKETCH) FOR HOW IT LACES AT STERN. WITHOUT A COVER - PUT 4 OARS, 1 LARGE & 1 SMALL WATERBREAKER PLUS 2 SQUARE AND 2 CYLINDRICAL GREY CANVAS - COVERED RATION (& FIRST AID) CONTAINERS INSIDE IT.

PORT MOORING
HAWSER (IF TO PORT)
WINCH

LKR. STACK LKR.

STBD. MOORING (IF TO ST')

H'WS'R (BD.)

CHOCK

20 mm.

DIAGRAM SHOWING HOW WINCH WAS USED NOT ONLY TO RAISE AND LOWER WHERRY, BUT ALSO TO ASSIST TAK-ING UP SLACK ON 'MIDSHIPS MOORING HAWSERS WHILE DOCKING.

BRKT.(2)

BOOM BOSS

(STACK BASE)

PADEYE & RING FOR 18' BOAT BOOM TACKLE (ON C)

LARGE DIAM. WATER TUBE (APPROX. 5")

DECK WELD LINES (REF.)

BASE

DECK

MOTOR

INBOARD →
WINCH

NOTE:
ALTHOUGH NO DETAILED SKET-CHES OR MEAS-UREMENTS WERE MADE OF THE WINCH, IT CAN BE SEEN FROM PLATE 21 AND PHOTO BELOW THAT IT WAS NO HIGHER THAN THE SQUARISH LOCKER MOUNTED ANGULARLY JUST FORWARD OF IT WHICH WAS 2'5" HIGH OFF THE DECK.

(9)

DARK (DECK) BLUE

←APPROX. 8 1/2' LONG→

(ANGLED LOCKER)

ONE-PIECE CANVAS WINCH COVER

(CHOCK)

U.S.S. PC-543
NOT TO SCALE

Plate No. 22

DRAWN BY
Robert K. Baldwin

GANGWAY: STORED BETW'N WHERRY AND TWO 20mm. READY AMMO. LOCKERS

20mm LOCKER

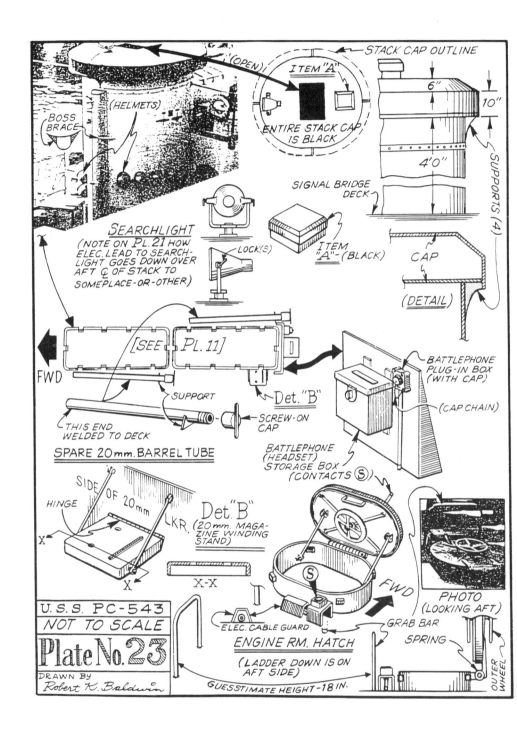

STACK CAP OUTLINE

(OPEN)

ITEM "A"

ENTIRE STACK CAP IS BLACK

6"

10"

4'0"

SUPPORTS (4)

(HELMETS)

BOSS BRACE

SIGNAL BRIDGE DECK

SEARCHLIGHT

(NOTE ON PL. 21 HOW ELEC. LEAD TO SEARCH-LIGHT GOES DOWN OVER AFT ℄ OF STACK TO SOMEPLACE-OR-OTHER)

LOCK(S)

ITEM "A"- (BLACK)

CAP

(DETAIL)

[SEE PL. 11]

FWD

SUPPORT

Det. "B"

SCREW-ON CAP

BATTLEPHONE PLUG-IN BOX (WITH CAP)

(CAP CHAIN)

THIS END WELDED TO DECK

SPARE 20 mm. BARREL TUBE

BATTLEPHONE (HEADSET) STORAGE BOX (CONTACTS Ⓢ)

SIDE OF 20 mm

HINGE

LKR.

Det. "B"
(20 mm. MAGA-ZINE WINDING STAND)

X

X

X-X

Ⓢ

FWD

PHOTO (LOOKING AFT)

U.S.S. PC-543

NOT TO SCALE

Plate No. 23

DRAWN BY
Robert K. Baldwin

ELEC. CABLE GUARD

ENGINE RM. HATCH

(LADDER DOWN IS ON AFT SIDE)

GUESSTIMATE HEIGHT -18 IN.

GRAB BAR

SPRING

OUTER WHEEL

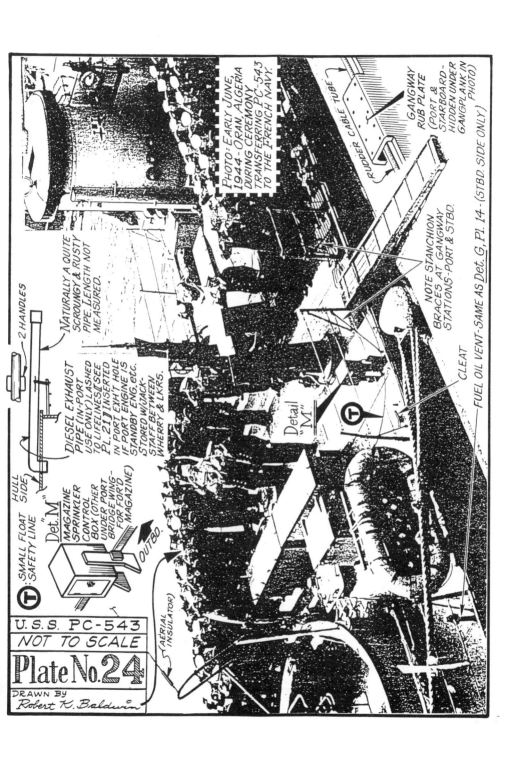

PHOTO: EARLY JUNE, 1944 - ORAN, ALGERIA DURING CEREMONY TRANSFERRING PC-543 TO THE FRENCH NAVY.

2 HANDLES

HULL SIDE

Det. "M"

NATURALLY A QUITE SCROUNGY & RUSTY PIPE. LENGTH NOT MEASURED.

DIESEL EXHAUST PIPE (IN-PORT USE ONLY) LASHED TO LIFELINES (SEE PL. 21) INSERTED IN PORT EXHT. HOLE IF PORT ENGINE IS STANDBY ENG. etc. STORED W/JACK-STAFF BETWEEN WHERRY & LKRS.

⊤: SMALL FLOAT SAFETY LINE

MAGAZINE SPRINKLER CONTROL BOX (OTHER UNDER PORT BRIDGE WING - FOR FORD MAGAZINE)

OUTBD.

AERIAL INSULATOR)

U.S.S. PC-543

NOT TO SCALE

Plate No. 24

DRAWN BY
Robert K. Baldwin

Detail "M"

⊤

(RUDDER CABLE TUBE)

GANGWAY RUB PLATE (PORT & STARBOARD - HIDDEN UNDER GANGPLANK IN PHOTO)

NOTE STANCHION BRACES AT GANGWAY STATIONS - PORT & STBD.

CLEAT

FUEL OIL VENT - SAME AS Det. G, Pl. 14 - (STBD. SIDE ONLY)

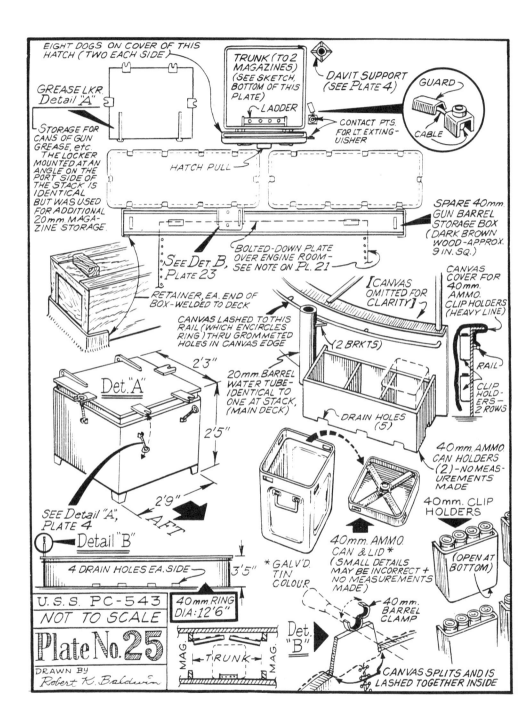

EIGHT DOGS ON COVER OF THIS HATCH (TWO EACH SIDE)

TRUNK (TO 2 MAGAZINES) (SEE SKETCH, BOTTOM OF THIS PLATE)

DAVIT SUPPORT (SEE PLATE 4)

GREASE LKR. Detail "A"

GUARD

LADDER

CONTACT PTS. FOR LT. EXTINGUISHER

STORAGE FOR CANS OF GUN GREASE, etc. THE LOCKER MOUNTED AT AN ANGLE ON THE PORT SIDE OF THE STACK IS IDENTICAL BUT WAS USED FOR ADDITIONAL 20mm MAGAZINE STORAGE.

CABLE

HATCH PULL

SPARE 40mm. GUN BARREL STORAGE BOX (DARK BROWN WOOD-APPROX. 9 IN. SQ.)

See Det. B, Plate 23

BOLTED-DOWN PLATE OVER ENGINE ROOM—SEE NOTE ON PL. 21

[CANVAS OMITTED FOR CLARITY]

CANVAS COVER FOR 40mm. AMMO. CLIP HOLDERS (HEAVY LINE)

RETAINER, EA. END OF BOX-WELDED TO DECK

CANVAS LASHED TO THIS RAIL (WHICH ENCIRCLES RING) THRU GROMMETED HOLES IN CANVAS EDGE

(2 BRKTS)

RAIL

CLIP HOLDERS- 2 ROWS

2' 3"

Det. "A"

20mm. BARREL WATER TUBE-IDENTICAL TO ONE AT STACK, (MAIN DECK)

DRAIN HOLES (5)

40mm. AMMO. CAN HOLDERS (2) -NO MEASUREMENTS MADE

2' 5"

40mm. CLIP HOLDERS

2' 9"

AFT

SEE Detail "A", PLATE 4

Detail "B"

40mm. AMMO. CAN & LID * (SMALL DETAILS MAY BE INCORRECT + NO MEASUREMENTS MADE)

(OPEN AT BOTTOM)

4 DRAIN HOLES EA. SIDE

3' 5"

* GALV'D. TIN COLOUR.

40mm. BARREL CLAMP

U.S.S. PC-543

NOT TO SCALE

40mm. RING DIA: 12'6"

Det. "B"

Plate No. 25

DRAWN BY Robert K. Baldwin

MAG.   TRUNK   MAG.

CANVAS SPLITS AND IS LASHED TOGETHER INSIDE

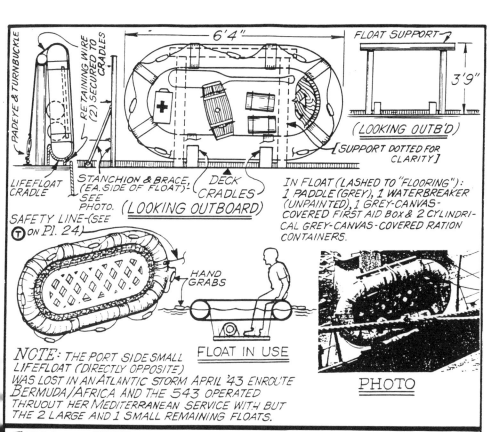

PADEYE & TURNBUCKLE

RETAINING WIRE (2) SECURED TO CRADLES

6'4"

FLOAT SUPPORT

3'9"

(LOOKING OUTB'D)

[SUPPORT DOTTED FOR CLARITY]

LIFEFLOAT CRADLE

STANCHION & BRACE, (EA. SIDE OF FLOAT): SEE PHOTO.

DECK CRADLES

(LOOKING OUTBOARD)

SAFETY LINE-(SEE (T) ON Pl. 24)

IN FLOAT (LASHED TO "FLOORING"):
1 PADDLE (GREY), 1 WATERBREAKER (UNPAINTED), 1 GREY-CANVAS-COVERED FIRST AID BOX & 2 CYLINDRICAL GREY-CANVAS-COVERED RATION CONTAINERS.

HAND GRABS

FLOAT IN USE

NOTE: THE PORT SIDE SMALL LIFEFLOAT (DIRECTLY OPPOSITE) WAS LOST IN AN ATLANTIC STORM APRIL '43 ENROUTE BERMUDA/AFRICA AND THE 543 OPERATED THRUOUT HER MEDITERRANEAN SERVICE WITH BUT THE 2 LARGE AND 1 SMALL REMAINING FLOATS.

PHOTO

CARRIED ON PORT LARGE LIFEFLOAT: 3 CANOE-TYPE OARS (SEE SMALL FLOAT DWG-TOP OF THIS PLATE), 2 LARGE WATERBREAKERS, 1 FOLDED CANVAS TARPAULIN, 2 CYLINDRICAL EMERG. RATION CONTAINERS AND 1 SQUARE FIRST AID BOX (W/RED CROSS THEREON)-LAST THREE ITEMS COVERED W/GREY CANVAS.

CARRIED ON STBD. LARGE LIFEFLOAT: 3 OARS (SAME), 2 WATERBREAKERS, 1 LARGE RECTANGULAR & 1 CYLINDRICAL RATION CONTAINER PLUS A FIRST AID BOX & A FOLDED TARPAULIN. ALL ITEMS LASHED INBOARD (TOP OF FLOAT'S "FLOORING") SO THAT WHEN FLOAT IS RELEASED OVERBOARD ITEMS WILL BE ACCESSIBLE TO OCCUPANTS.

As two seamen man the gun, another winds up the magazine for the 20mm AA cannon aboard a PC. The winding operation results in the shells being forced into the breech, thus keeping the gun firing.

(PHOTO FROM "OUR NAVY" MAGAZINE)

WINDING LEVER

U.S.S. PC-543
NOT TO SCALE

Plate No. 26

DRAWN BY
Robert K. Baldwin

20mm. MAGAZINE IN A WINDING STAND SUCH AS THAT SHOWN ON EITHER PLATES 11 OR 23.

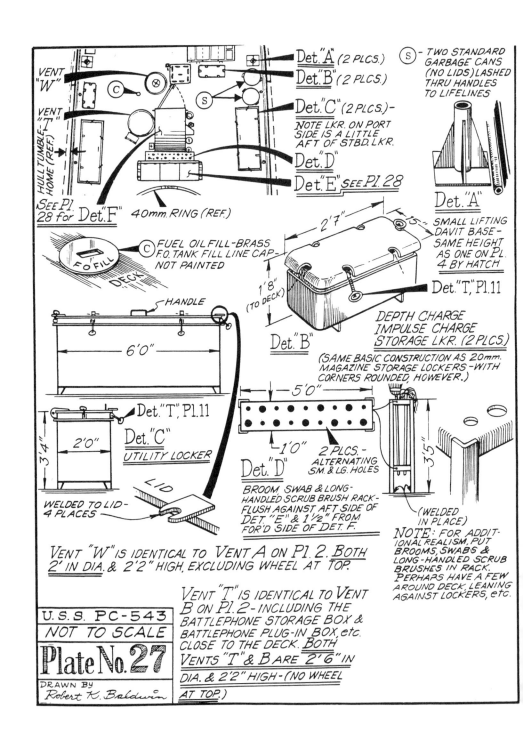

VENT "W"

VENT "T"

HULL TUMBLE-HOME (REF.)

(C)

(S)

Det. "A" (2 PLCS.)

Det. "B" (2 PLCS.)

Det. "C" (2 PLCS.) -
NOTE LKR. ON PORT SIDE IS A LITTLE AFT OF STBD. LKR.

Det. "D"

Det. "E" SEE Pl. 28

SEE Pl. 28 for Det. "F"

40mm. RING (REF.)

(S) - TWO STANDARD GARBAGE CANS (NO LIDS) LASHED THRU HANDLES TO LIFELINES

Det. "A"

SMALL LIFTING DAVIT BASE - SAME HEIGHT AS ONE ON Pl. 4 BY HATCH

(C) FUEL OIL FILL - BRASS F.O. TANK FILL LINE CAP - NOT PAINTED

F O FILL

DECK

2' 7"

1' 8" (TO DECK)

Det. "B"

Det. "T", Pl. 11

DEPTH CHARGE IMPULSE CHARGE STORAGE LKR. (2 PLCS.)

(SAME BASIC CONSTRUCTION AS 20mm. MAGAZINE STORAGE LOCKERS - WITH CORNERS ROUNDED, HOWEVER.)

HANDLE

6' 0"

Det. "T", Pl. 11

Det. "C"
UTILITY LOCKER

3' 4"

2' 0"

WELDED TO LID - 4 PLACES

LID

5' 0"

1' 0"

Det. "D"

2 PLCS. - ALTERNATING SM. & LG. HOLES

BROOM, SWAB & LONG-HANDLED SCRUB BRUSH RACK - FLUSH AGAINST AFT SIDE OF DET. "E" & 1½" FROM FOR'D SIDE OF DET. F.

3' 5"

(WELDED IN PLACE)

NOTE: FOR ADDITIONAL REALISM, PUT BROOMS, SWABS & LONG-HANDLED SCRUB BRUSHES IN RACK. PERHAPS HAVE A FEW AROUND DECK, LEANING AGAINST LOCKERS, etc.

VENT "W" IS IDENTICAL TO VENT A ON Pl. 2. BOTH 2' IN DIA. & 2' 2" HIGH, EXCLUDING WHEEL AT TOP.

VENT "T" IS IDENTICAL TO VENT B ON Pl. 2 - INCLUDING THE BATTLEPHONE STORAGE BOX & BATTLEPHONE PLUG-IN BOX, etc. CLOSE TO THE DECK. BOTH VENTS "T" & B ARE 2' 6" IN DIA. & 2' 2" HIGH - (NO WHEEL AT TOP.)

U.S.S. PC-543

NOT TO SCALE

Plate No. 27

DRAWN BY
Robert K. Baldwin

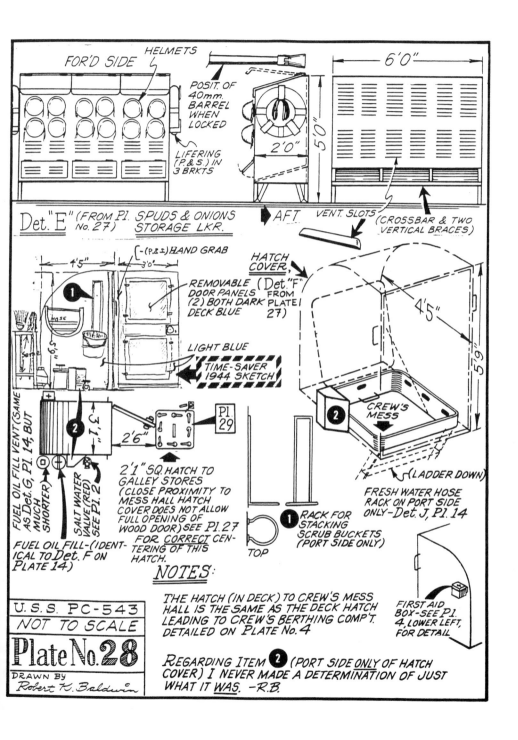

FOR'D SIDE

HELMETS

POSIT. OF 40mm. BARREL WHEN LOCKED

LIFERING (P.&S.) IN 3 BRKTS

2'0"

50"

6'0"

AFT

VENT. SLOTS (CROSSBAR & TWO VERTICAL BRACES)

Det. "E" (FROM Pl. No. 27) SPUDS & ONIONS STORAGE LKR.

—(P.&S.) HAND GRAB

4'5"

3'0"

1

HATCH COVER

REMOVABLE DOOR PANELS (2) BOTH DARK DECK BLUE

(Det. "F" FROM PLATE 27)

4'5"

5'9"

LIGHT BLUE

TIME-SAVER 1944 SKETCH

CREW'S MESS

2

5'9"

2

3'1"

2'6"

Pl. 29

(LADDER DOWN)

FUEL OIL FILL VENT (SAME AS Det. G, Pl. 14, BUT MUCH SHORTER)

SALT WATER VALVE (RED) SEE Pl. 2

2'1" SQ. HATCH TO GALLEY STORES (CLOSE PROXIMITY TO MESS HALL HATCH COVER DOES NOT ALLOW FULL OPENING OF WOOD DOOR) SEE Pl. 27 FOR CORRECT CEN- TERING OF THIS HATCH.

FRESH WATER HOSE RACK ON PORT SIDE ONLY–Det. J, Pl. 14

FUEL OIL FILL–(IDENT- ICAL TO Det. F ON PLATE 14)

TOP

1 RACK FOR STACKING SCRUB BUCKETS (PORT SIDE ONLY)

FIRST AID BOX–SEE Pl. 4, LOWER LEFT, FOR DETAIL.

NOTES:

THE HATCH (IN DECK) TO CREW'S MESS HALL IS THE SAME AS THE DECK HATCH LEADING TO CREW'S BERTHING COMP'T. DETAILED ON PLATE No. 4

U.S.S. PC-543

NOT TO SCALE

Plate No. 28

DRAWN BY Robert K. Baldwin

REGARDING ITEM **2** (PORT SIDE ONLY OF HATCH COVER) I NEVER MADE A DETERMINATION OF JUST WHAT IT WAS. –R.B.

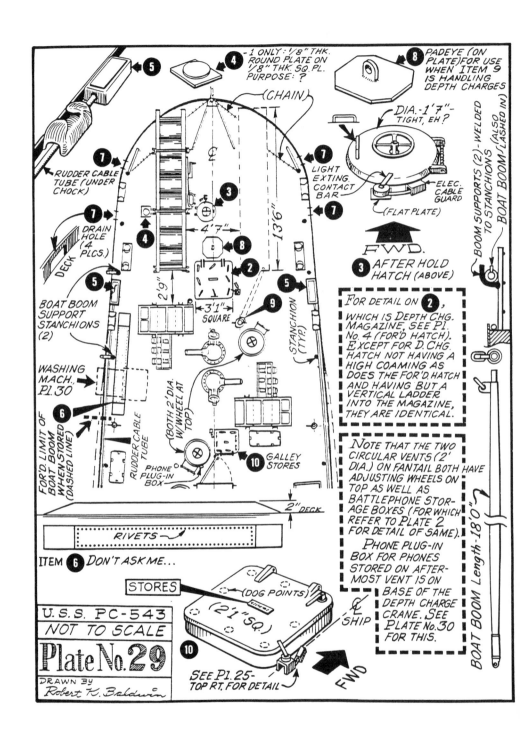

⑤

④ — 1 ONLY: 1/8" THK. ROUND PLATE ON 1/8" THK. SQ. PL. PURPOSE: ?

(CHAIN)

⑧ PADEYE (ON PLATE) FOR USE WHEN ITEM 9 IS HANDLING DEPTH CHARGES

DIA.-1'7"- TIGHT, EH?

⑦ RUDDER CABLE TUBE (UNDER CHOCK)

⑦

⑦ LIGHT EXTING. CONTACT BAR

⑦

ELEC. CABLE GUARD

(FLAT PLATE)

③

④

DRAIN HOLE (4 PLCS.)

DECK

4'7"

13'6"

⑧

FWD.

③ AFTER HOLD HATCH (ABOVE)

BOOM SUPPORTS (2) — WELDED TO STANCHIONS

BOAT BOOM (LASHED IN) (ALSO

⑤

BOAT BOOM SUPPORT STANCHIONS (2)

2'9"

②

3'1" SQUARE

⑤

⑨

STANCHION (TYP.)

FOR DETAIL ON **②**, WHICH IS DEPTH CHG. MAGAZINE, SEE PL. No. 4 (FOR'D HATCH). EXCEPT FOR D. CHG. HATCH NOT HAVING A HIGH COAMING AS DOES THE FOR'D. HATCH AND HAVING BUT A VERTICAL LADDER INTO THE MAGAZINE, THEY ARE IDENTICAL.

WASHING MACH. Pl. 30

⑥

FOR'D. LIMIT OF BOAT BOOM WHEN STORED (DASHED LINE)

(BOTH 2' DIA. W/ WHEEL AT TOP)

RUDDER CABLE TUBE

PHONE PLUG-IN BOX

⑩ GALLEY STORES

NOTE THAT THE TWO CIRCULAR VENTS (2' DIA.) ON FANTAIL BOTH HAVE ADJUSTING WHEELS ON TOP AS WELL AS BATTLEPHONE STORAGE BOXES (FOR WHICH REFER TO PLATE 2 FOR DETAIL OF SAME).

2" DECK

RIVETS

ITEM **⑥** DON'T ASK ME...

PHONE PLUG-IN BOX FOR PHONES STORED ON AFTERMOST VENT IS ON BASE OF THE DEPTH CHARGE CRANE. SEE PLATE No. 30 FOR THIS.

BOAT BOOM Length-18'0"

STORES

(DOG POINTS)

(2'1" SQ.)

⑩

SHIP

U.S.S. PC-543
NOT TO SCALE
Plate No. 29
DRAWN BY
Robert K. Baldwin

SEE Pl. 25- TOP RT. FOR DETAIL

FWD

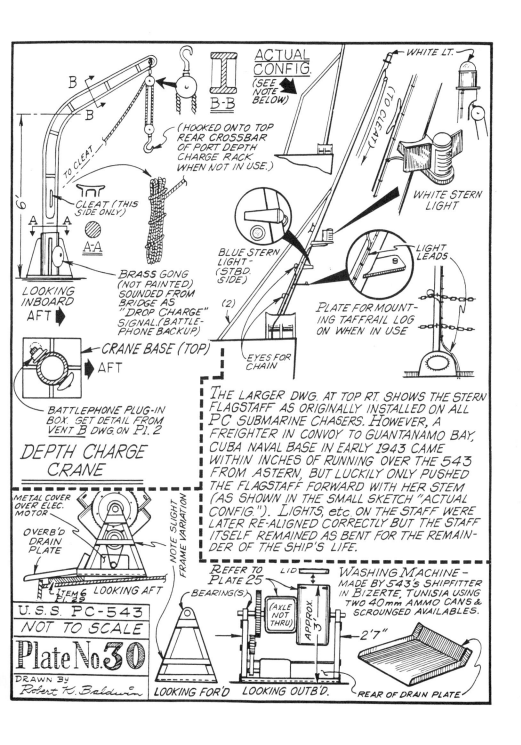

ACTUAL CONFIG. (SEE NOTE BELOW)

B-B

B B

WHITE LT.

(TO CLEAT)

WHITE STERN LIGHT

(HOOKED ONTO TOP REAR CROSSBAR OF PORT DEPTH CHARGE RACK WHEN NOT IN USE.)

TO CLEAT

CLEAT (THIS SIDE ONLY)

A A

A-A

6'

LOOKING INBOARD AFT

BRASS GONG (NOT PAINTED) SOUNDED FROM BRIDGE AS "DROP CHARGE" SIGNAL. (BATTLE-PHONE BACKUP)

BLUE STERN LIGHT - (STBD. SIDE) (2)

EYES FOR CHAIN

LIGHT LEADS

PLATE FOR MOUNT-ING TAFFRAIL LOG ON WHEN IN USE

CRANE BASE (TOP)

AFT

BATTLEPHONE PLUG-IN BOX. GET DETAIL FROM VENT B DWG. ON Pl. 2

DEPTH CHARGE CRANE

THE LARGER DWG. AT TOP RT. SHOWS THE STERN FLAGSTAFF AS ORIGINALLY INSTALLED ON ALL PC SUBMARINE CHASERS. HOWEVER, A FREIGHTER IN CONVOY TO GUANTANAMO BAY, CUBA NAVAL BASE IN EARLY 1943 CAME WITHIN INCHES OF RUNNING OVER THE 543 FROM ASTERN, BUT LUCKILY ONLY PUSHED THE FLAGSTAFF FORWARD WITH HER STEM (AS SHOWN IN THE SMALL SKETCH "ACTUAL CONFIG."). LIGHTS, etc. ON THE STAFF WERE LATER RE-ALIGNED CORRECTLY BUT THE STAFF ITSELF REMAINED AS BENT FOR THE REMAIN-DER OF THE SHIP'S LIFE.

METAL COVER OVER ELEC. MOTOR

OVERB'D DRAIN PLATE

NOTE SLIGHT FRAME VARIATION

ITEM 6 Pl. 29 LOOKING AFT

U.S.S. PC-543

NOT TO SCALE

Plate No. 30

DRAWN BY
Robert K. Baldwin

REFER TO PLATE 25

LID

BEARING(S)

(AXLE NOT THRU)

APPROX. 3'

WASHING MACHINE - MADE BY 543'S SHIPFITTER IN BIZERTE, TUNISIA USING TWO 40mm AMMO CANS & SCROUNGED AVAILABLES.

2'7"

LOOKING FOR'D

LOOKING OUTB'D

REAR OF DRAIN PLATE

APPENDIX C

Sixteen Shipyards that Built World War II PCs

The following sixteen shipyards built PCs during World War II.

Albina Engine and Machinery Works, Inc., Portland, Oregon
Brown Ship Building Co., Houston, Texas
Commercial Iron Works, Portland, Oregon
Consolidated Ship Building Corp., New York, New York
Defoe Shipbuilding Company, Bay City, Michigan
       (Formerly the Defoe Boat and Motor Co.)
Dravo Corp., Pittsburgh, Pennsylvania
Dravo Corp., Neville Island, Pennsylvania
Gibbs Gas Engine Co., Jacksonville, Florida
Jacobson Shipyard, Inc., Oyster Bay, Long Island, New York
Jeffersonville Boat and Machinery Co., Jeffersonville, Indiana
George Lawley, and Sons, Neponset, Massachusetts
Luders Marine Construction Co., Stamford, Connecticut
Nashville Bridge Co., Nashville, Tennessee
Penn-Jersey Ship Building Corp., Camden, New Jersey
Leathem D. Smith Coal and Ship Building Co., Sturgeon Bay, Wisconsin
Sullivan Dry Dock and Repair Co., Brooklyn, New York.

APPENDIX D

PCs Built at Sixteen Shipyards During World War II

This Appendix includes Tables D-1 through D-16 that include the significant dates for each ship.

The "keel laid" dates are actually beginning of construction because the keel came last on the hull. See Chapter 3.

Table D-1: PCs Built at the Albina Engine and Machinery Works

PC Number	Keel Laid	Launched	Commissioned	Deactivated	Disposition
569	9/11/41	1/22/42	5/9/42	6/14/61	Sold
570	9/11/41	1/5/42	4/18/42	12/52	Thailand
571	9/27/41	2/12/42	5/26/42	5/9/60	Sold
572	9/27/41	2/28/42	6/19/42	1/61	Venezuela
578	12/20/41	4/29/42	7/15/42	4/14/48	Sold
579	1/5/42	4/29/42	8/25/42	5/31/61	Sold
580	1/22/42	4/29/42	9/26/42	3/60	Indonesia
581	2/12/42	7/8/42	10/9/42	3/60	Indonesia
582	2/21/42	7/15/42	10/22/42	6/62	Venezuela
815	10/10/42	12/5/42	4/20/43	9/28/45	Sunk by collision
816	12/5/42	1/8/43	6/9/43	7/1/48	Maritime Commission
817	1/8/43	3/4/43	7/13/43	12/14/59	Sold
818	3/4/43	3/30/43	8/3/43	6/7/48	Maritime Commission
819	3/30/43	5/19/43	8/28/43	6/8/48	Maritime Commission
820	5/19/43	8/2/43	9/30/43	7/48	Mexico
1077	2/18/42	7/29/42	12/14/42	1/61	Venezuela
1078	4/29/42	8/8/42	2/5/43	5/54	China
1079	4/29/42	8/25/42	3/7/43	3/31/61	Sold

1080	4/29/42	8/27/42	3/29/43	1/16/47	Sold
1081	7/29/42	8/29/42	4/16/43	4/25/61	Sold
1082	8/29/42	10/10/42	5/8/43	11/13/46	Sold
Total = 21					

Table D-2: PCs Built at the Brown shipbuilding Co.

PC Number	Keel Laid	Launched	Commissioned	Deactivated	Disposition
565	8/14/41	2/27/42	5/25/42	6/62	Venezuela
566	8/14/41	3/21/42	6/15/42	1/61	Venezuela
567	9/15/41	4/11/42	6/27/42	1963	Air force
568	9/15/41	4/25/42	7/13/42	3/68	Philippines
608	1/8/42	5/16/42	8/18/42	7/48	Mexico
609	1/8/42	5/30/42	9/7/42	5/47	Thailand
610	2/24/42	6/19/42	9/28/42	6/7/50	Destroyed
611	2/24/42	6/29/42	10/26/42	7/1/48	Maritime Commission
1251	6/8/42	9/12/42	2/27/43	5/18/61	Sold
1252	6/8/42	9/30/42	3/27/43	1/61	Venezuela
1253	6/11/42	10/14/42	4/1/43	6/52	Thailand
1254	6/22/42	10/31/42	4/13/43	5/54	Taiwan
Total = 12					

Table D-3: PCs Built at the Commercial Iron Works

PC Number	Keel Laid	Launched	Commissioned	Deactivated	Disposition
596	4/18/42	8/8/42	1/23/43	11/1146	Sold
597	5/9/42	9/7/42	2/15/43	1957	Disposed of
598	5/23/42	9/7/42	3/5/43	11/29/46	Sold
599	8/2/42	9/26/42	5/15/43	4/14/48	Maritime Commission
776	8/10/42	10/27/42	3/28/43	8/59	Sold
777	9/7/42	11/11/42	4/8/43	8/59	Sold
778	9/7/42	11/26/42	4/30/43	4/1/59	Disposed of
779	9/26/42	12/7/42	5/31/43	4/1/59	Disposed of
780	10/27/42	12/16/42	6/19/43	4/1/59	Disposed of
781	11/11/42	12/24/42	6/19/43	4/1/59	Disposed of
782	11/26/42	12/31/42	7/19/43	4/1/59	Disposed of
783	12/7/42	1/13/43	8/14/43	6/16/48	Maritime Commission
784	12/16/42	1/18/43	9/17/43	3/17/48	Maritime Commission
785	12/24/42	1/23/43	10/9/43	4/1/59	Disposed of
786	12/31/42	2/6/43	10/30/43	7/54	China
787	1/13/43	2/12/43	11/13/43	6/7/48	Indonesia
788	1/18/43	3/5/43	2/15/44	7/8/48	Maritime Commission
789	1/23/43	3/13/43	3/6/44	7/14/48	Maritime Commission
790	2/6/43	3/22/43	3/ /44	6/7/48	Cuba
791	3/13/43	4/17/43	3/28/44	6/7/48	Maritime Commission

792	3/22/43	4/24/43	4/10/44	7/1/48	Maritime Commission
793	4/17/43	5/22/43	5/10/44	7/1/48	Maritime Commission
794	4/24/43	5/29/43	5/25/44	6/48	Mexico
795	5/22/43	7/24/43	6/10/44	6/7/48	Maritime Commission
796	5/29/43	7/3/43	6/19/44	6/48	France
797	7/17/43	8/21/43	7/5/44	7/48	France
798	7/3/43	8/14/43	7/19/44	6/48	France
799	7/24/43	8/14/43	8/3/44	7/48	Korea
800	7/31/43	8/28/43	9/23/44	4/19/48	Maritime Commission
801	8/21/43	9/18/43	12/20/44	7/1/48	Maritime Commission
802	8/14/43	9/25/43	1/6/45	7/48	Korea
803	8/16/43	10/2/43	1/23/45	7/1/48	Maritime Commission
804	8/28/43	10/16/43	1/6/45	7/14/48	Maritime Commission
805	9/18/43	10/27/43	11/29/44	2/13/48	Foreign Liquidation Commission
806	9/27/43	10/30/43	12/13/44	2/13/48	Foreign Liquidation Commission
807	10/2/43	11/6/43	2/20/45	7/2/48	Maritime Commission
808	10/16/43	11/27/43	11/7/45	8/59	Sold
809	10/27/43	12/4/43	3/20/45	3/48	Portugal
810	10/30/43	12/11/43	4/3/45	7/48	Mexico
811	11/6/43	12/18/43	4/17/45	3/48	Portugal
812	11/27/43	2/11/44	5/ /45	3/48	Portugal

813	12/11/43	3/27/44	5/ /45	6/48	Mexico
814	2/11/44	5/13/44	6/5/45	12/12/45	Destroyed
1586	7/31/41	2/21/42	7/28/42	3/18/49	Maritime Commission
1587	8/18/42	3/12/42	8/15/42	3/18/49	Maritime Commission
1588	12/3/41	4/6/42	9/2/42	5/6/48	Maritime Commission
1589	1/28/42	4/18/42	9/5/42	12/3/47	War Assets Administration
1590	2/21/42	5/9/42	9/21/42	9/17/54	Struck from the Naval Register
1591	3/12/42	5/23/42	10/10/42	3/18/48	Maritime Commission
1592	4/6/42	6/20/42	10/27/42	12/19/47	War Assets Administration
Total = 50					

Table D-4: PCs Built at the Consolidated Ship Building Corp.

PC Number	Keel Laid	Launched	Commissioned	Deactivated	Disposition
483	12/31/40	10/25/41	3/12/42	4/61	Venezuela
484	4/7/41	12/6/41	4/3/42	4/61	Venezuela
485	5/1/41	12/20/41	4/23/42	1/52	Korea
486	10/25/41	1/25/42	5/14/42	12/14/59	Sold
487	12/6/41	2/28/42	6/2/42	7/61	Venezuela
563	12/20/41	3/17/42	6/17/42	11/29/46	Sold
564	1/25/42	4/12/42	7/2/42	1/64	Korea
600	2/28/42	5/9/42	8/18/42	1/52	Korea
601	3/17/42	5/23/42	9/1/42	3/13/61	Sold
602	4/12/42	6/13/42	9/16/42	3/13/61	Sold
603	5/9/42	6/30/42	10/1/42	5/31/61	Sold
1191	5/23/42	7/25/42	11/2/42	4/1/59	Disposed of
1192	6/13/42	8/8/42	11/26/42	6/18/48	Maritime Commission
1193	6/30/42	8/29/42	1/21/43	4/1/59	Disposed of
1194	7/25/42	9/19/42	2/8/43	6/21/48	Maritime Commission
1195	8/28/42	10/3/42	3/23/43	6/7/48	Maritime Commission
1196	8/29/42	10/24/42	4/7/43	4/1/59	Disposed of
1197	9/19/42	11/14/42	4/22/43	6/21/48	Maritime Commission
1198	10/3/42	12/12/42	5/3/43	4/1/59	Disposed of
1199	10/24/42	1/2/43	5/17/43	6/18/48	Maritime Commission

1200	11/16/42	1/23/43	5/29/43	10/21/49	Destroyed
1201	12/12/42	2/14/43	6/11/43	4/1/59	Disposed of
1202	1/2/43	2/27/43	6/23/43	12/47	Dominican Republic
1203	1/23/43	3/14/43	7/ /43	11/4/49	Destroyed
1204	2/27/43	4/14/43	8/6/43	6/18/48	Maritime Commission
1205	3/14/43	4/29/43	8/26/43	7/1/48	Maritime Commission
1206	6/9/43	7/21/43	10/27/43	7/7/48	Maritime Commission
1207	6/26/43	8/18/43	11/12/43	6/23/48	Maritime Commission
1208	7/21/43	9/15/43	11/25/43	7/54	China
1209	8/18/43	10/7/43	5/1/44	4/1/59	Disposed of
1210	9/15/43	10/30/43	5/5/44	6/48	Mexico
1237	2/14/43	4/3/43	7/26/43	12/14/59	Sold
1238	4/3/43	5/15/43	9/6/43	5/47	Foreign Liquidation Commission
1239	4/14/43	6/9/43	9/27/43	2/5/46	Destroyed
1240	5/15/43	6/26/43	10/13/43	12/14/59	Sold
1264	10/7/43	11/28/43	4/25/44	3/24/48	Maritime Commission
1265	10/30/43	12/19/43	5/12/44	12/3/46	Maritime Commission
1546	11/28/43	1/30/44	6/5/44	11/60	Korea
1547	12/4/43	2/8/44	7/7/44	1957	Disposed of
1548	12/19/43	2/13/44	7/1/44	12/27/45	Destroyed
1549	1/30/44	12/9/44	7/25/44	6/30/48	China

1550	2/13/44	4/11/44	12/1/44	6/16/49	Foreign Liquidation Commission
1551	3/12/44	5/7/44	12/2/44	6/30/48	China
1552	4/11/44	5/25/44	11/22/44	11/24/47	Greece
1553	5/7/44	6/25/44	12/23/44	11/24/47	Greece
1554	5/25/44	7/16/44	12/5/44	12/2/47	War Assets Admin.
1555	7/25/44	8/13/44	1/18/45	12/2/47	War Assets Admin.
1556	7/16/44	9/6/44	2/3/45	12/11/47	Greece
1557	8/13/44	9/25/44	2/24/45	6/30/48	China
1558	9/6/44	10/28/44	3/19/45	12/24/45	Destroyed
1559	9/25/44	11/19/44	4/9/45	12/8/47	Greece
Total = 51					

Table D-5: PCs Built at the Defoe Shipbuilding Company

PC Number	Keel Laid	Launched	Commissioned	Deactivated	Disposition
451	9/25/39	5/23/40	8/12/40	12/5/46	Maritime Commission
452	3/14/40	8/23/41	7/26/43	1/27/47	Maritime Commission
471	4/21/41	9/15/41	11/3/41	6/9/44	France
472	7/1/41	11/14/41	12/9/41	6/30/44	France
473	8/18/41	11/19/41	12/9/41	7/7/44	France
474	8/20/41	12/5/41	2/11/42	6/1/44	France
475	9/11/41	12/16/41	2/7/42	6/23/44	France
476	10/2/41	1/1/42	3/18/42	7/1/48	Maritime Commission
477	11/21/41	1/29/42	3/30/42	1/17/47	Sold
478	12/17/41	2/20/42	4/1/42	11/14/46	Sold
479	1/14/41	3/10/42	4/30/42	12/5/46	Maritime Commission
480	1/22/42	3/25/42	4/30/42	7/21/44	France
481	2/3/42	3/31/42	4/30/42	6/16/44	France
482	2/16/42	4/9/42	5/23/42	7/15/44	France
542	2/26/42	4/20/42	5/25/42	9/30/44	France
543	3/11/42	4/24/42	5/30/42	6/8/44	France
544	3/24/42	4/30/42	6/6/42	9/24/42	Brazil
545	3/31/42	5/8/42	6/27/42	10/17/44	France
546	4/9/42	5/14/42	7/8/42	10/3/44	France
547	4/16/42	5/22/42	1942	9/24/42	Brazil
548	4/24/42	5/29/42	8/2/42	4/19/48	Maritime Commission

549	5/1/42	6/6/42	8/2/42	4/23/48	Maritime Commission
583	5/8/42	6/12/42	9/2/42	7/9/48	Maritime Commission
584	5/14/42	6/18/42	8/22/42	12/14/45	Destroyed
585	5/22/42	7/8/42	9/6/42	7/9/48	Maritime Commission
586	5/29/42	7/15/42	10/5/42	9/1/59	Sold
587	6/5/42	8/1/42	9/19/42	4/12/48	Maritime Commission
1119	6/12/42	8/18/42	12/18/42	1957	Disposed of
1120	6/19/42	8/24/42	12/18/42	1/25/60	Sold
1121	6/30/42	8/27/43	12/10/42	7/2/48	Philippines
1122	7/11/42	9/7/42	1/1/43	7/2/48	Philippines
1123	7/22/42	9/7/42	2/5/43	8/27/47	Foreign Liquidation Commission
1124	8/4/42	10/1/42	5/24/43	10/17/45	Destroyed
1125	8/20/42	10/15/42	5/26/43	12/14/59	Sold
1126	8/29/42	10/31/42	5/27/43	12/24/45	Destroyed
1127	9/7/42	11/2/42	5/29/43	7/1/48	Maritime Commission
1128	9/14/42	11/19/42	5/31/43	3/9/46	Destroyed
1129	9/23/42	12/7/42	6/3/43	1/31/45	Sunk by Japanese suicide Boat
1130	10/8/42	12/10/42	6/19/43	9/28/50	Indochina, then Viet Nam
1131	10/22/42	12/17/42	7/28/43	7/2/48	Philippines
1132	11/5/42	12/29/42	8/10/43	5/20/48	Destroyed
1133	11/25/42	1/9/43	8/24/43	7/2/48	Philippines
1134	12/4/42	1/18/43	9/11/43	7/2/48	Philippines
1135	12/11/42	2/3/43	10/7/43	1/60	Sold

1136	12/17/42	3/5/43	11/16/43	3/60	Sold
1137	12/29/42	3/29/43	11/18/43	3/60	Sold
1138	1/9/43	4/19/43	9/17/43	3/60	Sold
1139	1/25/43	5/10/43	11/18/43	9/28/50	Indochina
1140	2/8/43	6/14/43	1/22/44	3/13/61	Sold
1141	3/12/43	6/22/43	12/28/43	10/58	Indonesia
1142	3/31/43	8/20/43	6/3/44	7/57	China
1143	4/17/43	9/25/43	5/16/44	3/2/51	Indochina, then Viet Nam
1144	5/7/43	10/4/43	5/20/44	3/2/51	Indochina, then Viet Nam
1145	6/2/43	10/27/43	6/1/44	11/60	Korea
1146	9/21/43	11/21/43	7/13/44	3/2/51	Indochina, then Viet Nam
1147	10/11/43	12/2/43	8/12/44	4/30/48	Foreign Liquidation Commission
1148	10/25/43	12/19/43	10/25/44	11/24/47	Greece
1149	11/6/43	1/11/44	6/22/44	7/57	China
Total = 58					

Table D-6: PCs Built at the Dravo Corp., Pittsburgh, Pennsylvania

PC Number	Keel Laid	Launched	Commissioned	Deactivated	Disposition
490	5/9/41	10/18/41	5/12/42	8/27/48	China
491	5/9/41	12/6/41	4/13/42	2/13/48	Foreign Liquidation Commission
492	6/25/41	12/29/41	5/5/42	6/30/48	China
493	8/9/41	1/24/42	5/28/42	5/10/47	Foreign Liquidation Commission
494	8/9/41	1/24/42	5/23/42	2/11/48	Foreign Liquidation Comm
495	6/10/41	12/30/41	4/23/42	12/52	Thailand
573	10/14/41	3/5/42	6/13/42	6/23/48	Maritime Commission
574	12/30/41	3/30/42	7/2/42	11/6/46	Sold
575	2/24/42	5/5/42	8/8/42	3/47	Thailand
576	4/3/42	6/13/42	9/10/42	7/21/48	Maritime Commission
577	5/6/42	7/25/42	10/15/42	11/12/48	Destroyed in tests
592	3/31/42	6/27/42	11/28/42	9/1/59	Sold
593	4/21/42	8/22/42	12/26/42	8/27/48	China
594	5/1/42	9/7/42	3/9/43	12/3/47	Disposed of
595	5/19/42	10/9/42	4/30/43	6/30/48	China
Total = 15					

Table D-7: PCs Built at the Dravo Corp., Neville Island, Pennsylvania

PC Number	Keel Laid	Launched	Commissioned	Deactivated	Disposition
1593	11/24/42	3/28/42	8/31/42	9/16/46	Maritime Commission
1594	12/26/41	4/25/42	8/31/42	7/29/46	Maritime Commission
1595	1/16/42	5/26/42	9/15/42	10/21/46	Maritime Commission
1596	1/31/42	6/12/42	10/1/42	7/30/46	Maritime Commission
1597	2/26/42	7/11/42	10/22/42	11/8/46	Dominican Republic
Total =5					

Table D-8: PCs Built at the Gibbs Gas Engine Co.

PC Number	Keel Laid	Launched	Commissioned	Deactivated	Disposition
612	6/30/42	9/7/42	5/1/43	3/25/48	Maritime Commission
613	7/7/42	10/27/42	6/2/43	12/10/47	Dominican Republic
614	7/7/42	12/23/42	7/9/43	3/17/48	Mexico
615	7/7/42	2/17/43	7/16/43	6/21/48	Maritime Commission
1181	10/5/42	4/15/43	9/17/43	4/1/59	Disposed of
1182	10/9/42	6/14/43	10/27/43	7/54	China
1183	10/27/42	7/7/43	12/7/43	6/48	Indonesia
1184	1/8/43	8/4/43	1/24/44	6/12/48	Maritime Commission
1185	3/26/43	8/27/43	4/24/44	6/48	Thailand
1186	4/20/43	9/27/43	6/9/44	4/1/59	Disposed of
1187	6/18/43	11/26/43	7/18/44	7/1/48	Maritime Commission
1188	7/12/43	1/31/44	9/5/44	3/24/48	Maritime Commission
1189	8/10/43	4/14/44	11/24/44	10/24/45	Destroyed
1190	9/1/43	6/29/44	2/6/45	6/10/48	Maritime Commission
Total = 14					

Table D-9: PCs Built at the Jacobson Shipyard Inc.

PC Number	Keel Laid	Launched	Commissioned	Deactivated	Disposition
1598	12/19/41	5/10/42	12/11/42	6/11/47	Maritime Commission
1599	5/11/42	9/7/42	2/5/43	3/18/48	Maritime Commission
Total = 2					

Table D-10: PCs Built at the Jeffersonville Boat and Machinery Co.

PC Number	Keel Laid	Launched	Commissioned	Deactivated	Disposition
559	10/14/41	2/12/42	5/21/42	10/6/44	France
560	11/25/41	3/17/42	6/17/42	1957	Disposed of
561	1/30/42	5/1/42	7/11/42	11/30/43	Brazil
562	2/13/42	6/4/42	8/ /42	6/30/44	France
624	3/19/42	7/4/42	11/20/43	11/22/44	France, disposed of 1949
625	5/2/42	7/22/42	1942	10/16/44	France
626	6/5/42	8/18/42	9/26/42	11/11/44	France
627	7/6/42	9/7/42	11/5/42	10/28/44	France
Total = 8					

Table D-11: PCs Built by George Lawley, and Sons

PC Number	Keel Laid	Launched	Commissioned	Deactivated	Disposition
461	7/10/41	12/23/41	3/19/42	1957	Disposed of
462	7/22/41	1/24/42	4/15/42	2/20/47	Maritime Commission
463	8/1/41	2/27/42	4/29/42	7/53	Sunk as a target
464	8/8/41	2/27/42	5/15/42	1/12/47	Sold
465	8/19/41	3/28/42	5/25/42	4/61	Venezuela
466	9/1/41	4/29/42	6/3/42	3/13/61	Sold
467	10/22/41	4/29/42	6/20/42	9/16/42	Norway
468	1/1/42	5/30/42	7/10/42	8/6/42	Netherlands
469	1/30/42	6/10/42	7/13/42	6/49	Sunk as a target
470	2/27/42	6/27/42	7/31/42	3/13/61	Sold
616	2/27/42	7/4/42	8/19/42	6/4/42	Thailand
617	3/29/42	7/18/42	8/28/42	1957	disposed of
618	4/29/42	8/1/42	9/7/42	11/1/65	Struck from the Naval Register
619	4/29/42	8/15/42	9/16/42	7/61	Venezuela
1083	8/15/42	9/7/42	8/16/43	12/19/46	Maritime Commission
1084	9/7/42	10/31/42	8/31/43	8/19/46	Maritime Commission

1085	1/6/43	3/27/43	10/19/43	12/10/46	Maritime Commission
1086	2/13/43	4/24/43	1/19/44	3/2/51	Indochina, then Cambodia
1087	4/12/43	8/21/43	5/22/44	7/57	China
1088	8/31/43	1/18/45	4/24/45	6/30/48	China
1089	1/19/45	4/12/45	6/14/45	6/30/48	China
1090	4/12/45	6/15/45	8/9/45	6/30/48	China
1091	6/15/45	7/31/45	10/11/45	6/30/48	China
Total = 23					

Table D-12: Dates for PCs Built at the Luders Marine Construction Co.

PC Number	Keel Laid	Launched	Commissioned	Deactivated	Disposition
556	10/1/41	6/23/42	9/1/42	10/19/44	France
557	10/31/41	8/2/42	9/17/42	10/27/44	France
558	10/31/41	9/13/42	11/ /42	5/9/44	Sunk by Torpedo
604	2/16/42	10/24/42	3/10/43	6/11/43	Brazil
605	3/20/42	11/19/42	5/3/43	6/11/43	Brazil
606	4/14/42	1/8/43	8/7/43	1957	Disposed of
607	7/1/42	2/11/43	8/27/43	10/19/43	Brazil
1211	8/11/42	3/12/43	8/16/43	10/16/46	Maritime Commission
1212	9/26/42	4/23/43	9/18/43	4/1/59	Disposed of
1213	11/7/42	5/22/43	10/6/43	4/1/59	Disposed of
1214	2/22/43	6/28/43	10/28/43	4/12/51	Destroyed
1215	3/22/43	7/29/43	11/26/43	6/28/48	Maritime Commission
1216	4/29/43	8/29/43	12/31/43	4/1/59	Disposed of
1217	5/26/43	9/26/43	4/27/44	3/24/48	Maritime Commission
1218	7/2/43	10/24/43	5/29/44	6/48	Thailand
1219	8/2/43	11/21/43	7/1/44	4/5/48	Maritime Commission
1220	9/7/43	12/22/43	7/29/44	6/8/48	Maritime Commission
1255	9/29/43	1/23/44	/ /44	4/7/45	Sunk by Mine
1256	10/28/43	5/21/44	10/27/44	3/48	Portugal
1257	11/24/43	7/23/44	12/21/44	3/48	Portugal
1258	28/43	9/23/44	1/24/45	6/21/48	Maritime Commission
1259	1/28/44	10/7/44	3/6/45	3/48	Portugal
Total = 22					

Table D-13: PCs Built at the Nashville Bridge Co.

PC Number	Keel Laid	Launched	Commissioned	Deactivated	Disposition
620	2/27/42	8/12/42	1/8/43	1957	Disposed of
621	3/4/42	5/22/42	12/4/42	10/31/44	France
622	5/22/42	9/7/42	3/9/43	6/10/44	Greece
623	6/23/42	9/24/42	4/10/43	11/26/46	Sold
1241	9/4/42	12/24/42	5/28/43	7/2/48	Philippines
1242	9/22/42	1/25/43	7/12/43	5/60	Sold
1243	12/9/42	3/15/43	9/12/43	8/27/47	Foreign Liquidation Commission
1244	1/20/43	5/8/43	10/5/43	5/19/61	Sold
1245	3/9/43	5/29/43	10/30/43	2/48	France
1246	5/4/43	7/3/43	11/29/43	1957	Disposed of
1247	5/28/43	8/7/43	12/20/43	9/48	China
1248	6/29/43	9/18/43	43	1/18/44	France
1249	8/4/43	11/6/43	44	2/9/44	France
1250	9/14/43	12/18/43	44	3/9/44	France
1600	10/15/41	2/28/42	9/9/42	6/15/48	Maritime Commission
1601	10/18/41	3/5/42	10/12/42	6/15/48	Maritime Commission
Total = 16					

Table D-14: PCs Built at the Penn-Jersey Ship Building Corp.

PC Number	Keel Laid	Launched	Commissioned	Deactivated	Disposition
1221	5/29/42	8/29/43	4/19/44	7/28/48	Maritime Commission
1222	10/26/42	9/25/43	7/7/44	6/22/47	Maritime Commission
1223	9/26/43	1/9/44	11/13/44	11/26/46	Sold
1224	8/31/43	7/9/44	1/8/45	6/48	Mexico
1602	10/21/41	5/29/42	4/10/43	6/15/48	Maritime Commission
1603	11/19/41	9/7/42	6/16/43	10/24/45	Destroyed
Total = 6					

Table D-15: PCs Built at the Leathem D. Smith Coal and Ship Building Co.

PC Number	Keel Laid	Launched	Commissioned	Deactivated	Disposition
496	4/24/41	11/22/41	2/26/42	6/4/43	Sunk by a mine
550	6/6/41	3/8/42	5/5/42	6/13/44	France
551	7/22/41	4/12/42	5/19/42	10/19/43	France
588	11/22/41	5/3/42	6/22/42	3/11/60	Sold
589	3/9/42	6/7/42	7/23/42	3/60	Sold
590	4/14/42	7/4/42	10/5/42	2/23/46	Destroyed
591	5/8/42	8/2/42	10/26/42	10/18/44	France
821	9/1/43	10/23/43	6/23/44	6/7/48	Maritime Commission
822	10/26/43	12/27/43	6/2/44	12/14/59	Sold
823	11/8/43	1/15/44	7/24/44	2/11/46	Maritime Commission
824	3/6/44	5/10/44	8/28/44	6/8/48	Maritime Commission
825	3/27/44	5/28/44	9/20/44	6/8/48	Maritime Commission
1171	3/12/43	5/15/43	9/24/43	3/4/51	Indochina, then Cambodia
1172	3/29/43	6/5/43	10/6/43	1960	Disposed of
1173	4/21/43	6/26/43	11/1/43	1970	Disposed of
1174	5/18/43	7/22/43	11/5/43	1957	Disposed of
1175	6/8/43	8/7/43	12/1/43	7/15/57	China
1176	6/28/43	8/28/43	11/20/43	6/62	Venezuela

1177	7/24/43	9/18/43	12/20/43	1960	Disposed of
1178	8/11/43	10/2/43	1/22/44	11/1/59	Disposed of
1179	9/20/43	11/6/43	1/22/44	1960	Disposed of
1180	10/5/43	11/27/43	2/10/44	1960	Disposed of
1225	6/10/42	9/7/42	1/12/43	1957	Disposed of
1226	7/7/42	9/7/42	2/12/43	11/6/44	France
1227	8/5/42	10/17/42	2/23/43	11/18/44	France
1228	9/7/42	11/18/42	5/21/43	1957	Disposed of
1229	9/7/42	12/19/42	6/11/43	1957	Disposed of
1230	12/20/42	3/10/43	7/15/43	1/25/60	Sold
1260	10/20/42	1/16/43	4/24/43	5/9/60	Sold
1261	11/20/42	2/28/43	1943	6/6/44	Sunk by shell fire
1262	1/21/43	3/27/43	6/29/43	6/54	Taiwan
1263	3/2/43	4/19/43	7/28/43	7/59	Taiwan
1560	11/29/43	2/3/44	1944	4/15/44	France
1561	12/28/43	2/23/44	1944	6/5/44	France
1562	1/17/44	3/4/44	1944	6/5/44	France
1563	2/4/44	3/24/44	6/29/44	7/2/48	Philippines
1564	2/24/44	4/19/44	8/4/44	7/2/48	Philippines
1565	5/11/44	7/16/44	11/29/44	12/11/47	Greece
1566	5/29/44	8/12/44	12/27/44	4/7/47	Maritime Commission
1567	7/18/44	9/23/44	1/17/45	7/50	China
1568	8/14/44	10/14/44	2/9/45	10/27/47	Disposed of
1569	9/26/44	12/9/44	3/14/45	11/60	South Viet Nam
Total = 42					

Table D-16: PCs Built at the Sullivan Dry Dock and Repair Co.

PC Number	Keel Laid	Launched	Commissioned	Deactivated	Disposition
488	3/7/41	12/20/41	8/12/42	3/13/46	Sold
489	3/17/41	12/20/41	7/14/42	11/5/48	Maritime Commission
552	5/20/41	2/13/42	7/29/42	12/5/46	Maritime Commission
553	12/20/41	5/30/42	10/12/42	1957	Disposed of
554	12/20/41	5/2/42	9/2/42	10/29/43	Brazil
555	2/13/42	5/30/42	2/6/43	2/12/47	Sold
1167	4/3/43	7/3/43	12/3/43	3/2/51	Indochina, then Viet Nam
1168	4/3/43	7/3/43	12/31/43	5/54	China
1169	7/3/43	10/16/43	1/26/44	7/57	China
1170	7/3/43	10/16/43	2/21/44	1960	Disposed of
1231	9/1/42	12/12/42	7/13/43	5/31/61	Sold
1232	9/8/42	12/12/42	8/18/43	6/54	Taiwan
1233	9/21/43	1/11/43	9/24/43	7/54	Taiwan
1234	12/12/42	4/3/43	43	5/2/44	Uruguay
1235	12/12/42	4/3/43	43	10/26/44	France
1236	1/11/43	4/24/43	43	11/15/43	Brazil
Total = 16					

APPENDIX E: Construction Program, PC 451 Through PC 1603 – Table E-1, Page 1 of 2.

Number of PCs	Mann	Friedman	Baker	Fahey	Turner	Elliott	Silverstone
PC Hull Numbers Originally Identified for World War II Ships and Used, reclassified, or Canceled	1142						
PCs Ordered		618	405	369	419	399	
PCs Canceled	60	60	60	60	60	45	143
PC Hull Numbers Reclassified as SC[1]	481	480					
PC Hull Numbers Reclassified as PCE[2]	150	150					
PC Hull Numbers Reclassified as PCS[3]	90	90					
Ships Built on PC Hulls during World War II	361			362			
PCs Built					359	354	317
Ships Converted from PC to PGM and Commissioned as PGM	24	24	24	24	24	24	24
Ships Converted from PC to AM and Commissioned as AM	18	18		18		18	18
PC Hulls Initially Commissioned as PCs[4]	319			320		286	
Ships Reconverted from AM to PC	16	16				18	
Ships Reconverted from AM to PC then to PCC	2	2					
Ships Converted from PC to PCC but Commissioned as PC	32	35*			35	36	35
Ships Reconverted from PCC to PC	16						
Ships commissioned as PC but converted from PC to Auxiliary[5]	3					2	
PCs Delivered on Lend-Lease		46	46		44	44	
PCs Transferred to Other Countries During WW II[6]	45						42
PCs Transferred to Other Countries After WW II	110	111					

**APPENDIX E: Construction Program, PC 451 Through PC 1603
Table E-1, Page 2 of 2.**

1. 33 SCs were canceled
2. 82 PCEs were canceled
3. 30 PCSs were canceled
4. Friedman does not give commissioning dates
5. PC 624 to YW-120, PC 1124 to IX-206 (*Choucura*), PC 488 to IX-221 (*Eureka*)
6. This number includes PC 624 as YW-120
* This number includes AM 1599, AM 1601 and PC 466 (not shown as a PCC by Mann)

Mann, Earl, "Dictionary of American Naval Fighting Ships, Volume VI," Rough Draft, private communication from CDR Earl Mann, 4 January 1971.

Friedman, Norman, *U.S. Small Combatants*, (Naval Institute Press, Annapolis, Maryland, 1987).

Baker, A. D., III, "Historic Fleets," Naval History, Page 62, U. S. Naval Institute, December 1995.

Fahey, James C., *Ships and Aircraft of the United States Fleet* (Ships and Aircraft, New York, 1945).

Turner, *Patrol Craft Sailors Association History Book* 1995, Page 19 (Turner Publishing Co., Paducah, Kentucky, 1995).

Elliott, Peter, *Allied Escort Ships of World War II* (Macdonald and Jane's Publishers, Ltd., London, 1977).

Silverstone, Paul H., *U.S. Warships of World War II* (Doubleday & Company, New York, 1965).

APPENDIX F

Rates of Enlisted Men Aboard World War II PCs

The enlisted mens' rates aboard a PC included:

Boatswain
Ship's Cook
Coxswain
Electrician
Fireman
Gunner's Mate
Motor Machinist's Mate
Pharmacist's Mate
Quartermaster
Radarman
Radioman
Seaman
Shipfitter
Signalman
Soundman
Officer's Steward
Storekeeper
Yeoman

APPENDIX G

Decorations and Awards Won by PCs During World War II

The Navy gave many informal citations and commendations to various ships and individual crew members. In addition, PCs and their crew members received many ribbons, medals, and special Commendations including those listed below.

1. American Theater Campaign Medal
2. European, African, Middle-Eastern Theater Campaign Medal
3. Asiatic-Pacific Theater Campaign Medal
4. Navy Occupation Service Medal
5. Battle Stars for all campaigns
6. World War II Victory Medal
7. Occupation Service Medal, Asia
8. China Service Medal
9. Navy and Marine Corps Medal
10. Navy Unit Commendation Medal
11. Philippine Republic Presidential Unit Citation Badge
12. National Defense Service Medal
13. Purple Heart
14. Bronze Star
15. Letters of Commendation

APPENDIX H
The Story Behind
PC 1264

I put this account of the history of events leading up to PC 1264 in an appendix not because it is less important to the history of PCs but because it is of special importance. It deserves to stand alone to get special recognition.

The account of this ship is important for two reasons. First, this was the first United States Navy ship to have an all black crew. Second, it was the first ship to which the United States Navy assigned a black commissioned officer. Because those men performed their tasks so competently their actions made a significant contribution to the breakdown of segregation in the United States Navy.

In 1944 the United States Navy selected a PC for, what was at the time, a unique and controversial social experiment. The experiment was to use black sailors to operate a Navy ship. Though the Navy selected a DE as the first ship with an almost all black crew, a PC was the first United States Navy ship to go to sea with an all black crew. Also, it was the first United States Navy ship to have a black officer assigned to it.

Many persons in the Navy, at that time, thought that the experiment would fail, but it succeeded beyond expectations of even those who initiated and supported it. The crew of PC 1264 functioned as well as or better than other Navy crews, carried out their missions with success, and contributed to the war against U-boats. The experiment on the PC showed that the crew could operate and fight a naval ship. Its success altered the United States Navy of 1944 and changed the Navy of the future. This test was a major step that broke the color barrier in the Navy, and it contributed to an integrated Navy.

When the United States entered World War II, the armed forces, like much of the country, segregated white sailors from other enlisted men. Nonwhite men served only as Officer's Cooks and Officer's Stewards. The Navy did not hold these men in high regard. For example, the requirements for entry into U. S. Navy enlisted mens' service schools listed a mark no lower than seventy in the General Classification Test. For Officer's Cooks and Stewards, the score was only fifty. For the BUNAV Standard Test in Arithmetic, the numbers were fifty for most rates but only twenty-five for Officers Cooks and Stewards.[1]

Of the hundreds of thousands of men who had served and were serving in the Navy before 1942 there were no black officers or enlisted men with general rates. President Roosevelt changed that situation after the attack on Pearl Harbor. He decreed that, starting on 1 June 1942, they could enlist for general rates. Despite the decree, segregation still ruled relationships between whites and "colored" people in most of the United States. The Navy mirrored the idea of segregation though it let black men attain other rates. The position for segregation in the Navy was that white sailors would rebel against the authority of higher rated non-whites. They could become rated, but the Navy would still segregate them.

Training of black recruits began at Camp Robert Smalls, a part of the Great Lakes Naval Training Center for recruit training. This camp was a separate part of the training center and was isolated from the main part where white recruits trained. The operation was almost clandestine. White recruits (including the author) at the training center saw these recruits marching on their separate drill field. Some white recruits started scuttlebutt that the Navy was training them for a secret night operation.

A group of persons championed their cause. They believed

that if these enlisted men could function as other than Officer's Cooks and Stewards they could relieve other sailors from shore duty. Or they could serve in construction battalions, or on small coastal vessels. The Navy could then send those other men, they relieved, to sea on the larger ships. Most naval authorities did not consider black sailors capable of general shipboard duty. They did allow though that if they succeeded in lesser positions, then maybe they would try them for shipboard duty later. The experiment would proceed one step at a time. The experiment with enlisted men to train them in general rates, came first. The next step was to employ them in shore-based operations but still segregated. Then the Navy might assign them to small vessels, but still segregated. Integration might come later.

Two years after Pearl Harbor and President Roosevelt's decree, 100,000 black men were in the United States Navy. Thousands of them had earned deck and engine room rates, but none was serving aboard ships except on a few small harbor craft. Segregation kept them off fleet ships, and many senior Navy officers continued to insist that they would not make competent sailors.

Opponents of this position lobbied for employment of them aboard ships. They showed evidence that blacks had done well in shore billets and on harbor craft and could man ships of the fleet. To determine if that opinion were correct, the Navy decided to fit out two ships with black enlisted crews but with white officers. At that time the Navy had only white officers.

It was not until 1944, after thousands of men had been selected for Naval Officer Candidate School (OCS), that black men were selected as officer candidates in a special program. Only sixteen were chosen. Of those sixteen, thirteen completed the special program and the Navy commissioned twelve Ensigns and one Warrant Officer. They were called the "Golden Thirteen."[2]

In large part, due to the efforts of five men in the Navy who were sympathetic to the issue, black sailors would get their chance. Lt. j. g. Christopher Smith Sargent took charge of the Special Programs Unit. He had two assistants. They were Lt. Charles M.

Dillon, USNR and Lt. Donald O. Van Ness, USNR. Van Ness was formerly the Officer-in-Charge of Recruit Training at Camp Robert Smalls at the Great Lakes Naval Training Center. Captain H. G. Hopwood recommended that the Navy assign a Captain as Assistant to the Chief of Naval Personnel for the program. Captain Thomas F. Darden, USN, assumed that billet. Because of the actions of these five men, the Navy agreed to experiment with two ships, USS *Mason*, DE 529, and patrol craft PC 1264.

In 1944, the Navy manned these two new ships with black sailors who had general rates except the leading enlisted rates and commissioned officers. Those would be men who had previous sea duty. The intent was that in time those leading rates would transfer off the ship. The first ship, USS *Mason*,[3] the Navy had already commissioned on 20 March 1944. The second ship was the patrol craft USS PC 1264. It had a commissioning crew of five white officers, eight white senior petty officers, and fifty-two black enlisted men of various rates. Prophetically, PC 1264 slid down the launching ways at the Consolidated Ship Building Corporation on the Harlem River in New York City.

At Pier 42 in New York City on 25 April 1944, the men of PC 1264 raised aloft the ship's commissioning pennant. That action not only started a new United States man-of-war but also the experiment that proved they could operate and fight a Navy ship. Lt. Eric S. Purdon, USNR, the PC's first Captain, memorialized the ship in his book about PC 1264.[4]

The DE retained its white leading rates, therefore, the experiment on it did not attain all its goals. On the PC, however, the leading white rates transferred off the ship as the other men earned promotions. Only seven months later, after the crew of the PC had justified itself, the Navy transferred off the leading petty officers. The remaining crew operated the ship as well as before. The experiment to show that they could operate a ship was an outstanding success.

In May 1945 an Ensign, Samuel L. Gravely, Jr. reported aboard PC 1264 as Communications Officer. For the first time

Stewards fed a black man a meal in the wardroom of a United States Navy ship instead of his serving one. Gravely had trained as an enlisted man at the Great Lakes Naval Training Center and was a Fireman in 1943. He then became the first black person commissioned from a college Naval Reserve Officer's Training Course (ROTC). In May 1945, he was the first officer to integrate the wardroom of a United States Navy ship. He remained in the Navy after World War II, succeeded to command of naval ships, and became the first black Admiral in the United States Navy.

Later, other black officers came aboard PC 1264, and they, with the enlisted men, proved beyond doubt that they were as capable as any crew to operate a Navy ship. From their achievements followed more opportunities and complete equality for all persons in the United States Navy.

Because of the leadership of the commanding officers, Eric S. Purdon, Ernest V. Hardman, and Jack W. Sutherland, and the hard work, devotion to duty, and ability of the crew of PC 1264, the experiment succeeded. The successes of that crew resulted in the Navy integrating all persons into all aspects of Navy life. Vice Admiral Gravely wrote, "This little ship, the PC 1264, deserves a special place in the annals of U. S. Navy history. It completed a big mission with flying colors."[5]

REFERENCES

1. *The Bluejackets' Manual,* United States Navy, Tenth Edition, Page 120 (United States Naval Institute, Annapolis, MD, 1940).

2. Stillwell, Paul, Editor, "The Golden Thirteen," U.S. Naval Institute Proceedings, 113/5/1011, 146, May 1987. Also see *The Golden Thirteen: Recollections of the First Black Naval Officers* (U S Naval Institute Press, Annapolis, MD, 1993).

3. Kelly, Mary Pat, *Proudly We Served : The Men of the USS Mason* (Naval Institute Press, Annapolis, MD, 1995). Kelly, Mary Pat, "Memories of the Mason," US Naval Institute Proceedings, page 26 (US Naval Institute, Annapolis, MD, February 1995). Also see Emanuel, Edward R. Comments on "Memories of the Mason," Naval Institute Proceedings, page 22, April 1995.

4. Purdon, Eric, *Black Company,* Page 109 (Robert B. Luce, Inc., N.Y., 1972). Also see Purdon, Eric, Navy Times, 13 January 1986 and Roy C. Smith, III, "USS PC-1264: Forgotten Groundbreaker," Naval History, Vol. 12, No. 1, January/February 1998.

5. Gravely, Samuel L., Jr., VADM USN (Ret), "The PC 1264: A Small Ship With a Big Mission,"*Patrol Craft Sailors Association History Book*, Page 56 (Turner Publishing Company, Paducah, Kentucky, 1990).

APPENDIX I

PC Crew Casualties

The Bureau of Naval Personnel of the United States Navy maintains a list of casualties resulting from enemy action during World War II on Navy ships and stations (including the Armed Guard). It was done in 1947 and is on an IBM printout. The list is arranged chronologically by the campaigns that are listed in the Navy and Marine Corps Awards Manual of the Secretary of the Navy. For each campaign, the ships involved are listed alphabetically, then the individual personnel are listed alphabetically by last name. Other data given are service number, rank or rate, type of casualty, and date of casualty.

These records are at the Military Reference Branch, National Archives, Washington, DC 20408. Also, they are available on six reels of microfilm labeled NRS-1980-1 and on sixty-one sheets of microfiche labeled F-457.

A separate microfiche labeled F-454 lists officers and enlisted men who were prisoners of war. The data include name, rank or rate, date of capture, and Prisoner of War camp.

Either record may be purchased from the Department of the Navy, Operational Archives Branch, Naval Historical Center, 901 M Street, SE, Washington, DC 20374-5060.

In addition to these United States Government lists of casualties, another one may be found at large university or depository libraries. They may be obtained on interlibrary loan from local libraries. The list is from the US Navy Office of Information and is titled Combat Connected Naval Casualties of World War II by States, 2 volumes, Washington Office of Information, 1946.

APPENDIX J

Patrol Craft Sailors Association Museum

To preserve the history of the PC and other types of Patrol Craft of World War II the Patrol Craft Sailors Association established a museum. It contains written material, photographs, drawings, paintings, and naval artifacts that PCSA members donated. Because not all the items can be displayed at one time, they are maintained in an archive that also functions as a library. The material in the archives may be viewed or used for research by making arrangements with the museum curator.

The museum is housed in the Historical Museum of Bay County in Bay City, Michigan. In 1919, the Bay County Historical Society founded the museum, and in 1987 located it in the former National Guard Armory. The armory is listed on the Michigan State Historical Register and awaiting certification on the National Historical Register.

When the members of the PCSA dedicated the museum on 10 June, 1994, the museum established a display for patrol craft that ran through the summer. After completing renovations of the building, the museum intends to set up a permanent display of patrol craft artifacts.

To submit items to the PCSA museum, for more information, to visit the museum, or to arrange to see research data, address requests to Curator, Historical Museum of Bay County, 321 Washington Avenue, Bay City, Michigan 48708 or call (517)893-5733.

NOTES

1. Gannon, Michael *Operation Drumbeat* (Harper and Row, New York, 1990); Beach, Edward L. "Down By Subs," U.S. Naval Institute Proceedings, 117, no. 4, April 1991.

2. Churchill, Winston S., *The Second World War* (Houghton Mifflin Company, Boston, 1948).

3. Silverstone, Paul H., *U. S. Warships of World War II*, Page 232 (Doubleday & Company, Inc., New York, 1965).

4. Baker, A. D., III, "Historic Fleets," Naval History, Page 62, U. S. Naval Institute, January-February 1996.

5. Lewis, David D., CDR, USN, *The Fight for the Sea*, Page 143 (The World Publishing Company, New York, 1961).

6. Naval Orientation, NAVPERS 16138-A, Page 378, Bureau of Naval Personnel, Washington, D. C., 1948.

7. Werner, Herbert A., *Iron Coffins* (Holt, Rinehart and Winston, New York, 1969).

8. Gannon, and Beach.

9. Hoyt, Edwin P., *U-boats Offshore - When Hitler Struck America*, Pages 55, 120, and 171 (Stein and Day Publishers, New York, 1978).

10. Veigele, Wm. J. "The Patrol Craft - History Provides a Lesson," National Defense LXIX, 65, March, 1985.

11. Hoyt, Page 45.

12. Fahey, James. C., *The Ships and Aircraft of the United States Fleet, 1945*, four volumes, Reprint (Naval Institute Press, Annapolis, Maryland, 1976.); *Janes'*

Fighting Ships of World War II, 1939-1945, reprint (Studio Editions, Ltd., London, 1989.); Friedman, Norman, *U. S. Small Combatants* (US Naval Institute, Annapolis, Maryland, 1987).

13. Morison, Samuel E., *History of United States Naval Operations in World War II, Vol. I, The Battle of the Atlantic, September 1939 - May 1943,* Pages 230 and 231 (Little Brown and Co., Boston, 1947).

14. Fahey, James. C., *The Ships and Aircraft of the United States Fleet,* Victory Edition (Ships and Aircraft, New York, 1945).

15. Friedman, Norman, *U. S. Small Combatants* (Naval Institute Press, Annapolis, Maryland, 1987). Fahey, James C., *The Ships and Aircraft of the U. S. Fleet* (U. S. Naval Institute, Annapolis, Maryland, 1973).

16. Mann, Earl, CDR, Head, Ship's Histories, Department of the Navy, Appendix to *Dictionary of American Naval Fighting Ships, Vol. VI*, Office of CNO, Naval History Division, Washington, D. C., 4 January 1971, private communication.

17. The family of ship types considered as patrol craft include: DE (destroyer escort), PF (patrol frigate), PC, PGM (motor gunboat), PCE (patrol craft escort), PCS, SC, YMS, AM (minesweeper), and YP.

18. The phonetic alphabet used: Able, Baker, Charlie, Dog, Easy, Fox, George, How, Item, Jig, King, Love, Mike, Nan, Oboe, Peter, Queen, Roger, Sugar, Tare, Uncle, Victor, William, Xray, Yoke, and Zebra.

19. Elliott, P., *Allied Escort Ships of World War II* (Macdonald and Jane's Publishers Limited, London, 1977). This book contains different data about Mousetraps.

20. Various sources quote different numbers because of cancellations, conversions, and transfers. See Chapter 3 and Appendix E for a summary of the PC construction program.

21. Thale, Jack, "Miami-Trained Crews Licking subs," Miami Herald, Sunday, 13 February 1944.

22. Werner.

23. Dönitz, Karl, Grand Admiral, *Memoirs: Ten Years and Twenty Days* (World Publishing Company, Cleveland, Ohio, 1959).

24. Lodmell, Joseph, "It Only Takes One," U. S. Naval Institute Proceedings, Page 32, December 1996. This estimate came from Soviet Admiral Gorshkov.

25. Werner.

26. Thale.

27. *Submarine Chaser Manual*, Second Edition, Page VII, U. S. Navy Dept., Restricted. Declassified Library of Congress F. A. C. File Number 642, November 14, 1957, U. S. Navy Department (United States Government Printing Office, Washington, D. C., 1942).

28. Morison, Samuel E., *History of United States Naval Operations in World War II, Vol. XI, The Invasion of France and Germany,* Appendix III (Little, Brown and Company, Boston, 1957).

29. Described here is PC class 461. More PCs were in this than any other class. See Appendix A for ship characteristics and hull numbers of class 461 and other classes of PCs.

30. *Submarine Chaser Manual,*, Page 119. Morison, Samuel E., *History of United States Naval Operations in World War II, Vol. I, The Battle of the Atlantic, Sept. 1939-May 1943* , Page 209 (Little, Brown and Co., Boston, 1947).

31. Elliott. This book contains different data about Mousetraps.

32. Roberts, Douglas L., *Rustbucket 7, Chronicle of the USS PC 617 During the Great War, 1942 - 1946* (Mill Pond Press, New Castle, Maine, 1995).

33. The complement varied slightly among PC classes and individual ships within each class.

34. Friedman, Norman, *U.S. Small Combatants*, Page 71 (Naval Institute Press, Annapolis, 1987).

35. Furnas, J. C. "Catfish Navy," Saturday Evening Post, Volume 215, Page 10, 1942.

36. Elliott.

37. For brief histories of the Defoe Shipyard see, Gluntz, Marvin H., "Harry Defoe, Shipbuilder Extraordinary," Inland Seas, Quarterly Journal of the Great Lakes Historical Society, Volume 16, Number 2, Summer 1960. Swanson, A. F., "Development of the Defoe Shipbuilding Company," address to the Society of Naval Architects & Marine Engineers, Bay City, Michigan, May 21, 1964. Hardy, Richard, "Defoe made a big splash during, after war," The Bay City Times, Sunday, July 24, 1988.

38. Defoe, William M., Chairman of the Board, (Retired), Defoe Shipbuilding Company, Address Delivered at the Patrol Craft Sailors Association (PCSA) Library, Archive, and Museum Dedication Ceremony in Bay City, Michigan on 10 June 1994.

39. Defoe, William M., Private communication.

40. "Guest Speaker," Patrol Craft Sailors Association News, Issue Number 15, Page 7, January-March 1992. This article gives a brief biography of John (Jack) Hazard who commanded PC 452 and another PC in the Pacific.

41. *United States Naval Chronology, World War II*, Naval History Division, Office of the Chief of Naval Operations, Navy Department, Washington, D.C., 1955.

42. Furnas

43. Furnas

44. Mann, Earl, Appendix to *Dictionary of American Naval Fighting Ships, Vol. VI*, Office of CNO, Naval History Div., Washington, D.C. Rough Draft, Private Communication from CDR Earl Mann, 4 January 1971.

45. Friedman, Norman, *U.S. Small Combatants*, Page 67 (Naval Institute Press, Annapolis, MD, 1987).

46. Private communication from William Defoe and Robert W. Daly, Sr., 14 November 1996.

47. Proposed 175 foot Patrol Ships – 2nd ten ships, Defoe Shipyard, 26 January 1946. Courtesy of the Institute for Great Lakes Research.

48. Production of PCs for and by other countries continued after the war. Between 1955 and 1957, France built nine PCs. In 1956 and 1957 Portugal built two. In 1965 Turkey built one, and in 1966 Denmark completed a PC. In addition to these PCs constructed in other countries, during 1964 and 1965 shipyards in the United States built five PCs for Turkey.

49. The Navy commissioned two ships as AM 86 and AM 97, converted them to PC 1599 and PC 1601. See Table 3-3. Then it converted them to PCC 1599 and PCC 1601.

50. Buffington, Bill, "Ship's Insignia," Patrol Craft Sailors Association News, Issue Number 10.

51. Buffington. Also, Amaral, George, "WW II Journal of the U.S.S. PC-546 and Memorabilia," 1996.

52. Morison, Samuel Eliot, *History of United States Naval Operations in World War II, Volume I, The Battle of the Atlantic September 1939-May 1943*, Page 217 (Little, Brown and Co., Boston, 1947).

53. *Submarine Chaser Manual*, Second Edition, Declassified Library of Congress F. A. C. File Number 642, Nov. 14, 1957, U. S. Navy Department, U. S. Government Printing Office, Washington, D. C., 1942.

54. Morison, Samuel Eliot, *The Two-Ocean War*, Page 128 (Little, Brown and Company, Boston, 1963.)

55. Morison.

56. Shalett, S., "Our School of Death-to-U-Boats," The New York Times Magazine, February 19, 1944.

57. Williamson, John A., U.S. Naval Institute Proceedings, Page 112, U. S. Naval Institute, Annapolis, MD, July 1979 and Page 89, October 1979. Paulo Bracy Gama da Silva, "Which Williamson Turn?" U. S. Naval Institute Proceedings, Page. 106, March 1981.

58. Morison, Page 232.

59. Grundman, Vernon, H., "It's Rugged," Our Navy, 1 May 1945. This article is a humorous account of life on a PC.

60. "Man Overboard," The Miami Herald, December 3, 1943. Submitted by James Kisselburgh to the Patrol Craft Sailors Association News, Issue Number 23, Page 9, January - March 1994.

61. Emanuel, Ed, PC 555. PCSA Newsletter, Issue Number 23, January-March 1994.

62. On Navy ships tradition dictated that watch relievers arrive fifteen minutes early. This insured that they would be on time and to exchange information with the man they relieved.

63. Templeton, William B. and L. W. Owings, "The Rugged PC's The Roughest Escort Vessels Afloat," Our Navy, 1 July 1943.

64. Templeton, William B. and L. W. Owings, "Combat," *Patrol Craft Sailors Association History Book,* Page 16 (Turner Publishing Co., Paducah, 1990).

65. Grundman.

66. Cooper, Joe, "General History," *Patrol Craft Sailors Association History Book,* Page 12 (Turner Publishing Co., Paducah, KY, 1990).

67. Nolan, Thomas, "The Last Cruise of USS PC 1213," Patrol Craft Sailors Association News, Issue Number 33, Page 11, July-Sept. 1996.

68. Welling, Robert, *Patrol Craft Sailors Association History Book,* Page 101 (Turner Publishing Co., Paducah, KY, 1995).

69. Mager, Herb, "PC 1246," Patrol Craft Sailors Association News, Issue Number 8, Page 1, January 1990.

70. Fetridge, William H., Editor, *The Navy Reader*, Page 258 (The Bobbs-Merrill Co., NY, 1943).

71. Morison, Samuel Eliot, *History of U.S. Naval Operations in WWII, Victory in the Pacific Volume XIV*, Page 143 (Little Brown and Co., Boston, 1960).

72. Some material in this section is from Morison, Samuel Eliot, *History of U.S. Naval Operations in WWII, Volumes. II, VII - XIV* (Little Brown and Co., Boston, 1947, 51, 53, 54, 56 - 60).

73. Elliott.

74. Silverstone, Paul H., *U. S. Warships of World War II*, Page 233 (Doubleday & Company, Inc., New York, 1965).

75. *The Bluejackets' Manual* (United States Naval Institute, Annapolis, MD, 1950).

76. Eastern Sea Frontier Reports. Also see Hoyt, Edwin P., *U-boats Offshore*, Page 116 (Stein and Day, Publishers, New York, 1978).

77. Eastern Sea Frontier Reports. Also see Hoyt, Page 171.

78. Peck, Joe, "German U-boat Sinks Two More Ships," PCSA Newsletter, Issue Number 20, Page 1, April-June 1993.

79. Kerr, Donald M., Commanding Officer, PC 577, private communication, 1 September 1978. Kane, Peter F., Lt. j. g., "Voyage Report of S. S. Minotaur, Torpedoing of," February 15, 1943.

80. Thompson, Earle, R., *Patrol Craft Sailors Association History Book*, Page 99 (Turner Publishing Co., Paducah, KY, 1995).

81. Bagnasco, Erminio, *Submarines of World War II* , English language edition (United States Naval Institute Press, Annapolis, Maryland, 1977).

82. Werner, Herbert A., *Iron Coffins* (Holt, Rinehart and Winston, NY, 1969). The numbers include U-505 and U-570 which were captured, not sunk.

83. Roberts, Douglas L., Private communication, 9 January 1992. For a brief account of Q-ships in World War II see Roberts, Douglas L., *Rustbucket 7, Chronicle of the USS PC 617 During the Great War, 1942 - 1946* (Mill Pond Press, New Castle, Maine, 1995). Also see, Morison, Samuel Eliot., *History of United States Naval Operations in World War II, Volume I, The Battle of the Atlantic September 1939-May 1943*, Page 284 (Little, Brown and Co., Boston, 1947).

84. Roberts.

85. Eastern Sea Frontier Reports. Also see Hoyt, Page 226.

86. Gentile, Gary, *Track of the Gray Wolf, U-Boat Warfare on the U.S. Eastern Seaboard, 1942-45* (Avon Books, The Hearst Corp., NY, 1989). Samuel Eliot Morison, *History of United States Naval Operations in World War II, The Atlantic Battle Won, May 1943 - May 1945*, Volume X, Page 181 (Little, Brown and Company, Boston, 1956).

87. "History of the USS PC 1209," Office of Naval Records and History, Ship's Histories Branch, Navy Department, 2 September 1948.

88. Morison, Samuel Eliot, *History of United States Naval Operations in World War II, The Atlantic Battle Won, May 1943 - May 1945*, Volume X, Page 297 (Little, Brown and Company, Boston, 1956).

89. "How did she ever stay afloat??," PCSA Newsletter, Issue Number 34, Page 4, Oct.-Dec., 1996.

90. Reedy, B. D., Commanding Officer, "U.S.S. PC-1217 - Storm Damage - report of," To: Commander Eastern Sea Frontier, 25 September 1944.

91. Kirk, A. G., Commander U. S. Naval Forces, France, Second endorsement to letter to Commander-in-Chief, United States Fleet, CTG 125.2 Secret Ser., 00200 of 13 March 1945.

92. Welby, Richard E., "A Special Kind of Hero," *Patrol Craft Sailors Association History Book* (Turner Publishing Co., Paducah, KY, 1990).

93. Purdon, Eric, *Black Company,* Page 157 (Robert B. Luce, Inc., N.Y., 1972).

94. Roberts.

95. "Operation Mulberry Was No Bowl of Cherries." Private communication from Ray Goin, 1996.

96. Kisselburgh, J. F., "PC 1213," PCSA Newsletter, Issue Number 20, Page 10, April-June 1993.

97. "Statement of operations of PC-616 compiled from entries in Panama Sea Frontier War Diary October 1942 - December 1943," World War II Command File,

23 October 1963.

98. Amaral, George, "WW II Journal of the U.S.S. PC-546 and Memorabilia," 1996.

99. Dowdell, James S., "Subchaser Commander Saved as P. C. 496 Goes Down." Courtesy of Carter Barber.

100. Stafford, Edward P., *Subchaser*, Page 105 (Warner Books, Inc., NY, 1988).

101. Navy Department Press and Radio Release, August 27, 1943.

102. Karig, W., Earl Burton, and L. Freeland, *Battle Report, the Atlantic War, Appendix B* (Farrar & Rinehart, Inc., NY, 1946).

103. Brown, John J. and Carter Barber, "The PC 496 Lived Again," Patrol Craft Sailors Association News, Issue Number 8, Page 4.

104. Whitcomb, Lester, "PC 627," Patrol Craft Sailors Association News, Issue Number 7, Page 5, 1989.

105. Morison, Samuel Eliot, *History of United States Naval Operations in WWII, Volume IX, Sicily – Salerno – Anzio, January 1943 - June 1944*, Page 86 (Little, Brown and Company, Boston, 1954).

106. Amaral.

107. Stafford, Page 152.

108. Silverstein, M. W., Lt. j. g., "PC 543 Action Report of 10 July 1943."

109. Morison, Page 163.

110. "PC 556 History," U. S. Navy, Confidential. Private communication from Ed Emanuel, 15 October 1996 and Courtesy of Ken Tito.

111. Stafford, page 192.

112. Morison, Page 41.

113. Stafford, Page 193.

114. "History of USS PC 546," Ship's Data Section, Office of Public Information, Navy Department, 19 January 1948.

115. "USS PC 559 Gets Navy Unit Commendation," Newspaper Release, Navy Department, 12 April 1947.

116. Hyde, Latimer B. "Commence Firing," PCSA Newsletter, Issue Number 19, Page 4, January-March 1993 and "Commence Firing," *Patrol Craft Sailors Association History Book*, Page 68 (Turner Publishing Company, Paducah, Kentucky, 1995).

117. Morison, Pages 366 and 376.

118. "USS PC 619 Sank Nazi Sub U-986," private communication from Ray Goin on 17 September 1996.

119. "PC-558 Sinks Two One-Man Subs," Navy Department Press and Radio release, 12 June 1944.

120. PC 558, "Report of Action Against One-Man Submarine," 23 April 1944.

121. Morison, Page 372.

122. *United States Naval Chronology, World War II*, Naval History Division, Office of the Chief of Naval Operations, Navy Department, Washington, D.C., 1955.

123. Roberts, Douglas L., "Patrol Craft Squadron Number One, D-Day and Beyond," RFD #1, Box 241, Newcastle ME 04553, 1991.

124. Morison, Samuel Eliot, *History of United States Naval Operations in WWII, Volume XI, The Invasion of France and Germany, 1944 - 1945* (Little, Brown and Company, Boston, 1957).

125. Veigele.

126. Patrol Craft Sailors Association News, Issue Number 10, Page 1, 1990. Also see *Dictionary of American Naval Fighting Ships, Vol. IV*, Office of CNO, Naval History Div., Page 358 (Washington, D.C., 1969).

127. Barrett, Halsey V., "Experiences Aboard the First Ship Sunk in the D-Day Invasion of France," Patrol Craft Sailors Association News, Issue Number 10, Page 12, 1990.

128. PCSA Newsletter, Issue Number 24, Page 9, April-June 1994. Article taken from Lou Mio, Staff Writer, Cleveland Ohio Plain Dealer, June 6, 1986.

129. Emery, L. Warren, "Action at Normandy," Patrol Craft Sailors Association News, Issue Number 18, Page 6, Oct.-Dec. 1992.

130. Crook, Richard, "Action on D-Day - Omaha Beach (Easy Red Sector)," PCSA Newsletter, Issue Number 24, Page 1, April - June 1994. USS PC 553, Report of Operations 4 June - 17 June 1944, Declassified.

131. Roberts, Page 125.

132. Mahar, Ted, "Sailor Floats Idea of Navy PC," The Sunday Oregonian, May 30, 1993. Reprinted in the Patrol Craft Sailors Association News, Issue Number 21, Page 7, July - September 1993.

133. "US Patrol Boat of Invasion Fame in Bermuda for Peace-Time Role," Bermuda Newspaper, November or December 1945. Submitted by Bill Worstenholm to the Patrol Craft Sailors Association News, Issue Number 26, Page 9, October -December 1994.

134. Padelford, Philip S., Private communication to Ray Goin, 11 May 1994. Courtesy of Philip Padelford and Ray Goin.

135. Butler, Rick, "Jersey WWII vet finds friend in German flier he once guarded," The Star Ledger, Tuesday, June 4, 1991.

136. Roberts.

137. Roberts.

138. Kay, T., Mel Dewitt, Neal Smith, and Wes Johnson, "Torpedoing of the *Leopoldville*," Patrol Craft Sailors Association News, Issue Number 6, Page 7, June 1989.

139. In July 1984, Clive Cussler, with the National Underwater & Marine Agency (NUMA), led an expedition to search for the Confederate raider *Alabama*, sunk by the Union frigate *Kearsage* near where *Leopoldville* sank. After a five hour search they echo ranged off the hull of *Leopoldville* sixty feet from the bottom at 49^0 44' 42" North by 01^0 36' 20" West about five miles north of Cherbourg. Clive Cussler, private communication to Wesley Johnson, 25 September 1986. Courtesy of Wesley Johnson. In 1986 Cussler wrote a book titled *Cyclops* and dedicated it "To the eight hundred American men who were lost with the Leopoldville . . . ."

140. Morison, Samuel Eliot, *History of United States Naval Operations in WWII, Volume XI, The Invasion of France and Germany, 1944 - 1945*, Page 306 (Little, Brown and Company, Boston, 1957).

141. Bryans, Peter, editor, *Channel Islands Occupation Review*, 1987, (Channel Island Occupation Society, Jersey Branch, May 1987). See the chapter "The Missing Link - U. S. S. PC 564" by Margeret Ginns.

142. Sandell, Percy, "Statement of Percy Sandell, USNR, Commanding Officer of the PC-564, 10 March 1945," Patrol Craft Sailors Association News, Issue Number 10, Page 15.

143. Elliott, Bob, "Dear Friends," *Patrol Craft Sailors Association History Book*, Page 53 (Turner Publishing Co., Paducah, KY, 1990).

144. Kirk, A. G., United States Naval Forces, France, "Action off and at Granville night 8-9 March 1945 - Report of," CTG 125.2 Secret Ser., 00200 of 3/13/45, File no.: A16-3, Serial 00188, 23 March 1945.

145. "History of PC-474," Ship's History Section, Division of Naval History (OP 09B9), Office of the Chief of Naval Operations, Navy Department.

146. Bell, Art, *Peter Charlie - The Cruise of the PC 477* (Courtroom Compendiums, Woodland Hills, CA, 1982). For PC 479 see Clyde H. Morton, Jr., *Patrol Craft Sailors Association History Book,* Page 89 (Turner Publishing Co., Paducah, 1995).

147. "History of USS PC 581," Office of Naval Records and History, Ship's History Section, Navy Department, 10 August 1948.

148. Garfield, B., *The Thousand Mile War: World War II in Alaska and the Aleutians* (Doubleday and Co., NY, 1969). Morison, Samuel Eliot, *History of the United States Naval Operations in World War II, Volume VII, Aleutians, Gilberts and Marshalls, June 1942 - April 1944,* Revised, Page 57 (Little, Brown and Company, Boston, 1984). *The Campaigns of the Pacific War United States Strategic Bombing Survey (Pacific)*, Naval Analysis Division, Appendix 31, Page 93, U. S. Government Printing Office, Washington, D. C., 1946. The latter two sources list the submarine incorrectly as I-9. The USS *Frazier* (DD 607) sank I-9 in the Aleutians three days later on 13 June 1943.

149. Bagnasco.

150. Brown, David L., "The Untimely Death of The YP-281," *Patrol Craft Sailors History Book*, Page 55 (Turner Publishing Co., Paducah, KY, 1990).

151. "United States Naval Chronology, World War II" (Naval History Division, Office of the Chief of Naval Operations, Navy Department, United States Government Printing Office, Washington, D. C., 1955).

152. Deck log of PC 1125, Saturday 17 June 1944. Declassified, 21 September 1989. Courtesy of Ed Emanuel.

153. Green, Lester R., *Patrol Craft Sailors Association History Book,* Page 77 (Turner Publishing Co., Paducah, 1990).

154. Craig, Joseph, "PC 623 War Diary - Rescue, Taffy 3 Survivors, U.S.S. PC 623, Flagship, 25 October 1944 (Declassified)." Patrol Craft Sailors Association News, Issue Number 33, Page 6, July - Sept. 1996.

155. Levy, Allison M., private communication, 2 November 1996.

156. Kurtz, Len, "More Taffy 3 Rescue," Patrol Craft Sailors Association News, Issue Number 33, Page 10, July - Sept. 1996.

157. Donohue, Philip Edward, *Patrol Craft Sailors Association Memory Book,* Page 73 (Turner Publishing Co., Paducah, 1990).

158. Morison, Samuel Eliot, *History of United States Naval Operations in World War II, Volume XIII, The Liberation of the Philippines, Luzon, Mindanao, the Visayas, 1944-1945*, Page 191 (Little, Brown, and Company, Boston, 1959.)

159. O'Quin, Herbert W., "The Saga of a Gallant Little Ship: U.S.S. PC 1129," 1989. Private communication 25 March 1997.

160. Truemper, William G., "WW II Memoirs." Private communication 10 September 1996.

161. "Sub Chaser PC-1119 is Little Ship With Big War Record," Press and Radio Release, Navy Department, 16 October 1945.

162. Other invasions included: Nambier, 7/4/44; Cape Sansapor, 7/30/44; Moratai Island, 9/15/44; Leyte, 10/20/44; Pegun Island, Maple Island Group, 11/15/44; Igi Island, Asia Group, 11/19/44; Linguyen Gulf, 1/9/45; San Antonio, Luzon, 1/29/45; Grande Island, 1/30/45; Bataan, 2/16/45; Corregidor, 2/17/45; Mindanao, 3/8/45; Cebu, 3/27/45; Mindanao, 4/17/45; Davao, 4/30/45; Morotai Island, 6/11/45; San Pedro Bay, 6/45; and Subic Bay, 6/28/45.

163. "History of USS PC-1133," Ship's History Section, Division of Naval History (OP 0939), Office of the Chief of Naval Operations, Navy Department, 8 February 1960.

164. Kurtz, Leonard, "Everything But Sub Chasing," Patrol Craft Sailors Association News, Issue Number 20, Page 6, April-June 1993. "Letter of Appreciation," U.S.S. *Gambier Bay*, 22 November 1944. "Performance of Duty," U. S. Pacific Fleet, Commander Transport Div. Thirty-Eight, 5 February 1945. Commendation from Commander Flotilla One, FE25-SF1/P15, 24 February 1945.

165. Morrissey, Fred and Joseph B. Whitman, "An Unlucky Day for the 1124," PCSA Newsletter, Issue Number 31, Page 1, Jan.-Mar. 1996.

166. Meseroll, Richard, "Follow-up on PC 1124," PCSA Newsletter, Issue Number 32, Page 5, April-June 1996.

167. PCs 569, 572, 670, 673, 777, 778, 780, 781, 784, 786, 788, 792, 793, 817, 818, 819, 820, 1411, 1422, and 1459. These ships were listed in the log of PC 793.

168. Fletcher, Frank, Jack, VADM, "Announcement to All Ships and Sectors North Pacific," from Radio Adak, Alaska, 14 August 1945.

169. Fuller, Alton J., PCSA Newsletter, Issue Number 16, Page 5, April-June 1992.

170. Fisher, Arthur, "I'll Never Forget Iwo Jima - Part Two," PCSA Newsletter, Issue Number 19, Page 5, January-March 1993.

171. Newby, David E., "PC 469 — Iwo Memories," PCSA Newsletter, Issue Number 22, Page 9, Oct.-Dec. 1993.

172. Emanuel, Edward, R., "USS PC 555 Duty in the Pacific," Patrol Craft Sailors Association News, Issue Number 7, Page 5, 1989.

173. Morison, Samuel Eliot, *History of United States Naval Operations in World War II, Vol. XIV, Victory in the Pacific, 1945*, Page 115 (Little, Brown and Company, Boston, 1960).

174. "USS PC 1128," Press and Radio Release, Navy Department, 16 July 1945.

175. Morison, Page 318.

176. Sutherland, J. W., "USS PC 586 - Jezebel, A Fighting Ship," Patrol Craft Sailors Association News, Issue Number 8, Page 3, 1990.

177. Young, Albert, "The Ship That Would Not Die," Patrol Craft Sailors Association News, Issue Number 14, Page 3, October 1991.

178. Young, Albert W., "PC 1603 Follow-Up," Patrol Craft Sailors Association News, Issue Number 16, Page 6, April-June 1992. Albert Young, private communication, 21 November 1996.

179. Secor, Gordon, LT, USNR, "Advance copies of ASW -1 reports, Submission of," Antisubmarine Action by Surface Ship, 13 May 1945.

180. "History of PC 594," Division of Naval History, Ship's History Section, Navy Department, 8 June 1955.

181. "History of USS PC 1546," Division of Naval History, Ship's History Section, Navy Department, 7 June 1955.

182. Kennedy, Kenneth, "First PC to enter Tokyo Bay," Patrol Craft Sailors Association News, Issue Number 29, Page 3, July-Sept., 1995.

183. Blair, Donald R., "50 years ago – the last World War II POW," PCSA Newsletter, Issue Number 34, Page 1, Oct. - Dec., 1996.

184. Boone, E. E., HA1c, USS *Mona Island* (ARG9), "The Last Cruise of the USS PC 590," 15 October 1945. Loss of the PC 590, "USS PC-590 Founders in Okinawa Typhoon." Crew members wrote these accounts of their ordeal when PC 590 ran aground and broke in half during the typhoon on 9 October 1945.

185. Fuller, Alton J., PCSA Newsletter, Issue Number 16, Page 5, April-June 1992.

186. Hale, Emil and Bob Daly, "PGM 27 Meets Typhoon Louise — and Loses!," Patrol Craft Sailors Association News, Issue Number 22, Page 4, Oct. - Dec. 1993.

187. Dunlap, Robert B., "Fate of USS PC 1238," Patrol Craft Sailors Association News, Issue Number 10, Page 21.

188. *United States Naval Chronology, World War II* (Naval History Division, Office of the Chief of Naval Operations, Navy Department, United States Government Printing Office, Washington, D. C., 1955). For PC 584 see Kellay, Cassius J., *Patrol Craft Sailors Association History Book,* Page 83 (Turner Publishing Co., Paducah, KY, 1990). *Patrol Craft Sailors Association History Book,* Page 19 (Turner Publishing Co., Paducah, KY, 1995). PCSA Newsletter, Issue Number 32, Page 8, April-June 1996 for PC 814. Also, private communication with Robert Daly, 26 February 1996 for information on the French PCs.

189. Many historians did not include the losses of PCs and their crew members in their writing. For example Brown, David, *Warship Losses of World War Two* (Naval Institute Press, Annapolis, MD, 1990) does not list any of the PCs that were casualties.

190. A Press and Radio Release by the Navy Department on 2 October 1945 gives this date as 21 May 1945.

191. "United States Naval Vessels Lost During the War," Press and Radio Release, Navy Department, 2 October 1945. Jane, Fred T., *Jane's Fighting Ships, 1944/5,* (Arco Publishing Company, Inc., New York, 1945). Various other sources.

192. Boone.

193. Of the 361 PCs, PGMs, and AMs that the Navy built on PC hulls during World War II in the United States, 45 were transferred to other countries during World War II and 16 were sunk or destroyed.

194. Pease, Edgar C., Chief Quartermaster on PC 542, private communication, 21 July 1978.

195. Hays, Oliver, *Patrol Craft Sailors Association History Book,* Page 78 (Turner Publishing Co., Paducah, 1990).

196. Belmore, Brainard J., "PC 550, PGM 32, ...," Patrol Craft Sailors Association News, Issue Number 7, Page 1, 1989.

197. Bryans, Peter, editor, "Channel Islands Occupation Review, 1987, (Channel Island Occupation Society, Jersey Branch, May 1987). See the chapter "The Missing Link - U. S. S. PC 564" by Margeret Ginns.

198. Mann, Earl, CDR, Head, Ship's Histories, Department of the Navy, private communication, 4 January 1971. Also in an Appendix to *Dictionary of American Naval Fighting Ships, Vol. VI*, Office of CNO, Naval History Div., Washington, D.C.

199. Mann.

200. Vessel History Card, Navships 3817 (7-50).

201. "Portland Built PC in Action," PCSA Newsletter, Issue Number 20, Page 7, April-June 1993.

202. Office of Naval Attache, Embassy of the Republic of Korea, Washington, D. C., 11 February 1994. Also, Daly, Robert W., Sr., private communication, 13 January 1996.

203. Almeida, James E., "PGM – 13 . . . . 'Lucky 13,'" PCSA Newsletter, Issue Number 18, Page 4, October - December 1992.

204. Morgan, James F., "PC 1141 (U. S. S. Pierre)," Patrol Craft Sailors Association News, Issue Number 12, Page 10, April 1991.

205. "History of USS PC 1172," Division of Naval History, Ship's History Section, Navy Department, 27 April 1955.

206. Daly, Robert W., Sr., "Duffy Remembers the 1172," Patrol Craft Sailors Association News, Issue Number 33, Page 10, July - Sept. 1996.

207. Johnson, George E. Q., "Corrected Log Of The PC 1243," Patrol Craft Sailors Association News, Issue Number 18, Page 10, October - December 1992.

208. "History of USS PC 1243," Patrol Craft Sailors Association News, Issue Number 13, Page 8, July 1991.

209. *Dictionary of American Naval Fighting Ships, Volume 4*, page 358, Office of CNO, Naval History Div., Washington, D.C., 1969.

210. Silverstone, Paul, H., *Warships of the U. S. Navy Since 1945* (U. S. Naval Institute, Annapolis, MD, 1987).

211. Hunter, Bob, *Warrior's of the Rainbow* (Holt, Rinehart & Winston, NY, 1979). Also see Daly, Robert W., Sr., "From a WWII warship to derelict — the saga of PC 1120."

212. Sager, Charles, Catellus Development Corp., Berkeley, CA., private communication, March 1991.

213. Hartmann, Joseph, in O'Heir, Jeff, "Seven Navy buddies take a melancholy look at PC 1217, fifty years after they piloted her through the stormy waters of World War II," Advance South Shore Bureau, Staten Island Advance, Staten Island, New York, 10 June 1995. Reprinted by Reinhold, Frank G. and Walter J. Mackey, PCSA Newsletter, Issue Number 30, Page 3, Oct.-Dec. 1995.

214. O'Heir.

215. Humphrey, B., "Naval History," Volume 5, Number 2, Page 71, Naval Institute Press, Annapolis, MD, Summer 1991. Also see "Naval Institute Guide to Maritime Museums of North America," Naval Institute Press, Annapolis, 1990.

216. This number 361 includes 24 ships commissioned as PGMs and 18 ships commissioned as AMs.

217. Ward, Patrick and Wes Johnson, letter to "Dear PC Sailor, Veteran, and Friends," November 1986.

218. Veigele, Wm. J., "Too Good to be Forgotten," Naval History, Page 8, 1989. Also see *Patrol Craft Sailors Association History Book,* Page 16 (Turner Publishing Co., Paducah, KY, 1995).

219. Johnson, Wesley G., Letter to "Directors of the PC Squadron," 24 June 1987. The Board of Directors consisted of Harry Ayres, Art Bell, Ollie Durham, Tom Gaffney, Wes Johnson, Joseph Kelliher, James Morgan, Eric Purdon, Charles Sheppard, James Spencer, Thomas Tait, William Veigele, Patrick Ward, and Alban Weber.

220. For membership and other information about the Patrol Craft Sailors Association contact Mr. Joe Kelliher (PC 1122), Membership Secretary, 14 Hickory Hill, Spring Lake Village, Southington, CT 06489-3445. Telephone 860-276-8243.

221. The museum is in the former National Guard Armory next to the City Hall in Bay City. Upon completion of renovation of the building, the PCSA will have a permanent exhibit, library, and research archive. Funds to operate the museum and/or contributions of patrol craft items may be sent to the Curator, PCSA Exhibit, The Historical Museum of Bay County, 321 Washington Avenue, Bay City, MI 48708. Telephone (517) 893-5733.

222. Other notables at the ceremony included State Senator Joel Gougeon; the Honorable Michael Buda, Mayor of Bay City; the Honorable Edward Rivet, Chairman of the Bay County Board of Commissioners; Brig. Gen. Richard DeMara, USA (Ret), Bay County Veteran's Council; Thomas Hickner, Bay County Exec.; Gene Kramer, V. P., Bay County Historical Society; Mrs. Gay McInerney, Museum Director; Ron Bloomfield and Jeanne Feyedelem, Museum Curators; Gay McGee, Museum volunteer. Reverend Frank Toste, CSC, former Signalman 3/C on PCE 869, gave the Invocation and Benediction, and Rhonda O'Laughlin sang the National Anthem.

223. *Patrol Craft Sailors Association History Book* (Turner Publishing Co., Paducah, KY, 1990 and 1995).

224. Bell, Art, *Peter Charlie - The Cruise of the PC 477* (Courtroom Compendiums, Woodland Hills, CA, 1982).

INDEX

A

Adsmond, Roy 189
Albert, Eddie 57
Alcazar 83, 97
Alchiba 205
Aleutian 59, 128, 138, 143, 202, 204, 207, 208, 216, 223, 239
Alexander, George 160
AM 63, 65, 137, 180, 208, 218
AM 82 65
AM 95 65
Andrews, Adolphus, RADM 27, 29, 153
APC Pills 112
archive 282-284
armament on PCs 29, 30, 37-39, 41, 43, 61, 64, 67, 149, 293
Atik, USS 155
B

Baldwin, Robert K. 37, 171, 175, 179, 297
Barber, Carter 172, 173
Bargsten, Klaus 158
Barrett, Halsey V. 184, 185
Bell, Art 205, 206, 285
Belmore, Brainard J. 51, 249, 272
Bering Sea 59, 141
Big Horn, USS (AO 45) 155, 156
Birmingham City 153
birthplace of PCs 56, 57, 283
Black Company 159
Black, John 161
Blair, Donald 225, 226
Bluejackets' Manual 139
Brazil 69, 84, 153, 254-256
Bronson, Charles 57
Buffington, William 134, 281
Buzz bombs 162, 163
Byington, D. A. 214

C

Cain, John R. 179
Cambodia 69, 259, 260, 262
canceled, PCs 57, 61, 63, 356
Cape Warwick 151
Caribbean 26, 30, 32, 59, 139, 152, 153, 159, 166, 205, 224, 250
Carlinville 264, 265
casualties 233, 239, 243, 366
CAT fever 112
Chadron (USS), former PC 564 .... 79, 94, 249, 264
characteristics of PCs 293
Childress, James Rudolph 188
Chile 69, 261, 262
Chilore 152
China 68, 69, 210, 224, 225, 251, 253, 257-262
Churchill, Winston 21, 22, 24, 31
classes of PCs 28, 37, 60, 61, 293
Clifton, Ray 158
Collingsworth (SS) 153
Commemorative Community Program 284, 285, 289
Commercial Iron Works 55, 251
complement 89, 101, 277
control ship 63, 128, 137, 165, 170, 179, 182-188, 210, 214, 220
converted, PCs 61, 63-65, 67, 68, 203, 247, 356
Coolbaugh, Lt. j. g. 215
Cooper, Gary 57
Cooper, Joe 123
Cornell, Wallace Gordon 207
Cornwallis (SS) 162
corvettes 24, 153
cost, to build PCs 56, 61, 250
Coventry City (HMS) 151
Cuba 69, 153, 157, 160, 161, 187, 224, 252, 258, 262, 266
Cyane (USCG) 223, 224

D

Daly, Robert W. 51
DD 165, 174, 183, 186, 207, 210, 240
D-day 182-187, 195, 198
DE 58, 100, 211, 220
Defoe, Harry 56, 57, 71

Defoe Shipbuilding Company 28, 29, 55-58, 60, 61, 71, 205, 283
Defoe, William 283
depth charge attacks . . . 25, 140, 151, 154-160, 178, 181, 194, 205, 209, 218, 220
Der Blaue Engel 187, 188
destroyed, PCs 68, 173, 233-235, 240-243
destroyer escorts 23, 100, 186
Dickie, Jim 79, 94
diesel 28, 37, 42, 43, 51, 52, 56, 60, 65, 105, 116
Dione (USCG) 151
disposed of, PCs 68, 246-248, 265
Dixie Line 186
Dominican Republic 69, 84, 258, 260-262
Donald Duck Navy 79, 81, 90, 99, 100, 160, 280
Dönitz, Karl 22, 23, 30, 31, 82, 152, 155
Dowdell, James S. 172, 173
Duffy's Tavern 117, 135
Durham, J. Ollie 281
E
Eagle boats 27
Eastern Sea Frontier 27, 162-163, 170, 250
Ellis (USS) 151
English Channel 141, 164, 170, 171, 182, 187, 190, 191, 235
Ensign Whitehead 251
Everglades 83, 97
E-boats 170, 186, 191, 240, 242
F
Fletcher, Frank Jack, VADM 216
Flynn, W. T. 157
Fort, Squire 189
Fowler (USS DE 222) 142, 194
France 69, 84, 144, 164, 165, 171, 179, 180-191,194,195,240,241,
                                                         249, 253-256,258, 260, 262
fresh water 28, 42, 106, 108, 122, 123
frigates 23
Fuller, Alton 238
G
Gambier Bay (USS CVE 73) 210
Gleaner 247, 252, 271
Goff (USS DD) 153, 154
Goggins, GM1/C 180

Goin, Ray 188
Goldenbaum, Hermann 188
Gomez (BM1/C) 162
Granville 191-194
Gravely, Samuel L., Jr., VADM 363, 364
Gray Ghost (PC 1232) 187
Greece 69, 253, 255, 256, 259, 261, 262
Greenpeace 265, 266, 274
Greer, Jane 57
Grundman, Vernon H. 122
Guadalcanal 142, 202, 205
Gulf Dawn (SS) 155
gunboats 27, 63, 64, 192, 193, 210

H
Haag, Walter 131
Halligan (USS DD) 219
Hazard, John W. (Jack) 57
hedgehogs 39, 61, 88
Hitler, Adolph 23, 24, 31, 32, 82
Hoel (USS DD 533) 210
Hollywood movie of a PC 57
Hoover, Elmer (Scrappie) 192
hull numbers of PCs 61, 63, 64, 67
hurricanes 45, 59, 128, 160, 161, 241-243, 266, 267
Hyde, Latimer B. 180, 135

I
Icarus (USCG) 164
Indochina 69, 70, 259, 260, 262, 263
Indonesia 69, 252, 257-260, 262
iron coffins 31
Italy 125, 143, 144, 164, 171, 174, 179, 181, 203, 240
I-32 143
I-53 220

J
James, Henry J. 163
James M. Sprunt 153
Johnson, Wesley G. 280, 281
Jones, Cliff 267
Jones, Paul. 223
Jordan, Larry 193

Jordan, Matthew 161
K
Kaiser, Karl 180
Kelliher, Joseph F. 281
Kennedy, James F. 123, 188
Kennedy, Ken 225
Kerr, Donald M. 154
Klinger, Russell 193
Knapp, Dave 214
Korea 67, 69, 249, 251, 252, 257-259, 261, 262, 278
L
Laugh (USS DE) 211
launching of PCs 55, 58, 59, 185, 225
LCI 125, 138, 210, 211, 218
LCT 179, 183, 188, 191
Leopoldville (SS) 189, 190
Levy, Allison 211
Lewis, Everitt D. 214
library, PCSA 282-284
Louise, typhoon 236, 240, 241
Lowther, R. D. 177, 178
LSM 218, 220
LST 138, 174, 175, 187, 214-217
Lyons (Mess Cook) 206
M
Mackey, Walter J. 267
Maddox (USS DD622) 174, 175
mail call, on PCs 110, 116, 118, 142, 195, 236
man hours needed to build a PC 62
Manlove (USS DE 36) 143, 209
Maritime Commission 27, 67, 68, 247, 251
Marvin. Lee 57
Mason (USS DE529) 159, 363
McAllister 83, 97
McCormick (USS DD) 151
McDaniel, Eugene Field 82, 83, 86-89, 96
Mediterranean 137-139, 141, 144, 170-174, 177, 182, 194, 235, 240, 249
Meredith (USS DD 726) 183, 187
Mexico 56, 69, 211, 258, 260, 262
Meyer, Gerhardt, Oberleutnant 189

Mid-Ocean Meeting Point (MOMP) 25
Milledgeville (PC 1263) 253, 265
Miller, David C. 205, 206
minesweepers 65, 137, 219
Minotaur (SS) 153
Missouri (USS BB) 225
Moffett (USS DD 362) 165
Mona Island (USS ARG 91) 237, 238
Morison, Samuel Elliot 37, 137
Morrissey, Fred 216
mortars 61
mousetraps 30, 35, 38, 61, 64, 88, 156, 160, 223, 234
movies 111, 113, 117, 279
Mowinckle (SS) 152
Mulholland, Harry K. 16
museum, PCSA 281-284, 288, 367
N
names assigned to PCs 29, 254, 256, 263
Navy Memorial 282
Netherlands 69, 214, 254, 256
Newby, David E. 219
Newport News Shipbuilding 28
Niblack 175
ninety day wonders 78, 119
Noble, Ralph 185
Nolan, Thomas 123
Norfolk 84
North Atlantic 59, 82, 128, 138, 165, 182
Norway 69, 84, 254, 256
Nueva Viscaya 250, 257
O
O'Connor, William 131
Ohana Kai 266, 274
Okinawa 209, 217, 219-221, 224, 236, 238-241, 251
Omaha Beach 183, 185, 187, 188
Operation Drum Beat 22
Operation Paukenschlag 22, 32, 92, 164
O'Meara, Jack 178
P
Padelford, Philip 187, 188

Page, Raymond 224, 232
Panama Canal 152, 166, 202, 205, 224, 239, 252, 253
patrol craft escorts 23
Patrol Craft Sailors Association 277, 280. 281, 284, 285, 287, 367
Patrol Craft Sailors' Society 280
PC
68 151
449 27
451 .... 28, 29, 34, 56, 72, 73, 76
452 .... 28, 56, 57
458 152
460 239
461 .... 28, 37, 46, 60, 61, 263
462 .... 67, 151, 152
463 .... 67, 152, 220
466 .... 224, 225, 232, 247, 263, 270
467 .... 254, 256
468 .... 254, 256
469 .... 67, 159, 218, 220
471 .... 28, 29, 254, 256
472 .... 29, 254
473 .... 29, 239, 254
474 .... 142, 194, 254
475 .... 254, 256
476 205
477 .... 123, 138, 142, 144, 146, 205-207, 248, 285
478 .... 131, 141, 148, 247, 269
479 .... 144, 205, 283, 289
480 .... 152, 254, 256
481 254
482 .... 239, 254, 256
483 .... 86, 257, 263, 264
484 .... 182, 186, 257, 263, 264
486 .... 124, 264
487 .... 143, 207, 208, 227, 239, 257, 263, 264
490 .... 253, 257, 262
496 .... 153, 172, 173, 196, 240
542 .... 144, 171, 248, 254, 256
543 .... 37, 47, 144, 171, 174, 175, 179, 196, 197, 254, 256, 272, 273
544 .... 254, 256

545 . . . . 143, 180, 255
546 . . . . 41, 50, 79, 94, 171, 172, 174, 176, 178, 240, 255, 256
547 . . . . 255, 256
548 . . . . 54, 249
549 . . . . 55, 67, 153, 210
550 . . . . 153, 174, 179, 249, 255, 256, 272, 273
551 . . . . 56, 255, 256
552 . . . . 157, 182, 183, 186, 191, 192
553 . . . . 153, 182, 183, 186, 199, 264
554 . . . . 139, 147, 153, 255, 256
555 . . . . 67, 136, 144, 153, 210, 219
556 . . . . 99, 175, 176, 240, 255, 256
557 . . . . 153, 255, 256
558 . . . . 58, 143, 181, 240
559 . . . . 144, 179, 180, 255, 256
561 . . . . 255, 256
562 . . . . 174, 240, 255, 256
564 . . . . . 79, 94, 161, 165, 169, 182, 189-194, 240, 249, 257, 262, 264, 280, 281
565 . . . . 94, 143, 157, 158, 165, 168, 182, 257, 263, 264, 280
566 . . . . 86, 257, 263, 264
574 136
567 . . . . 165, 182, 183, 250, 264
568 . . . . 165, 182, 183, 250, 257, 263, 264
576 . . . . 154, 250
577 . . . . 153, 154, 171
578 . . . . 67, 240
581 . . . . 207, 210, 257, 262, 264
582 . . . . 67, 240, 257, 263, 264
584 . . . . 220, 239, 240
586 . . . . 221, 264
590 . . . . 236-238, 240, 244
591 . . . . 174, 255, 256
594 224
602 . . . . 153, 265
604 . . . . 255, 256
605 . . . . 255, 256
607 . . . . 255, 256
616 . . . . 166, 258, 263
617 . . . . 40, 144, 155, 156, 165, 182, 183, 186-188, 191, 265
618 . . . . 155, 165, 182, 183, 250, 265

619 .... 132, 143, 144, 165, 180, 182, 187, 188, 194, 199, 201, 258, 263, 265
621 .... 174, 240, 255, 256
622 .... 174, 255, 256
623 .... 144, 210, 211
624 .... 143, 174, 177, 178, 240, 241, 245, 255, 256
625 .... 174, 255
626 .... 143, 181, 255
627 .... 143, 173, 178, 180, 240, 255, 256
701 251
709 .... 249, 257
777 .... 204, 263
779 .... 50, 132, 217, 218, 232, 264
789 133
793 .... 13-19, 52, 53, 130, 204, 216, 223, 224, 232, 279, 286, 291
800 .... 217, 238
803 .... 67, 220, 225, 226
804 .... 67, 220
805 64
806 64
807 .... 67, 251
814 .... 55, 239, 240
815 240
818 .... 150, 151, 167
820 .... 48, 49, 52, 54, 204, 247, 258, 262, 270
823 251
877 240
1079 .... 67, 210, 264
1080 .... 67, 210
1088 .... 64, 259
1089 .... 64, 251, 259
1090 .... 64, 259
1091 .... 64, 259, 262
1119 .... 144, 210, 211, 213-215, 230, 240, 264
1120 .... 264-266, 274, 282
1121 .... 259, 262, 263
122 .... 150, 153, 259, 262, 263
123 .... 143, 212, 213, 229
124 .... 215, 216, 231, 240, 241, 245
125 .... 68, 94, 102, 129, 144, 210, 264, 283, 288
126 .... 68, 210, 238, 240

1127 . . . . 68, 210
1128 . . . . 144, 219, 220, 241
1129 . . . . 143, 211, 229, 241
1131 . . . . 129, 259, 263
1133 . . . . 144, 214, 215, 230, 241, 259, 263
1134 . . . . 144, 208-210, 228, 259, 263
1135 . . . . 143, 209, 264
1136 . . . . 68, 210, 264
1141 . . . . 57, 74, 252, 259, 262, 264
1148 . . . . 64, 259, 262
1149 . . . . 164, 260, 262, 265
1168 . . . . 57, 68, 260, 262
1171 . . . . 86, 260, 262
1172 . . . . 247, 252, 265, 271
1174 . . . . 76, 265
1176 . . . . 182, 183, 185, 186, 194, 260, 263
1177 . . . . 68, 224, 263
1181 . . . . 53, 264
1189 . . . . 64, 241
1191 . . . . 51, 264
1193 . . . . 86, 264
1196 . . . . 89, 264
1198 . . . . 149, 264
1207 133
1209 . . . . 138, 146, 158, 159, 264
1212 . . . . 159, 264
1213 . . . . 103, 123, 165, 166, 264
1217 . . . . 160, 161, 168, 169, 241, 265-267, 275, 276, 282, 287
1225 . . . . 94, 182, 186, 264
1226 . . . . 255, 256
1227 . . . . 255, 256
1228 . . . . 153, 264
1232 . . . . 165, 182, 187, 260, 263
1233 . . . . 165, 182, 260, 263
1234 . . . . 255, 256
1235 . . . . 181, 256
1236 256
1238 . . . . 239, 241, 244
1239 . . . . 239, 241
1242 . . . . 94, 264

1243	253
1246	125, 264
1248	256
1249	256
1250	256
1252	165, 182, 260, 263, 265
1255	64, 241
1261	165, 182-185, 198, 241
1262	165, 182, 186, 187, 261, 263
1263	182, 183, 253, 261, 263, 265
1264	47, 159, 160, 163, 164, 265, 267, 276, 282, 360
1546	224, 261, 262, 265
1548	64
1558	238, 241
1560	256
1561	256
1562	256
1565	65, 253, 261, 262
1568	64, 77
1588	65, 208
1590	66, 253
1599	66, 68, 241
1601	66, 68
1603	55, 56, 66, 74, 134, 221, 222, 241
PCC	63, 65-68, 128, 137, 203, 234, 356
PCE	23, 32, 45, 61, 140, 356
PCS	61, 356
PCSA	281-285, 289
PE	27
Peck, Joseph J.	153
Peru	84
Peterson, George	185
pets	102, 103, 129, 130
PF	29
PG	27
PGM	63, 64, 137, 203, 234, 238, 241, 249, 251, 253, 259, 261
PGM 9	64
PGM 13	251, 259
PGM 17	241
PGM 18	241

PGM 27 .... 238, 241
PGM 29 .... 253, 261
PGM 32 .... 64, 77, 249
Philippines . . 70, 143, 209, 211, 212, 215, 224, 240, 249, 252, 257, 259, 261-263
pitching, of a PC 37, 42, 108, 109, 121-123, 126, 162
poker 112, 113, 279
Pollock, Thomas A. 283
Portugal 70, 258, 261, 263
Purdon, Eric 163, 164
Pyle, Ernie 125, 221
Q
Q-ship 155, 156
R
range, of PCs 138, 142, 165
rates of enlisted men, on PCs 358
reclassified, PCs 61
Reeves, Joseph P. 189
reservists 78, 79, 93, 160, 165
Riley, Daniel 161, 169
river gunboats 27
roll, of a PC 37, 39, 42, 45, 59, 108, 109, 110, 121-123, 126, 127, 161, 237
Roosevelt. Franklin Delano 21, 22, 28
Russia 84
S
Safari (HMS submarine) 174, 175, 197
Samuel B. Roberts (USS DE 413) 210
San Diego 80, 81, 91, 166, 202, 207, 217, 240
Sandell, Percy 192, 193
SC 27, 29, 61, 126, 174, 215, 356
SC 530 174
Scaffe, Norman 161
SCTC 81-93, 96, 98, 103, 119, 154, 158
seasickness 118, 121, 126
Secor, Gordon 16, 223
Sentinel (USS AM 113) 174
Severn (USS AO 61) 215, 216
Sherburne (USS APA 205) 238
shipyards 30, 55-58, 60, 70, 247, 329, 330
Silverstein, M. W. 175
Skylark (USS AM) 219

small craft 27, 29, 84, 93, 190, 235, 237
snorkel 162
sold, PCs 69, 248, 250-252, 262, 265, 282
sound school 80, 90, 91, 93
South Pacific 100, 107, 108, 138, 141, 144, 208, 211, 215, 249
Spain 70, 260, 263
speed, of PCs 24, 36-38, 119, 140, 152, 157, 159, 223
Spencer, James 190
Spielman, James S. 191
Spry (USS DD) 152
steam engine 28, 56, 57
Stevens, Ralph 182
Stotzer, Lt. j. g. 173
stricken, PCs 67, 249, 262
Strive (USS) 178
subchasers 79, 86, 88, 90, 125
Submarine Chaser Manual 37, 80, 81, 87
Submarine Chaser Training Center 81, 90, 93, 95, 96, 98, 99, 102, 119
submarine chasers 27-29, 36, 81, 84, 87, 137
Sutherland, Ensign 221
Swift (USS AM 122) 180, 181
T
Taiwan 70, 252, 259-261, 263
Teakettle 57
Texas (USS BB) 183
Thailand 70, 257, 258, 260, 263
Thetis (USCG) 164
Thompson, Earle 154
Tokyo Bay 224, 225, 252
Tokyo Rose 203, 204, 226
Tombaugh, John 37, 297
transfer, of PCs 30, 61, 63, 64, 69, 171, 249, 252-254, 257, 262, 282, 356
trawlers 24, 151
Tull, Richard 161
Turaichi, Armando 133
typhoons 210, 236, 238-241, 243
U
Underhill (USS DE) 220
uniform 84, 90, 107
Uruguay 69, 84, 255, 256

USSR L-15 166
U-123 22
U-375 .... 143, 177, 178
U-486 189
U-518 159
U-1230 162
U-boats 21-27, 29-32, 140, 151, 154, 155, 162-164, 181, 242,
V
Venezuela 67, 70, 84, 257, 258, 260, 263
victory gardens 24
Vietnam 70, 278
V-J day 210, 246
Von Zell, Harry 57
W
Ward, Pat 280, 281
Wayne, John 214, 230
Weatherford (USS), former PC 618 .... 250, 265
Webb, Jack 57
Weber, Alban RADM 281
Weeks, Bob 206
Weidenheft, Bill 187
wherry 41, 61, 166
Whitcomb, Gabe 173
Williamson turn 89
wolf pack 26, 31, 155, 181
Y
Young, Albert 221
YP-281 .... 208, 209, 228